Lincoln Christian College

P9-CRR-081

GOD'S FRONTIERSMEN:

The Yale Band in Illinois

John Randolph Willis

University Press
of America™

Copyright © 1979 by

University Press of America, Inc.™

4710 Auth Place, S.E., Washington, D.C. 20023

All rights reserved
Printed in the United States of America

ISBN: 0-8191-0781-6
Library of Congress No.: 79-65011

PREFACE

This work would not have been possible if it had not been for the kind help and courtesy of many individuals and institutions that have aided the author in one way or another. Especially is he grateful to Dean Luther A. Weigle of the Yale Divinity School, who first suggested the topic to him for intensive research and who has spent many hours reading and correcting the manuscript. He is equally indebted to Dr. Kenneth S. Latourette, who has been very generous with both his time and his suggestions. These two men deserve his most sincere thanks.

The author would like also to acknowledge his indebtedness to Miss Anne S. Pratt and the staff of the Yale Library, Miss Evah Ostrander of the Hammond Library at Chicago Theological Seminary, Dr. Gary Hudson and Miss Norma Hammond of Illinois College, the Illinois State Historical Library, McCormick Theological Seminary, Swift Library at the University of Chicago, Dr. Robert Richardson of Beloit College, Wisconsin, and Mr. Frederick Kuhns, who was of invaluable assistance in locating source material.

Finally, I am indebted to Ms. Patricia L. Rogers for her expertise in typing the manuscript.

INTRODUCTION

There is no more fascinating chapter in American history than the story of the winning of the West. From the year 1740, when the first English trading posts were established west of the Alleghenies, until 1890 when the United States Census Bureau formally announced the disappearance of the frontier, a great wave of population swept over an area of three million square miles of prairie, forest, mountain, desert, and plain. From this great tract of land, thirty-one new states were carved and fused into one great nation. This was an achievement which had never before occurred in the annals of history.

By the middle of the eighteenth century, the Atlantic Seaboard had become fairly well filled with English settlements, and little groups of pioneers were beginning to spill across the Appalachian range. Checked at first by the French and Indian War, and then by the British occupation, the trickle of emigration by 1783 had become a torrent. Kentucky and Tennessee were the first to attain statehood, and then followed six more states in rapid succession -- Ohio, Indiana, Mississippi, Alabama, Missouri, and Illinois.

Characteristic of this great westward movement, although differing from other states in detail, was the growth and development of Illinois. Long before her admittance into the Union in 1818, settlers had been converging on Illinois from numerous directions. They came from North Carolina, Tennessee, Virginia, Kentucky, Maryland, Pennsylvania, New York and New England. The main stream of travel came from the Ohio River, later supplemented by the Cumberland Road, the great national highway from Wheeling on the Ohio across the states of Ohio and Indiana, and by other land routes.

All sorts of peoples and classes were to be found in the new Prairie State. The first Europeans to share the Indian's hunting ground had been the French, who in turn were supplanted by the British. Rough trappers and hunters were followed by the squatter, who stopped for a few years to improve his means, and then sold his cabin and his land to more permanent settlers and moved on. Squatters might become farmers however, developing their first living arrangements into homes comparable to those they had left behind. It was not long before enterprising young men, many of them college graduates, were coming to the frontier to seek a fortune in land or in trade. Ninian Edwards abandoned a Kentucky judgeship in 1809 to

1

become governor of Illinois Territory. Elias Kent Kane was a graduate of Yale who was eventually to become the Jacksonian leader in the State.

Other settlers soon arrived whose primary interest was not self-advancement, but the spread of the Christian Gospel. The Baptists were the first in the field, and they were soon followed by the Methodists. The Presbyterians and Congregationalists were not far behind. United, under the Plan of Union of 1801, they insisted on an educated ministry to preach Calvinistic theology. This work was facilitated by the establishment of the American Home Missionary Society in 1826.

In 1829, a little group of seven men at Yale College became interested in Illinois as a field for missionary enterprise. Their object was twofold: to spread Christianity through the new state of Illinois, and to found a college which would give the frontier an educated ministry. Originally seven in number, by 1833 the little group had grown to fifteen, and had become known as the Illinois Band.

The formation of the Illinois Band has been told by a number of historians, and the history of Illinois College has been ably written by Charles H. Rammelkamp, in his Illinois College, a Centennial History. But there is no single study which describes the entire work of each of the members of the Illinois Band. The aim of this study is to tell the complete story as far as it has been recorded. Beginning with the formation of the Band at Yale, the author will attempt to describe the work of the various men on the frontier. Particular notice will be paid to those men who were employed by the American Home Missionary Society as agents for the entire state. Since many of the members of the Illinois Band were teachers and educators as well as missionaries, a chapter will be devoted to their educational activities. Many of the members of the Band played an important role in the growth of Congregationalism in Illinois, and the disruption of the Plan of Union with the Presbyterians. This will be followed by an examination of the Band's attitude toward various social issues of the day, particularly the anti-slavery movement. The historical period covered begins with the year 1829, when the Band was first formed, and extends to the outbreak of the Civil War in 1861.

The most valuable mine of information and manuscript materials is the Hammond Library at Chicago Theological Seminary, Chicago, Illinois. The store

room contains literally thousands of letters written by
various men in the employ of the American Home Missionary
Society from all parts of the United States. More than
eight hundred were written by members of the Band. The
Hammond Library also contains hundreds of Letter Books,
duplicates of letters which the Society wrote to the
various missionaries in its employ. There are other
valuable manuscript materials also, such as the journals
of Flavel Bascom and Lemuel Foster. Many of the letters
which passed between Theron Baldwin and Julian Sturtevant are collected at Illinois College in the Baldwin-
Sturtevant correspondence. There are letters from other
members of the Band here also. Much valuable material
is at Sterling Memorial Library at Yale University in
New Haven, Connecticut. Other sources of aid were Beloit
College, McCormick Theological Seminary, and the Illinois
State Historical Library. The Home Missionary Journal
and the Journal of the Illinois State Historical Society
were invaluable. Other important sources such as the
Congressional Quarterly, and the Illinois Churches file
collected by Mr. Frederick Kuhns at Chicago Theological
Seminary, are too numerous to mention.

CHAPTER I

THE ILLINOIS FRONTIER

Father Jacques Marquette and Sieur Louis Joliet were the first white men to set foot on Illinois sod. In the spring of 1673, they entered the water of the Mississippi from the Wisconsin River, and floated down the Mississippi to the mouth of the Arkansas. The return voyage was made by way of the Illinois River, Marquette promising the Indians at Kaskaskia that he would soon come back to them and establish a mission. Two motives dominated the life of Marquette, the explorer's desire for knowledge, and the missionary's zeal for converting the Indians to Christianity.[1]

In fulfillment of this promise, Marquette and two companions returned from Wisconsin the following year, and spent the spring of 1674 with these Indians. On Easter Sunday he established the Mission of the Immaculate Conception. But as he preached to the Indians at Kaskaskia, he found that his strength was ebbing. He found it necessary to return to Canada, but he failed to reach the mission at St. Ignace, dying upon the eastern shores of Lake Michigan, near Ludington, May 18, 1675.[2]

Marquette's successor in Illinois was the imperialist Robert Cavelier, Sieur de la Salle. His aim was to establish posts to the south of the Great Lakes to link the fur trade of the region to Fort Frontenac, and to establish the Mississippi as a great trade outlet from the interior to the ocean. In January of 1680 he built Fort Crevecoeur at the Lake of Peoria among the Illinois tribes. In spite of foreclosures by his creditors, the sinking of his ships, repeated mutinies and desertions, and the hardship of life in the American wilderness, he succeeded in laying the foundations of a French colony in Illinois.[3]

The French colony in Illinois never became very strong. By the middle of the eighteenth century there

---

[1] Weigle, Luther Allan, _American Idealism, The Pageant of America_, Vol. X, p. 31.

[2] _Ibid._ _Cf._ also Waggener, Halley Farr, _Baptist Beginnings in Illinois_, S.T.M. dissertation in Swift Library, University of Chicago, p. 3.

[3] Pease, Theodore Calvin, _The Story of Illinois_, p. 8.

were probably not more than two thousand inhabitants, French and negroes, scattered mainly in the little villages of Kaskaskia, Prairie du Rocher, St. Philips, Fort de Chartres, and Cahokia. Yet this little population supplied grain to posts on the Ohio, Louisiana, and New Orleans as well.[4]

In 1763, after the close of the French and Indian War, France transferred her claims to the Illinois Territory to England, having the previous year secretly ceded all of her territory west of the Mississippi to Spain. Kaskaskia became the British capital as it had been the French, and a military garrison was maintained at Fort Chartres.[5]

When the English took over the territory, the number of French and half-breeds east of the Mississippi numbered about six thousand. Most of them were located in Cahokia and Kaskaskia. Cahokia boasted forty families in 1766, and at the outbreak of the Revolutionary War the number had increased to fifty; it was once the seat of a considerable fur trade. Kaskaskia contained about one hundred families in 1763, but after the capital was moved, its population and trade were greatly reduced, and in 1834 the number had dwindled to about fifty or sixty families. Kaskaskia possessed a brick court house, a Roman Catholic chapel, a nunnery and a female boarding school.[6]

The English were not blind to the value of their new possessions in the Mississippi Valley, but they erroneously thought that the wealth of the country lay in the fur trade. A proclamation was passed in 1763 which forbade colonization of the territory between the Ohio and the Mississippi Rivers. This attempt to exclude aggressive pioneers from establishing new homes turned out to be an abortive one. In 1778, thanks to the heroic invasion of George Rogers Clark, Illinois passed from English to American hands, and was created a county of Virginia.[7] At the close of the Revolutionary War,

---

[4] Pease, Theodore Calvin, The Story of Illinois, p. 16.

[5] Cf. Peck, John M., A Gazetteer of Illinois, pp. 236, 237.

[6] Peck, John M., A Gazetteer of Illinois, p. 268. When the Indians moved from their village on the Illinois to Kaskaskia, they moved their mission of the Immaculate Conception with them (1700).

[7] Pease, Theodore Calvin, The Story of Illinois, p. 13.

Virginia ceded her claims to the country lying to the north of the Ohio River to the United States.

In 1787, the United States organized the Northwest Territory by means of the Northwest Ordinance, which provided for the eventual formation of new states to be admitted into the Union. The Northwest Ordinance provided for trial by jury, granted freedom of worship, encouraged education by setting aside land for educational purposes, and prohibited slavery.[8]

In 1800, the population of Illinois was about 3,000. In 1809, when Congress set off the Territory of Illinois from that of Indiana, the population had risen to 12,282, and when Illinois became a state in 1818, the population exceeded 40,000. Two years later, the capital was moved from Kaskaskia, to a more central town in the state, Vandalia.[9]

One of the earliest missionaries from the East, who traversed the Illinois territory early in the nineteenth century, was Samuel J. Mills. In 1812-1813, with John F. Schermerhorn, and again in 1814-1815, with David Smith, he travelled altogether about ten thousand miles, inquiring into the moral conditions of the Great Valley, and the spiritual needs of its inhabitants, distributing Bibles and organizing Bible Societies wherever he went. He found that the Illinois Territory contained five Baptist churches with a total membership of one hundred and twenty, and six Methodist preachers with a following of six hundred members.[10]

Mills' visit to the West bore significant fruit. On May 6, 1816, the American Bible Society was formed in New York City, and in Washington on December 27 six months later, the American Colonization Society was established. Congregationalists and Presbyterians rose to meet the religious challenge of the American frontier.[11]

Mills was followed by Salmon Giddings, who came in 1815 to Missouri for the Missionary Society of Connecticut. With his headquarters at Saint Louis, and aided

[8]Moss, S.D., American History and Government, p. 25.

[9]Peck, John M., Gazetteer of Illinois, pp. 108-109.

[10]Weigle, Luther Allan, American Idealism, The Pageant of America, Vol. X, p. 239.

[11]Spinka, M., Kuhns, F., et al., A History of Illinois Congregational and Christian Churches, p. 322, fn. 10.

by the Reverend Timothy Flint, Giddings divided his time
between the territories of Missouri and Illinois, organizing the First Presbyterian Church of St. Louis in 1817,
and the Presbytery of Missouri in connection with the
Synod of Tennessee. Altogether, Giddings and his associates established seventeen Presbyterian churches in
Illinois by 1828, the most important ones being at Kas-[12]
kaskia, Edwardsville, Belleville, and Collinsville.

In the meantime, from 1815 to 1826, the Missionary
Society of Connecticut had been sending a succession of
itinerant ministers into southern Indiana, Illinois, and
Missouri. Under the Plan of Union, Congregationalists
and Presbyterians worked side by side. Yet, it became
increasingly apparent that resident missionaries were
needed if the Christian Gospel was to take permanent
root on the frontier.[13]

Such a man was John Milliot Ellis. Born in Keene,
New Hampshire, in 1793, he had been brought up in New
England in a family of deep piety. Although farmers,
the Ellis family was in comfortable circumstances, and
John enjoyed a college education at Dartmouth. He was
already over thirty when he was ordained to the ministry
in the Old South Church, Boston. His seminary training
had been taken at Andover, and in 1825 this "tall and
athletic" young man went west to devote his life and[14]
talents to missionary service.

Arriving in Kaskaskia, Ellis found that in spite of
seven years of statehood, the southern portion of Illinois was very sparsely settled, and the northern half of
the state was almost an unbroken wilderness. But the
population was rapidly increasing. Easterners from New
England and New York were gathering in small towns and
villages and moving north. Southerners were moving in

---

[12]Spinka, M., Kuhns, F., et al., A History of Illinois
Congregational and Christian Churches, p. 3. Kofoid,
Carrie P., gives twenty "Puritan Influences in the Form-
ative Years of Illinois History," Transactions of the
Illinois State Historical Society for the year 1905, 276.

[13]Spinka, M., Kuhns, F., et al., A History of Illinois
Congregational and Christian Churches, p. 4.

[14]Rammelkamp, Charles H., Illinois College, A Centennial
History, pp. 1, 3.

from Kentucky, Tennessee, and Missouri, settling mainly in the area around Saint Louis and Vincennes.[15]

Education was something of a foreigner on the frontier, and schools were almost unknown. Pioneers were usually too occupied with the struggle for existence to be concerned about giving their children an education. One of the early alumni of Illinois College who graduated in the class of 1837 describes the situation as follows:

During the early history of Illinois, schools were almost unknown in some neighborhoods, and in the most favored districts they were kept up solely by subscription, and only in the winter season, each subscriber agreeing to pay for his children pro rata for the number of days they should be in attendance. The teacher usually drew up articles of agreement, which stipulated that the school should commence when a specified number of scholars should be subscribed at the rate of $2, $2.50, or $3 per scholar for the quarter. In these written articles he bound himself to teach spelling, reading, writing and arithmetic as far as the double rule of three. Occasionally a teacher would venture to include English grammar. But in the early years of my youth I knew of no teacher who attempted to give instruction in grammar or geography. And such branches as history, natural philosophy, or astronomy were not thought of. Many parents were unwilling that their children should study arithmetic, contending that it was quite unnecessary for farmers. And what was the use of grammar to a person who could talk so as to be understood by everybody? I studied English grammar and all the later rules of arithmetic when about twelve years old without the aid of a teacher, and geography at a later age, when I had begun to prepare for college.

The mode of conducting schools was peculiar. All the pupils studied their lessons by spelling or reading aloud simultaneously, while the teacher usually heard each scholar recite alone; although in the opening of the school, a chapter of the

[15]Rammelkamp, Charles H., Illinois College, A Centennial History, p. 4.

9

Bible was read by the older scholars by verses, in turn, and at the close in the evening the whole school, except the beginners, stood up and spelled words in turn, as given out by the master.[16]

Newspapers were also a rarity on the frontier. Illinois probably had four papers in the year of Ellis' arrival. The Illinois Reporter succeeded the Kaskaskia Republican in 1826; it carried a few of Ellis' articles on the educational needs of the state. Thomas Lippincott, one of the founders of Illinois College, was one time editor of the Edwardsville Spectator. There existed also the Illinois Gazette and the Illinois Intelligencer.[17]

The earliest preachers on the frontier were usually unlearned men. They looked askance at education. Peter Cartwright, famous pioneer evangelist, once declared that he was glad he had not spent four years rubbing his back against the walls of a college. Some could not even read the Bible. What they lacked in information, they made up in vociferous speech and violent action. And yet it cannot be denied that they raised the moral standard of living among the people of the backwoods.

It was natural that the older preachers would feel a bit jealous of the new man coming to the state. They might easily be superseded by a more educated clergy. But the new men from the East proved to be just as rugged and hardy messengers of the Gospel. We shall have occasion later to examine some of the hardships which members of the Illinois Band had to meet when they acted as Agents for the American Home Missionary Society.

John Ellis was quick to see that religion could make little headway in Illinois unless it was aided by education. He early cast about for some means of establishing a "seminary of learning" to provide young men with a theoretical and practical training. In 1827 he outlined one such plan and published it in Kaskaskia's Illinois Reporter. In addition to courses in the classics, pro-

---

[16]Patterson, R.W., Early Society in Southern Illinois, pp. 23, 24.

[17]Rammelkamp, Charles H., Illinois College, A Centennial History, p. 6.

vision was made for farming, and even a savings bank.[18]

Encouragement for establishing such a school came from settlers at Shoal Creek, who had even organized a board of trustees for their proposed institution which was to be called the "Fairfield Literary and Theological Seminary." They were ready to go to work at once, but Ellis was advised by other friends to wait until several possible sites farther north had been examined. He therefore undertook an inspection of the neighboring counties with his close friend Thomas Lippincott.[19]

Lippincott was a pioneer Quaker who had come to Illinois in 1818. After making the hazardous trip from the East, he had opened a general store near Alton under the firm name of "Lippincott and Company." After some experience as a journalist, he served as clerk of the state senate in 1822, and shortly after was instrumental in defeating a scheme for making Illinois a slave state. Perhaps it was this experience that gave an impetus to his desire to raise the moral and educational level of the pioneer state.[20]

During the winter of 1827-1828, the two men made an exploratory trip for the site of the proposed college, but only gave serious consideration to Carrollton, Jacksonville, and Springfield. Struck by the apparent beauty of Wilson's Grove at Jacksonville, and sufficiently encouraged by the friends of education there, Ellis immediately purchased the land which is the present-day site of Illinois College.[21]

Opposition arose from this move. Many at Shoal Creek felt that Ellis and Lippincott had overstepped their bounds. Presbytery refused to give its endorsement, claiming that the College should be founded on the other side of the river.[22]

Ellis was not easily discouraged, however. Having determined on a site for the new College, he set about raising money by sending a subscription paper through Morgan County. He succeeded in raising a subscription of $1,913 and two tracts of land, although only $785 was payable in cash, the rest was to be in labor or produce.

---

[18] Rammelkamp, Charles H., Illinois College, A Centennial History, pp. 9-10.

[19] Ibid., pp. 10-12.

[20] Ibid.

[21] Ibid., pp. 13-14.

[22] Ibid.

Ellis had proposed to have a theological school in his seminary of learning, therefore it was somewhat embarrassing not to have the endorsement of presbytery. To prevent his theological plans from running amuck, he conceived the idea of having the Presbyterian clergymen within the state choose the professors of theology. This would create confidence in the orthodoxy of his new institution. While pursuing his plans, a stroke of good luck befell him. He was called to the pastorate of the recently organized Presbyterian church of Jacksonville. This change in pastorates must have been a tremendous advantage to him in his enterprise.[23]

In 1826 the American Home Missionary Society had been established in New York to aid Congregational and Presbyterian ministers in spreading the Christian gospel on the frontier. Those who were in the Society's employ frequently wrote letters and reports of their activities which were published in the Home Missionary. On September 25, 1828, Ellis wrote such a communication describing his work at the Presbyterian Church of Jacksonville. After emphasizing the need for more missionaries, he concluded with the following paragraphs:

A SEMINARY OF LEARNING

is projected, to go into operation next fall. The subscription now stands at between 2 and $3,000. The site is selected in this county, Morgan, and the selection made with considerable deliberation, by a committee appointed for that purpose; and is one in which the public sentiment perfectly coincides. The half quarter section purchased for the site, is certainly the most delightful spot I have ever seen. It is about one mile north of the celebrated Diamond Grove, at the east end of Wilson Grove, on an eminence overlooking the town and country for several miles around.

The object of the Seminary is popular, and it is my deliberate opinion that there never was in our country a more promising opportunity for any who desire it, to bestow a few thousand dollars in the cause of education, and of Missions. The posture of things now is such, as to show all the intelligent people,

---

[23]Rammelkamp, Charles H., Illinois College, A Centennial History, pp. 15-16.

12

the good effects of your society, and to secure their cooperation in a happy degree in
all the great benevolent objects of the day,
IF SUCH AID CAN NOW BE AFFORDED in the objects above mentioned.[24]

To a group of young men at Yale University, this
seemed like a direct answer to prayer. They had been
wondering how they might make their lives count for
something worthwhile in the world. Here was the opportunity which they had long been looking for. They immediately formed themselves into an Illinois Band,
pledging their lives to missionary and educational
service on the Western frontier. Who were these men?
In order to tell their story, we must shift our scene
to New England and life at Yale University.

---

[24]American Home Missionary Journal, Vol. I, p. 136.

CHAPTER II

THE FORMATION OF THE ILLINOIS BAND

When Timothy Dwight became president of Yale College in 1795, he was confronted by a situation which did not look very promising for the future of Christianity. The closing years of the eighteenth century were marked by a vogue of atheism and infidelity, not only at Yale, but also throughout the entire colonies. War has never been a friend of religion, and the War of Independence in America was no exception. Extreme inflation, crime and immorality were all after-effects of the war. Many churches had been damaged or destroyed; many had lost their leadership; and many were characterized by a cold and empty formalism. On top of all this, English Deism and French Skepticism were very much of a fad. Under the leadership of David Hume, Deism declared that Christianity was a reasonable religion. Its fundamental beliefs could be set forth in ways to convince the mind. Since the mind of man is the measure of all truth, what is not rationally convincing is untrue. It opposed the idea that there is any special action on the part of God tending to reveal Himself, His disposition and His will. This led to opposition to the church as the organized institution of Christian faith. One should first live reasonably. The English Deists were a far cry from the teachers of the Reformation.[1]

French Skepticism was less rational and more militant. Many colonists were pro-French because of French help during the Revolution, and also because France was now going through a similar struggle. Although French atheism was more of a fashion than a faith, nevertheless skepticism invaded the colleges. At Princeton, in 1782, there were but two students who professed to be Christians. In 1783, a revival at Yale had swelled the membership of the college church; but seventeen years later there were but five student members.[2]

This moral and spiritual depression, however, must not be overemphasized. By no means had the churches lost all their strength. From this threat of infidelity and atheism there arose a very remarkable recovery. It came in the form of the Second Great Awakening.

---

[1] Weigle, Luther Allan, American Idealism, The Pageant of America, Vol. X, p. 138ff.

[2] Ibid.

The Second Great Awakening made a tremendous impact on the entire nineteenth century. It affected the Congregational, Presbyterian and Baptist churches which were in the Calvinist tradition, saw the rise of Methodism, produced great revivals on the frontier, stimulated the growth of church membership and new denominations, was responsible for the impetus to home and foreign missions, stimulated the organization of philanthropic societies, multiplied Christian colleges, produced seminaries, and seriously concerned itself with the social problems of its day, such as slavery, temperance, education and war.

Timothy Dwight was one of the earliest heralds of this Second Great Awakening. He preached a series of sermons in chapel which gave an exposition of Christian theology, and at one of his baccalaureate addresses he talked on infidelity. He frequently discussed these subjects in informal meetings with seniors in debate class. In 1802 Yale College experienced a remarkable revival during the course of which more than one-third of the students professed conversion. Of this one-third, nearly one-half entered the Christian ministry. This revival was followed by a number of conversion years, 1808, 1812, 1813, 1815, 1825, 1831, 1835, 1841, and 1858 being the most notable.

One of the results of the Second Great Awakening was the great impetus given to domestic and foreign missions. The famous Haystack Prayer Meeting at Williams College which led eventually to the formation of the American Board of Commissioners for Foreign Missions is a familiar story. Nor is it necessary to trace the origins of similar organizations such as the London Missionary Society, the Baptist Missionary Society, and the Church Missionary Society. There soon developed an interest in home missions as well as foreign missions. This missionary enthusiasm was noticeably present at Yale. On April 6, 1797, a group of twenty-five students met in the County Court House and formed "themselves into a society for the promotion and preservation of morality among the members of this University to be known by the name of the Moral Society of Yale College."[3] The society was secret. Each candidate for membership had to subscribe to the following questions:

---

[3]Record Book, A Yale Moral Society--Art. I, Section 7 of the Constitution (Yale MS.).

16

"Will you endeavor to regulate your conduct by the
rules of morality contained in the Bible? Will you
endeavor, by all prudent means, to suppress vice and
promote the interests of morality in this seminary?
Will you, as long as you continue a member of this society, wholly refrain from every kind of profane language? Will you never be guilty of playing any game
in which property is concerned and will you refrain
entirely from playing cards whilst you continue a member of this society?" And later, "Will you, so long
as you continue a member of this society, abstain from
the intemperate use of spiritous liquor?"

The function of this society was largely to debate
various theological and ethical questions. The society
continued in existence for a good many years. In 1828
its name was changed to the Moral and Theological Society.
In 1834, it was changed to the Rhetorical Society and
seems to have consisted mainly of theological students.
In 1861, it became the Taylor Rhetorical Society, and
then after that date it disappears.[4]

Shortly after Jeremiah Day became President of the
College in 1818, a Society of Inquiry Regarding Missions
was formed. This was the first body of its kind at Yale.
The Society bore this name until 1852, when it was
changed to the Yale College Missionary Society.[5] It had
charge of the monthly concert and furnished religious
literature for the reading-room on Sundays. This Society lasted until the 1870s. Another movement at Yale,
growing out of the Second Great Awakening, was the Lycurgan Society for the Promotion of Simplicity in Life
and Morals. It set itself against extravagance of dress.
The Lycurgan Society was relatively short-lived, 1818-
1821. We are told that it died "as soon as it had exposed the follies of luxury, and simplicity had been
again restored."[6] During the 1820s, Yale College ex-

_____

[4]Shedd, Clarence P., _Two Centuries of Student Christian
Movements_, p. 31.

[5]Wright, Henry B., _Two Centuries of Christian Activity
at Yale_, pp. 76-77.

[6]_Ibid._, p. 77 (footnote).
    Of less importance but of considerable interest was
an organization called the "Blue Skin Club." Sturtevant
describes it in his Autobiography (Sturtevant, J.M., _An
Autobiography_, p. 96): "Our room was separated from the
chapel only by a narrow, open space. One night we were
[footnote continued on next page]

perienced a revival every year, with the exception of
the years 1826 and 1829. As a direct result of the
1825 revival, a Yale Temperance Society was started in
1826. It was reorganized in 1832 and various societies
bearing this name existed until 1870. The society in
existence in 1835 was founded on thoroughly cold-water
principles, and its members agreed to abstain from the
use of intoxicating liquors during their connection
with the college as undergraduates. "While there were
periods when such a society exerted a strong influence
upon the college, it is doubtful whether it was ever as
potent a force for temperance as other organizations
whose efforts in the same direction were more far-
reaching, though less conspicuous and direct."[7]

The year 1822 is important as marking the founding
of the Theological School, as it was then called. In
answer to a petition of fifteen young men, who were pursuing special theological studies under the private instruction of several of the academic professors, a

---

[footnote continued from previous page] startled from
our slumbers by a frightful explosion. At six o'clock
on a chill, cloudy, winter morning, the bell summoned
us to prayers in the chapel. But what a wreck did we
behold! The explosion had been produced by a large
package of gunpowder wrapped in a strong paper . . . .
    Immediately after prayers four persons met at our
room: the two occupants of the room, our friend Wright,
and Wyllys Warner, afterwards treasurer of the college.
We were of one mind. This could be endured no longer.
There was a term of reproach and ignomy which was
freely applied to anyone suspected of reporting to the
authorities. It was the custom to call him a "Blue Skin,"
and no one who was not in Yale College at the time, can
have any conception of the peculiar sting which the term
carried. We decided to disarm that scorpion. We sol-
emnly pledged ourselves to each other to communicate to
the authorities every violation of the order of the college of which we could get any information. We called
our league "The Blue Skin Club." With such a name and
such an aim, we determined to increase the membership as
fast as possible. We communicated our plan first to
those of whose approbation and co-operation we were sure.
Thus we widened the circle cautiously but rapidly, till
in a short time we had about a hundred pledged to co-operation, without having communicated our plan to anyone
not in sympathy with us."

[7]Wright, H.B., Two Centuries of Christian Activity at
Yale, p. 81.

18

special department was set aside. Three years later, a group of theological students started an organization called the Society for Christian Research. Beginning in 1825, this Society met regularly (about once a month) to hear reports from its various members on some particular phase of Christian service. There were four committees: one on Domestic Missions, one on Foreign Missions, a Committee of Correspondence with other Colleges and Seminaries, and a Committee on People of Color,[8] the latter being a reflection of the rise of the anti-slavery movement. In 1831, a Committee on Seamen was added.

With one or two exceptions, members of the Illinois Band were first members of this Society for Christian Research. Henry Herrick was a member in 1825. In 1827, Baldwin, Hale, Messenger, Turner and Sturtevant joined. In 1828, Barnes, Brooks, Foster, Grosvenor, Jenney and Kirby were added to the list. In 1830, Bascom joined; the following year he was elected president. On December 30, 1828, Sturtevant read a paper "on certain considerations which often influence a theological student in selecting his field of labor." On February 27, 1829 Brooks read a dissertation on home missions in the West. On June 30 of that same year Theron Baldwin was appointed to deliver the annual address in commencement week. On November 24, Brooks read another dissertation, this time "on the claims of this country on its Christian citizens." Most important of all, however, was Theron Baldwin's essay delivered on November 25, 1828.[9]

Baldwin's essay was entitled "The Encouragements to Active Individual Efforts in the Cause of Christ."[10] It was read before the "Society of Inquiry Respecting Missions." Baldwin had already pledged himself to the cause of home missions. His elder brother Abram had been a missionary in northern Vermont, but in 1826 he died at Montreal, and Theron had gone there to recover his remains. He discovered that his brother had preached with considerable success, and was greatly mourned by the people. Theron was therefore strongly tempted to continue his brother's work in Canada.[11]

---

[8] By-laws of the Society, article iii.

[9] Society for Christian Research (Yale MS).

[10] Sturtevant incorrectly says December in his Autobiography, p. 135.

[11] Sturtevant, J.M., "Life of Theron Baldwin," The Congregational Quarterly, April 1875, pp. 223-224.

The credit for the actual formation of the Illinois Band belongs to Mason Grosvenor. He had been strongly impressed by Baldwin's essay, and was very anxious to form a group of students which should devote its life to the cause of home missions. Some, who might be reluctant to go to a frontier state alone, might readily join a group and in that way strengthen the work of each other. This band of students would go to some frontier state, and establish churches, and an institution of learning. Sturtevant says that, "In consequence, probably, of my early frontier experience I was soon taken into the counsels of those most interested in this plan, and I co-operated with great enthusiasm in its development."[12]

In the December issue of the American Home Missionary Magazine (1828) appeared the announcement of John M. Ellis' "projected seminary of learning" which was to go into operation the following fall. Here was the very opportunity which the Band had been seeking -- a promising field of service, which contained great possibilities for missionary and educational work both. Mason Grosvenor lost no time in getting in touch with John Ellis.[13] He

_____

[12]Sturtevant, J.M., Autobiography, p. 136.

[13]Grosvenor to Ellis, New Haven, December 5, 1828.
"I trust you will not think it strange that I address you through a stranger as it respects personal acquaintance. I am at present a member of the Theological Department in this place. My object in writing is to obtain some information respecting the western country. The moral condition of its inhabitants is a subject which has occupied many of my thoughts and I trust called forth the feelings of my heart. To think of the present number of immortal souls within our own country -- living on trial for an endless destiny, is deeply affecting: But to think of their rapid increase in a situation where little or no light shines to invite them to the world of felicity or to warn them of that dark abyss to which they rapidly hasten is truly overwhelming. What more can be done to give them the light of the Gospel has for some time past been the subject of my investigations. Among a few in this Seminary the subject has been discussed and I think some plan of effort will soon be adopted by them. I will give you the outline of the one which has been somewhat discussed and in reference to which it is my present object to gain some information. We have thought of forming an association consisting of eight or ten, who may go out to the west, two or three the next autumn and the remainder the autumn succeeding. It would be their intentions to
[footnote continued on next page]

20

[footnote continued from previous page] select a spot the most favorable for exerting an influence with a view of taking up this abode for life. It would also be desirable for them to settle as near each other as circumstances would allow, with the expectation of having their number increased yearly. One of their first objects would be to establish a seminary of learning where in due time young men may acquire a thorough education both collegiate and theological, and thus be prepared for the ministry. They might each of them make it a special object to look out all the young lads who may or have become pious, and of proper qualifications, and put them upon a course of education. Some quantity of land also might be owned by the Seminary in order to afford manual labor for the students and also to prevent the impressive influence of their settling too near. In order to accomplish this object funds must be raised. But of the proclibility [sic] of raising funds in this region we feel little doubt. It will be necessary too that the individuals who engage in such an expedition together with the clergymen now on the ground should have the main control of the Seminary.

These Sir are the outlines of the plan under consideration. There are young men in this Seminary who sustain a high character for piety and talents, and who I think will be willing to enlist with all their souls in such a cause, and something I hope may be done with the blessing of Providence. Since turning our attention to this subject we have perused your letters directed to the Secretary of the Home Missionary Society together with that of the Layman from Jacksonville. From your statements, this section of the western country seems to strike our minds as a favorable spot for such efforts. I wish therefore that you would do me the favor of giving some information respecting this section of the country and also respecting the Seminary mentioned in your letter. First please to state particulars raised here to a considerable amount, this contemplated Seminary can be carried forward on the plan which I have suggested; or whether it is so under the control of others as to forbid this. And in the next place please to state respecting its location. What is its distance from the junction of the Illinois with the Mississippi, and in what part of Morgan County and how far distant from Jacksonville. I fear it is a little farther north than would be desirable. As it respects this, please to state your views. Also what is the climate and how it compares with the Southern part of Illinois. What kind of disease it is subject, and what the character of your winters? What would be the best season of the year for travelling? These are most of the subjects concerning which particular information would be a great favor. Whatever other [footnote continued on next page]

told him about the interest of some of his fellow students in frontier missions in the West, and how they were anxious to combine religious work with an educational project. He asked for additional information about Ellis' plans: the location of the "seminary," the climate of Illinois, the life of the churches, the best time for travelling, and what kind of diseases to expect. One point is of particular interest. Grosvenor was afraid that Jacksonville was too far north for the future home of Illinois College. Subsequent events were to show that the new institution of learning had been planted too far south.

Ellis was delighted to hear from Grosvenor, and on January 17, 1829 he replied to his letter, complimenting him on the formation of the "Association," and hastening to add the details about which Grosvenor had inquired. He assured him that the site for the Seminary was on a "commanding eminence uncommonly beautiful." He explained that the northern part of the state had "better land, water, climate everything" than the southern part, and was beginning to fill up rapidly.[14]

[footnote continued from previous page] considerations however which you may think to have any . . .(?) . . . (?) As you have an opportunity of extensive information respecting the western country, and considerations from yourself would be peculiarly valuable, all facts respecting the prosperity of your little churches and of the cause generally will be very interesting.

Thus, Sir, I have stated to you my views and wishes, and would request that you would not make known our views to any one until you may hear more about the subject.

Wishing you great prosperity in the cause of the Redeemer I subscribe myself your friend & Brother.

M. Grosvenor."

[14]Ellis to Grosvenor, Jacksonville, Morgan Co., Illinois. January 17, 1829; letter at Illinois College, Jacksonville, Illinois.

"Yours of December 5 has been duly received and read with uncommon interest. God grant that your communication may prove as the stars in the East for the salvation of the western country. Evangelical truth and education must go hand in hand to the work of the world's redemption. We must commence as the fathers of New England . . .(?) Bibles and tracts make their way but slowly, and to little purpose where the community do not read. The friends of the Bible and tract cause are a little preposterous perhaps in their Expectations with [footnote continued on next page]

[footnote continued from previous page] regard to this
country. The foreign Missionary establishes schools as
among his first work, and through them he expects his
principal success. For the same reason the cause of
Education is essentially connected with the success of
the benevolent operations in the western country.

With regard to the splendid project contemplated by
your "Association" it is my serious conviction that were
you here you would fix on the place we have chosen as
the field of your operations.

As to the plan (plan of this seminary) it gives me
pleasure to state that it was originally so framed as
to admit of the cooperation of the friends at the East;
and so as to give them all the control of the institution
they could desire if they want to furnish the fund.

As to the location, I can say it was selected by a
committee appointed by the Presbytery for that purpose.
Thomas Lippincott Esq formerly Editor of the Edwardsville Spectator now a Licentiate in our Presbytery together with myself, sufficient time was taken to examine
the country and to ascertain the opinion of gentlemen
whose judgment could be in any way serviceable in a decision of so much importance, and I am happy to say that
time has had the effect to confirm in every point of view
the choice originally made.

The site for the Seminary is about one mile west
of Jacksonville, at the east end of Wilson grove on a
commanding eminence uncommonly beautiful. Jacksonville
is near the center of this county about 20 miles from
the Illinois River and about sixty miles from its junction with the Mississippi. It is near enough to the
river for safety of health which must be an object never
to be lost sight of. You express fear that Morgan is a
little far north than would be desirable. In order to
exhibit proper evidence before you on that subject permit me to mention the following particulars. 1st. The
opinion of men on the ground, men every way interested
to fix on the best location and whose acquaintance in
the western country qualify them to judge correctly.
One of the subscribers of $400 from New England an elder
in our church living in Madison County nearly east of St.
Louis was so well satisfied that the northern part of the
state was best made it a condition of his subscription
that it should be in Morgan County. In the southern part
of the state there is little improvement. In the Northern
part, the land is far better, everything is better. The
northern part of Ind. Ill. and Mis. are the most important parts, settling faster on account of the better land,
water, climate everything."

It took about two months for a letter to go to Illinois and come back. In the meantime, the little association at Yale was growing. A number of students had become interested in it, although as yet no formal document had been signed.[15] A correspondence had also begun between Grosvenor and Absalom Peters, secretary of the American Home Missionary Society. "It was with all of us the grave problem of a life investment," says Sturtevant.

> The more it was considered, the more it grew in favor. My personal knowledge of the urgency of the work of home evangelization made the question comparatively easy. With the wants of the frontier so distinctly before me I could not think of going to a foreign field, or of seeking a settlement in any of the churches in the older states. I felt that Providence had selected the valley of the Mississippi for my home, and I dared not desert it in the emergency which I felt was upon it. I highly appreciated the advantages of the proposed association, for I dreaded the isolation of the frontier. It is proper also to state that my associates told me from the beginning that they would need my services as teacher in the new institution. This plan suited my tastes much better than entering the pastorate. . . .

> In my own case it may readily be supposed that as the happiness of two persons was involved, both were to be consulted before the decision was reached. The whole subject was laid frankly before Miss Fayerweather, and without the least attempt to conceal the trials incident to the location of our home five hundred miles west of civilization. She was far from being a romantic girl. At twenty-two years of age she was a woman of rare thoughtfulness and sobriety, and, judging correctly of the future, cheerfully approved the plan. I signed the compact, and that signature bound me to a lifework that continued while great states were born and nations rose and fell.[16]

---

[15]Sturtevant, J.M., _Autobiography_, p. 137.

[16]_Ibid._, pp. 136, 137.

On February 21, 1829, a solemn pledge or compact
was drawn up and signed by the seven members who composed the Illinois Association at that time. It is an
interesting and important document:

Believing in the entire alienation of the natural
heart from God, in the necessity of the influences
of the Holy Spirit for its renovation, and that
these influences are not to be expected without
the use of means; deeply impressed also with the
destitute condition of the western section of our
country and the urgent claims of its inhabitants
upon the benevolent at the East, and in view of
the fearful crisis evidently approaching, and
which we believe can only be averted by speedy
and energetic measures on the part of the friends
of religion and literature in the older states,
and believing that evangelical religion and education must go hand in hand in order to the successful accomplishment of this desirable object;
we the undersigned hereby express our readiness
to go to the state of Illinois for the purpose
of establishing a seminary of learning such as
shall be best adapted to the exigencies of that
country -- a part of us to engage as instructors
in the seminary -- the others to occupy -- as
preachers -- important stations in the surrounding country -- provided the undertaking be deemed
practicable, and the location approved by intelligent men -- and provided also the Providence of
God permit us to engage in it.

	Theron Baldwin
Theological Department	John F. Brooks
	Mason Grosvenor
Yale College	Elisha Jenney
	William Kirby
February 21, 1829	Julian M. Sturtevant
	Asa Turner, Jr.

The compact is endorsed as follows:

This certifies that the proposed establishment
of a Seminary of Learning in the State of Illinois, combined with the plan of Missionary
labor, has our entire and cordial approbation,
as one which is deemed of vital importance to
the best civil and religious interests of that
portion of our country, and promises to be more
efficiently useful by its early institution,
and by the enlarged and liberal views of its
patrons; and also, that the Gentlemen from

this Seminary, who propose to unite in the promotion of this object, are in our opinion, in a
high degree qualified for the undertaking in respect to ardent piety, discreet seal [sic] and
laborious perseverance, as well as by their
talents and literary acquisitions; and that an
equal number of young men, engaged in a preparatory course of Theological education, could
scarcely be selected, who promise to be better
prepared for the superintendence and instruction
of such a Seminary, and for the work of preaching the Gospel.

Yale College Feby. 23d, 1829.
            Nath. W. Taylor, Prof. Didact. Theol.
            Josiah W. Gibbs, Prof. Sacred Liter.

I fully concur in the above recommendations being
familiarly acquainted with a majority of the
Gentlemen and having satisfactory information
concerning the others.   [17]
            Jeremiah Day, Pres. Yale C.

Although the original Yale Band consisted of the
above seven members, the little group began to grow.
In addition to the original signers of the Compact, the
records of the Illinois Band include the names of William Carter, Benoni Y. Messenger, Henry Herrick, Albert
Hale, Romulus Barnes, Flavel Bascom, and Jairus Wilcox.
Lemuel Foster was also a member, although he did not
formally sign. [18]

---

[17]The original document is at Illinois College.

[18]Foster, Lemuel, Autobiography, pp. 1-2.   "Some of my
class at Yale, graduating in '28 were in t [the] company
there made up to come West as missionaries, & co-operated in starting a College at Jacksonville Illinois. I
was absent from t Theological Seminary there, when t
company was made up, in consequence of prostrated health,
& did not formally join t enterprise. But my heart was
in it, as to t missionary part, & as health improved
with relaxation & exercise, my arrangements were made
accordingly."

It was now necessary to make formal arrangements
with the American Home Missionary Society and Julian M.
Sturtevant was accordingly sent to New York to discuss
plans with the directors.

On March 7, 1829, a communication was sent to Ellis,
assuring him that "Illinois is the state which, of all
others, ought to be selected as the seat of our operations. . . . It becomes therefore, necessary that we
state to you fully and explicitly our views & wishes
in respect to the contemplated establishment. . . . We
proceed, therefore, to state the following principles
which we deem important to the success of a Seminary of
the higher order. 1st That there be a board of trustees,
of a limited number, who shall have the entire direction
of the concerns of the Seminary, independent of any ex-
traneous influence, except that they be sacredly pledged
to appropriate the donations which they may <u>choose</u> to
<u>accept</u> in accordance with the expressed wishes of the
donors. 2d That a majority of the board of trustees,
even after its organization have power to fill their own
vacancies."

"The Association at Yale volunteered to raise ten
thousand dollars for the institution, two thousand of it
to be furnished at once, and the remainder within two
years from that time."[19] The number of trustees would

---

[19] The rest of the letter to Ellis, dated March 7, 1829,
is as follows:
". . . [W]e have now laid before you the terms of
the proposed union and the opinions of men well qualified
to judge in respect to them. We further state it to be
our beleif [sic] that it is for the want of those fundamental principles we have laid down, that so many Seminaries for learning in the Eastern states, have been
transient in their prosperity. Many instances might be
adduced where this has been the true reason of their
failure. And such we beleive [sic] to be the state of
publick sentiment in this region, that no considerable
amount of funds could be raised for a Seminary, not
founded on these principles.
In respect to the terms of Union above stated, we
see not dear sir, why they might not be adopted. The
Second is the principal one, but this, as we suppose,
does not violate the principles stated in your communication. It gives the Stockholders in Illinois the
privilege of voting for Trustees in the first instance,
according to their shares of stock, while, at the same
[footnote continued on next page]

[footnote continued from previous page] time, it is far more favorable to those stockholders, that it would be, should we, with the funds which we promise to raise, proceed to elect Trustees, according to your principles of voting. This we wish not to do, for we are extremely desirous that the gentlemen in Illinois should have a full share in the management of the Institution. We know they are upon the ground, and are capable of judging. And we are very anxious that the whole plan of union should meet their unqualified approbation. For we do not feel like engaging in this enterprize without the full co-operation of yourself and other patrons of the Institution. We wish, therefore, that these proposals may be submitted to the stockholders, and their decision forwarded to us as soon as circumstances will permit. Please to state explicitly if there be any who are in the least dissatisfied with the terms of Union. If the decision of the stockholders cannot be obtained immediately, we shall be much obliged if you will consult, on the subject, with such gentlemen as may be at hand, and forward to us, without delay, your own and their opinion of the proposals, and the probable decision of the stockholders generally.

In respect to the location of the proposed Seminary, we have no reason to distrust it, but on the contrary, all the evidence we have goes to show it is the best that should have been selected. We are glad so far as to allow them to show its benefits, while at the same time we consider it in the highest degree desirable that it be, as it is, Presbyterian in its character. As to the objects designed to be accomplished by the Seminary, we approve of all which you have specified, and on condition that we become pledged to promote their accomplishment to the extent of our ability. We wish to see an Institution on that spot, where pupils can be fitted for college and for the various departments of active life, and where a thorough collegiate and ultimately professional education may be obtained. All this we do not suppose can be done in a day; but the object of our association will not be accomplished till all this shall be secured, and that too on a foundation so permanent as to be transmitted, as a rich legacy, to succeeding generations.

As we presume, sir, it has been your intention to erect, during the coming summer, a building, and make preparations for opening the school in autumn, we would express a wish that you would persist in doing so, suggesting, however, that it would be well to erect a building of considerable size, and containing several apartments, in order that it may answer our purpose for some time to come.

It is our present expectation that two, perhaps three of our number will be in Illinois in the month of October or Nov. next, when, if nothing objectionable. . ."(letter breaks off).

28

be limited to fifteen, only ten of which were to be chosen for the present. The Association realized that careful planning was necessary if the new project was to be a success. If there were any objections, they must be stated explicitly. "We wish to see an Institution there," they wrote, "in which pupils can be fitted for college and the various departments of life and in which a thorough collegiate and ultimately professional education may be obtained. All this we do not suppose can be done in a day; but the object of our association will not be accomplished until all this shall be secured and that too on a foundation so permanent as to be transmitted a rich legacy to succeeding generations."[20]

The terms of the Association were unanimously agreed on by the trustees in the west. With the assistance of John Ellis, who came east for the purpose, the $10,000 which had been pledged was raised with little difficulty.[21] Grosvenor was asked to accompany Peters and Ellis to Boston and Andover to present the project and help to raise funds. The project was received with hearty enthusiasm at Andover, and in New Haven, a public meeting was held one Sunday evening in one of the churches at which subscriptions amounting to some twelve hundred dollars were secured.[22] On April 14, 1829, the American Home Missionary Society formally appointed Sturtevant, Baldwin and Turner as missionaries to Illinois.[23] On Thursday, August 26, 1829, Baldwin and Sturtevant were ordained to the Christian ministry at Woodbury, Connecticut. The charge was given by Rev. Matthias Bruin of New York, as a representative of the American Home Missionary Society.[24] A few days later, Julian Sturtevant married Elizabeth Fayerweather and started west.

Born in 1805, in Warren, Connecticut, Sturtevant was one of a large family of thrifty New England farmers. As a boy, he heard the gifted preaching of Lyman Beecher, who "produced a powerful impression" on his mind. The War of 1812 brought economic depression to New England, and Sturtevant's parents decided to go west. On May 29, 1816, they began their long pilgrimage through New Jersey

---

[20] Grosvenor to Ellis. March 7, 1829. Hammond Library, Chicago Theological Seminary, Chicago, Illinois.

[21] Sturtevant, J.M., Autobiography, p. 142.

[22] Rammelkamp, C.H., Illinois College, A Centennial History, p. 30.

[23] Hall to Sturtevant, Letter Book C, Sept. 2, 1829, #128.

[24] Sturtevant, J.M., Autobiography, p. 142.

and Pennsylvania until they reached Tallmadge, Ohio. The rest of the summer was spent in building a log cabin, and by November, it was ready for use. Sturtevant says:

> Well do I remember the day we took up our abode in it. It was the 29th of November, 1816. The undergrowth only had been removed, leaving the giants of the forest, some of them more than a hundred feet in height, towering far above our frail shelter. Our chimney was constructed by cutting away a portion of the logs on one side of the cabin and building in the opening thus made a fireplace of stones laid in clay, and projecting outside the wall. Above the stone work, raised only high enough to avoid contact with the fire, the chimney was finished with sticks daubed with clay. The fireplace was very large, and I often stood partially within it and looked up the chimney at the tree tops which were waving far above it. Primitive as that habitation was, its rudeness was not its worst feature. It was entirely inadequate to protect us from the severities of such winters as those we found in northeastern Ohio. This was especially true of a house fresh built from green logs. That was a long and dreary winter. The rheumatism with which my father suffered and the colds of my mother and the rest of the family are painful to remember.[25]

In spite of the rigorous and exacting life of the frontier, the Sturtevants were anxious that their children should have educational opportunities, and so Julian and his older brother were sent to the academy at Tallmadge to study Latin and Greek, and prepare to enter Yale. When the time came for the boys to go east it was discovered that there was no money in the family treasury for the trip. "To us lads the plan seemed utterly impracticable," writes Sturtevant, "and we expected and even wished our parents to reject the proposition. I was especially averse to it, for the idea of going far from home among strangers, under circumstances so peculiar and so remote from the life to which I was accustomed, appeared intol-

---

[25]Sturtevant, J.M., _Autobiography_, pp. 47-48. _Cf_. also Bacon, Theodore D., _Leonard Bacon_, pp. 23ff. The town of Tallmadge was founded in 1805 by Leonard Bacon's father, David Bacon.

erable. . . . My vague and unreasoning dread was not removed, but my conscience was appealed to and the appeal
prevailed."[26]

In October, 1829, Julian and his bride said goodbye
to New England and started west for Illinois. It is not
necessary to go into a minute description of their trip.
From Albany they took the stage coach to Buffalo, being
careful to patronize the Pioneer Line, because "it was
managed on strictly Sabbath-keeping principles."[27] They
traveled from Schenectady to Utica by canal-boat. From
Buffalo to Erie they went by steamboat, and thence to
Cleveland by stage. After a short visit at Tallmadge,
they took the stage to Wheeling, and then sailed down the
Ohio, stopping at Cincinnati and Louisville. Eventually
they reached Saint Louis. Since there was no transporta-
tion between Saint Louis and Jacksonville, it was necessary to hire a "team and driver." Baldwin remained behind in St. Louis, while Sturtevant and the three ladies
proceeded on their way. It was Sunday morning, November
15, 1829, when the Sturtevants' long and tedious journey
was over, and they finally entered the village of Jacksonville.

The village was hardly impressive.

The people generally without capital, could yet
show few signs of thrift, and good lumber was
beyond the reach of any but the very wealthy.
There was no scarcity of timber, but it was hard
wood, mostly oak, unfit for finishing lumber.
Most of the houses were covered with boards
split from oak logs four feet in length, and
nailed on without shaving. Many roofs were
covered in the same way. Small houses and
many log cabins were built in hope that better
lumber would soon be accessible. The census
of 1830 gave Jacksonville a population of a
little over 600. This was the little town
that we saw in its somber robes on that Sabbath morning. . . .[28]

---

[26]Sturtevant, J.M., Autobiography, p. 55.

[27]Cf. Foster, Lemuel, Autobiography, p. 4. Hammond
Library, Rare Book Vault, Chicago Theological Seminary,
Chicago, Illinois.

[28]Sturtevant, J.M., Autobiography, p. 157.

During the next two months Sturtevant supplied the pulpit of John M. Ellis, who was away on missionary work. He also worked to complete the organization of the college. The building was not yet ready, but it was decided that college should be opened to students on the first Monday in January, and Sturtevant was to take entire charge. The ten thousand dollars had been raised, and more money was being deposited in the East, which the trustees could draw upon as the need arose. Samuel D. Lockwood, John P. Wilkinson and William C. Posey were elected as the three local trustees provided for in the agreement. At the same meeting the school was christened "Illinois College." "On Monday, the 4th of January, 1830, but one large room was ready for use. In it I found on that morning nine pupils assembled for instruction. It was the day of small things, but its inspiration was drawn from faith in God and the future. After reading from the Bible I briefly addressed the young men. The very spirit of our enterprise was expressed in my first sentence. 'We are here today to open a fountain where future generations may drink.' I then offered prayer committing the whole enterprise for the present and the long future to the care and protection of God."[29]

The work of the Yale Band in Illinois had begun.

---

[29]Sturtevant, J.M., _Autobiography_, p. 166.

CHAPTER III

AGENTS OF THE AMERICAN HOME MISSIONARY SOCIETY

Between the years 1833 and 1867, the American Home
Missionary Society employed five members of the Illinois
Band as agents for the Society in the State of Illinois.
Theron Baldwin was the first of this group to be appointed, accepting his commission in 1833. He was followed by Albert Hale, for a short time his co-worker,
then Flavel Bascom, William Kirby, and finally Elisha
Jenney, who resigned his commission in 1867. The special function of the Agent was to act as coordinator between the mission field and the Society. He was to visit
feeble and destitute churches and neighborhoods and encourage them to make efforts for the support of the Gospel. He was to communicate information and advice in
the locating of missionaries, promote the organization
of churches, investigate the claims of applicant congregations and preachers and report them to the Society.
And finally, he was expected to form auxiliary societies
and collect funds for the promotion of the Society's
work on the frontier.

To describe minutely the work of each Agent would
be unnecessary and tedious. We shall content ourselves
with a description of Theron Baldwin's agency as a
typical example, and then summarize briefly the work of
the other four members of the Illinois Band.

While Sturtevant was at Jacksonville, Theron Baldwin decided to settle at Vandalia as a pastor, where he
could labor to secure funds and a charter for the new
college. In many respects, Baldwin was the moving spirit
behind the Illinois Band. He was a man of indefatigable
energy. Born in Goshen, Connecticut, on July 21, 1801,
he grew up in a typical New England rural community.
Summers were spent on the farm. Winters were spent at
the Academy of the town. The family observed two traditional holidays every year, one at the end of the
corn-planting season, the other came at the end of haying time. Apparently the latter was a sort of literary
festival. The family gathered around the "Rostrum" --
a huge pile of boulders -- and heard one of the sons
deliver an oration. The Baldwin boys were in demand as
teachers, and three of them were engaged in teaching at
the same time in Goshen and adjacent towns. Theron,
however, was the quiet and thoughtful member of the
family, so that on one occasion his father remarked,
"Theron does not often speak, but when he does, he has

something to say worth hearing."[1]

Perhaps this gravity and seriousness was accentuated by his New England environment. The Baldwin family put much emphasis on religion, but Theron does not seem to have been particularly affected by it until the age of twenty. In April 1821, a revival occurred under Rev. Joseph Harvey and it was at the usual weekly prayer-meeting, during the singing of the hymn,

One only hope can now avail,
Christ has a weight to turn the scale,

that he made the commitment which was to mold his entire life. He was teaching school at the time, and "boarding around" as the custom was in those days. After hearing him lead family worship, Deacon Norton, an old friend, abruptly said to him: "You have a call to preach the Gospel. . . Do you know it?" A year later Theron decided to enter Yale College, and therefore secluded himself in the most retired room of his father's house to study Latin and Greek. In this, he was fortunate in having the assistance of his pastor, Rev. Joseph Harvey, to whose house he walked four miles twice a week. In 1823, his persistence was rewarded, and he was admitted to Yale College as a freshman. In a letter to a brother, just after he had entered college, he wrote, "Taking everything into consideration, I believe I am about as well fitted as could be expected from the manner in which I fitted. I guess it was not generally thought, when I first began to take my book under my arm, and stretch my solitary way over Ivy Mountain, that I should hold out long: but if we succeed in life, we shall have higher mountains to climb than Ivy Mountain."[2]

While in college, Baldwin distinguished himself as a student. He joined several debating societies and was elected to Phi Beta Kappa. He was energetic and industrious. "Do you know my cousin, Mr. Baldwin?" said a lady to one of his classmates. "Theron Baldwin? No; he has not been seen three feet from college since he entered it." It is to his credit that he stood high in his class, for one of his classmates was none other than Horace Bushnell.

---

[1] Sturtevant, J.M., "Life of Theron Baldwin," The Congregational Quarterly, April 1875, pp. 213ff.

[2] Ibid.

Sturtevant's description of the famous "Corollary Rebellion" is an excellent single example for an insight into Baldwin's character.

> In those times, perhaps it is still true, crises used sometimes to occur in college which put the moral principle and moral courage of the Christian student to a very severe test. Such crises did occur in his college life. One of them was that "Corollary Rebellion." It occurred in his class. The students claimed that they had received a promise from the tutors that certain corollaries in Conic Sections were to be omitted at the recitation; they were, however, required as part of the daily lessons. The greater part of the students in the class refused to recite unless these were omitted, and the thing was carried so far as to involve a large majority of the class in an open conflict with the government of the college. Mr. Baldwin's convictions of right would not allow him to join in the rebellion. To return to his home and thus escape from the excitement was only an indirect way of resisting the authorities of the college; for they could give no leave of absence under such circumstances. He had, therefore, no way open to him which satisfied his conscience but to attend recitations as usual, and face the storm of obloquy which assailed him from his classmates; this he therefore steadily persisted in doing. By experiences like this not only he, but many of his college friends, were in those times severely tried, and by the trial made stronger men for the rest of their lives. Colleges certainly were in those days admirable schools of virtue to those who would firmly resist temptation, but, like all the other conditions of human life, schools of vice to those who prefer lazily to float down the stream, rather than make progress upward towards the right, by bravely and stoutly rowing against the current of evil.[3]

It was during the summer of 1826 that Baldwin pledged himself to do missionary work, and Canada

---

[3]Sturtevant, J.M., "Life of Theron Baldwin," The Congregational Quarterly, April 1875, p. 219.

was the field he had chosen. He felt compelled to
finish his brother's work, cut short as it was by his
untimely death. With this thought in mind, he entered
Yale Theological Seminary in the fall of 1827. We have
already noticed his connection with the Society for
Christian Research, the reading of his famous essay,
and his resolution to go west with other members of the
Illinois Band. The fall of 1829 found him in Vandalia,
Illinois, which was then the capital of the state. Before coming west, however, he had been ordained toward
the end of August, 1829, by the Association of Litchfield South at Woodbury, Connecticut.[4] Then he made
the arduous journey west with his good friend Julian
Sturtevant.

According to the United States census for 1830, the
state of Illinois had a population of about 160,000.
The city of Chicago did not even exist. The bulk of
the population was in the southern part of the state,
clustered around Saint Louis in the west, and Vincennes
in the east. The northern half of the state was a
wilderness. Jacksonville was only a group of rudely
constructed dwellings. After spending a few days here,
Baldwin set off for the annual meeting of the State
Bible Society at Vandalia. He only intended to spend
the night at Vandalia, but he was induced to remain
until the Sabbath, when he preached at the communion
service of the little Presbyterian church. Early the
next week, he received an invitation from the church
to labor there as their pastor "for the winter and as
much longer as should suit his convenience." A church
building was under construction, but since it was not
finished, services were held in the State House. Two
hundred dollars would be subscribed for his support,
the other two hundred dollars coming from the American
Home Missionary Society. The town of Vandalia contained
only about four hundred people, but since it was the
capital of the state, it would exercise considerable
influence.[5] Another factor entered the picture. Illinois College needed a charter, and it soon became
apparent that a charter would not be obtained without
some difficulty. It was necessary, therefore, for
someone to keep in close touch with the Legislature.[6]

---

[4] A letter from Baldwin to Peters (American Home Missionary Society secretary) August 27, 1829 includes a line
from Noah Smith, a member of the Litchfield South Association.

[5] Baldwin to Peters, February 9, 1830 from Vandalia, Ill.

[6] Ibid, December 30, 1830 from Vandalia, Ill.

One of Baldwin's first acts was to establish a Sunday School. One Sunday he preached a sermon on the subject. Then he followed up his sermon by calling on everyone in the village. A school was soon organized, he becoming superintendent, librarian, and teacher.[7] It was at this time that the American Sunday School Union had announced its intention of establishing a Sunday School everywhere in the Mississippi Valley where it would be practicable. The first Illinois Sunday School Union was formed in a log school-house in Jacksonville. Baldwin was appointed secretary and made an extensive report at the first anniversary in Vandalia, December 8, 1830.[8]

The next seven years found Baldwin very active, especially in the cause of education. On May 21, 1830, he wrote,

> . . . Every step that I take here causes me to feel more and more the importance and necessity of education. I visited 27 families not long since in a section of this county in which there was not an individual who could read! There were in that part 52 families in all. I went to carry them the word of life, but they were unable to read it! They would gladly receive a bible but it was of no use to them! . . . <u>There is yet every thing to be done here on the subject of education.</u>[9]

---

[7] Baldwin to Peters, February 9, 1830.
"We have commenced a Sabbath School under very encouraging auspices, between 70 and 80 scholars the second Sabbath. Almost the entire influence of Vandalia is enlisted in its favor, and we hope and pray for happy results. Twenty four dollars have been subscribed for the purchase of a Library. A small but neat and commodious Meeting House is also nearly finished. The church consists of 12 members 4 males and 8 females, four of whom have been added by examination within a few weeks. There is also a Female Tract Society here and at their last meeting they passed a resolution to commence a monthly distribution of tracts. Meetings at present are well attended, considerable desire manifested to hear the Gospel preached and within a few weeks one individual has been led to make the anxious inquiry 'What shall I do to be saved?' We hope the Lord has mercy in store for this people."

[8] Baldwin to Peters, August 16, 1830 from Vandalia, Hammond Library, Chicago Technological Seminary, Chicago, Ill.

[9] Baldwin to Peters, May 21, 1830. A part of this letter [footnote continued on next page]

In the spring of 1831, the trustees of Illinois College appointed him to go east and raise funds for the institution. He went east again in 1832, 1833, and 1835. His first trip east enabled him to attend the "anniversaries" of the American Home Missionary[10] Society, at which he was invited to make a speech. In June, he took unto himself a wife, Miss Caroline Wilder, of Burlington, Vermont, who had been a close friend of his brother's.[11] Baldwin's work as agent for Illinois College and his struggle to secure a charter from the Legislature will be told in the chapter on education.

In October, 1831, Absalom Peters, secretary of the American Home Missionary Society was very anxious to appoint Baldwin as General Agent for the state of Illinois. The object of this appointment was

> that Mr. Baldwin may plead the cause of Domestic Missions in as many congregations as he may find it convenient to visit; that he may correspond with and visit the feeble and destitute churches & neighborhoods and encourage them to make efforts for the support of the Gospel, that he may assist by communicating information & advice in the location of missionaries, that he may promote the organization of churches, investigate the claims of applicant congregations and preachers, and report on the same to this Committee; that he may form Societies and associations auxiliary to the A.H.M.S., collect funds and pay them into the Treasury of the Auxiliary within whose bounds they may be contributed (except sums given directly to the Parent Society, for which he is to account to the Treasurer of the Same), and in other ways promote the great objects of the A.H.M.S., the enlargement of the church & the conversion of souls in these United States. . . .[12]

[footnote continued from previous page] was printed in the Home Missionary Journal for July 1830 (pp. 59-60). It is interesting to note how a missionary's letter would be edited carefully, and all comments excluded which might be offensive to the readers about whom he might be writing.

[10] Home Missionary Journal, June 1831, pp. 39-42.

[11] Sturtevant, J.M., Autobiography, p. 233.

[12] Letter Book E #222 October 25, 1831.

He was to be paid four hundred dollars and travelling expenses.

The position of Agent for the Society of a particular state was a job of considerable importance. The personality and character of the agent counted for much, and it was not easy to select a man who possessed the necessary rugged endurance which such an exhausting task required. At first, Baldwin travelled by horse, but this wore him out so, that he finally bought a small buggy, which a friend of his affectionately named "Pepper-box." As he travelled up and down the state, he would make a report of all he saw and did, and send it east to the American Home Missionary Society. Frequently his report was published in the Home Missionary Journal. In the summer of 1833, he and Albert Hale made an extensive tour in the northern part of the state, and in its November issue, the Society published his report in full.[13]

> In my last, I informed you of a contemplated tour through the northern part of this state. We returned a few days since, after an absence of seven weeks; having travelled more than 700 miles, and preached about 50 sermons.
>
> We were advised by some physicians not to attempt the tour, in consequence of the prevalence of the cholera; but a kind of Providence has preserved us. There has as yet been no cholera farther north than Morgan co;, except on the Mississippi river; so that the whole northern part, which we wished to visit, could be safely traversed, while the pestilence was spreading its ravages over the lower parts of this state, and different portions of Missouri. The cholera had just commenced its work of death, when we left Jacksonville, and had almost entirely passed off, at our return. An awful gloom has hung over this village for two months past; though the ravages of the pestilence have been light, compared with some other places. There have been about 50 deaths in all; no case here at present. At times during my absence, I had most serious apprehensions respecting the safety of my wife, as she was exposed, and frequently

---

[13] American Home Missionary Journal, November 1833, pp. 119-124.

raised the question whether it was not my duty
to return;   but the Lord appeared to be opening
the way for doing good;   and after having sol-
emnly committed the case to God, I resolved to
proceed, feeling that life and death were at
his disposal.   You have doubtless seen a notice
of the death of Mrs. Ellis and her two children,
all as it were by a single stroke!

Insufficient medical supplies and lack of adequate
sanitation facilities frequently cause fearful epidemics among pioneers.   One of the terrible scourges of
frontier life was the cholera, and during the summer
of 1833 there was a serious epidemic in Southern Illinois.   John M. Ellis was in Indiana at the time, and
it was several days before he received the sad news
about his family.[14]

Baldwin's report continues with an outline of his
tour.

I can only give you an outline of our tour.
From Jacksonville, we went to Quincy for the
purpose of holding a protracted meeting.   But
as we entered the place, one of the first
things that arrested our attention was the
preparation of coffins.   The cholera was there
in its most malignant form.   We remained but a
few hours.   There had been several deaths
since the previous morning.

Our route then lay through Hancock, M'Donough,
Fulton, Peoria, Tazewell, Putnam, La Salle, and
Cook Counties, to Chicago.

The first Sabbath we spent in Hancock co.   On
Saturday afternoon we had a 12 mile prairie
to cross, without even a trace to guide our
steps, and with very indefinite information
as to the point we ought to strike on the op-
posite side.   However, we missed our way but
a few miles, and about dark arrived at the
house of a gentleman recently from Connecticut, whose wife and sister are members of the
Presbyterian Church.   In the morning he sent
out messengers to give notice of preaching --

---

[14]Sturtevant, J.M., _Autobiography_, p. 201.

his nearest neighbour being one mile and three
fourths distant. He took pains, also, to yoke
his oxen, and bring and return one whole family; who lived about two miles from him. We
had a congregation of about 40, and at the close
of the service addressed the people with regard
to Sabbath Schools, and appointed a meeting for
the formation of one in that settlement. It has
since been formed. There was nothing of the kind
for 12 miles around.[15]

Missionaries frequently wrote about the perils of
travel. Since the American Home Missionary Society was
trying to lure young clergymen to the west, it was not
too anxious to give undue prominence to these trials and
difficulties. But every missionary had his share of them.

In consequence of recent and heavy rains, the
streams were very much swollen, and we employed
two or three hours in ineffectual attempts to
cross Crooked creek, about 12 miles from where
we spent the Sabbath. Br. Hale undertook to
swim one of the horses over, while I drove the
other in after him; but no sooner had his horse
reached the current, than he was overpowered, and
his rider plunged into the stream, and down they
were driven together towards a large drift of
wood that lay some distance below. This Br.
Hale with some difficulty succeeded in mounting,
and even then found the bridle around one arm.
He extricated himself, and the horses by powerful
struggles wheeled and swam out at the place of
entrance. For a little time, Br. Hale was in
great peril; but the Lord preserved him. The
next morning we succeeded in crossing some miles
above, by carrying our saddles across on a log,
and swimming our horses. In M'Donough we made
arrangements for a protracted meeting on our return.[16]

The explorers continued north along the Illinois,
Fox, and Dupage Rivers until they reached the little
town of Chicago.

Chicago is destined soon to be a place of great
importance. It is fast becoming a great thorough-
fare; furnishing as it does, the only harbour on
all that portion of the lake; especially when the

_____

[15]American Home Missionary Journal, November 1833, pp.
119-124.
[16]Ibid.

canal, or railroad is opened, there must be a
vast amount of business drawn to that point.
It has increased with astonishing rapidity the
present season. I was told, that since the
opening of spring, not far from 70 buildings
of all sorts, had been erected, or were under
way. There are more than 20 stores, of different kinds; and I regret to add, that, with
few exceptions, they traffic in ardent spirits.
I had been for some time desirous of visiting
that place with reference to the location of a
missionary; and we were delighted to find it
not only an important point for labour, but already occupied by one of your missionaries. We
remained there about a week, for the sake of a
little relaxation, preached five sermons, and,
of course, learn from brother Porter the particulars of his situation and prospects. I
saw nothing in Chicago to induce the belief
that the morals of the people generally were
below other new towns of a similar character.
No instance of intoxication, on the part of
the white man, fell under my notice.[17]

The missionary on the frontier, regardless of his
denomination, was out to save souls. That was his primary purpose for being on the frontier, and he addressed
his message to all races of people alike. One common
method of getting the attention of people on things spiritual was to hold a protracted meeting. Meetings would
be arranged to be held at convenient points in new counties, and they would be continued one, two or four days,
as the case might be, where scattered Christian families
who lived five, ten, or twenty miles away, could be
gathered together. If the region was "destitute," an
attempt would be made to establish a church, and if possible to locate a home missionary there. For the first
year or two, the American Home Missionary Society would
furnish most of the money necessary to support such a man.
But it would always insist that the people do something
to support their own minister. Gradually the society
would withdraw its aid until the newly-founded church
could support itself. By 1837, the Congretational and
Presbyterian churches of Illinois were almost self-supporting.[18]

---

[17] American Home Missionary Journal, November 1833, pp.
122-123.

[18] Baldwin to Peters, Alton, April 12, 1837; and April 19,
1837.

Baldwin was frequently faced with opposition of one kind of another. One of his duties as agent, was to assist and advise in the location of missionaries. A church would apply to the Society's Agent for financial aid. The Agent would then examine the request, and usually pen a brief note on the church's application, which he then sent to the home office in New York. There would be not a little prejudice against easterners. "Any preacher who cannot succeed in N.E. had better stay at home than come into this field," he wrote.[19]

> . . . the Eastern preacher . . . is not unfrequently the very "antipodes" of his audience, and sometimes even looked upon as a mysterious, suspicious being from another hemisphere or another planet. Since my residence in the State I have travelled 2000 miles or more in different directions, and it is my settled conviction that for the Eastern preacher who expects to settle permanently in this State, it is all important there be at first travel a great deal, and mingle with the people, acquaint himself with their manners and customs, their sentiments prejudices &c &c. He has as a general fact many points which must be knocked off before it is possible for him to come in close contact with this people, and if he is unable to do this where is the prospect of his usefulness? Any preacher in fact who is ignorant of the character of his audience, discharges his arrows "at a venture."[20]

Often there would be denominational rivalry, particularly between Old School and New School men. On at least one occasion, he had to remove suspicions and establish amicable relations with some Old School Presbyterians who were doing missionary work under the Assembly's Board. Cases of friction were frequent, and often the cry of heresy was raised.[21] Clashes would occur with regard to the proper method of conducting missionary enterprises. Old School Presbyterians were suspicious of the Society's activities. Baldwin says that they were trying to push

---

[19] Baldwin to Peters, December 15, 1830, from Vandalia, Illinois.

[20] Ibid., August 16, 1830, from Vandalia, Illinois.

[21] Cf. letters to Peters dated January 5 and January 8, 1831, and July 1, 1833.

the New School men into the northern half of the state
as much as possible.[22]

---

[22]Baldwin discussed the whole problem with Peters in a
letter dated January 5, 1831, from Edwardsville, Illinois.
". . . But to the real object of my letter. I was
unexpectedly thrown into Galeanda (?) where I found br.
B.F. Spellman who thinks that New School men can wander
but a few steps more from the Confession of Faith and
have any hope of salvation. He told me that the Rev.
W.R. Steward had been appointed Agent of the Assembly's
Board upon his recommendation, and that was given in consequence of my appointment. He would have me to understand that most of the churches in the Kaskaskia Presbytery were in harmonious action with the A.B. and expressed a desire that their quiet might not be disturbed
by the efforts of Home Missionary men. Brother Hale had
been warmly recommend(ed) also by him to take up the line
of his march northward till he had at least passed the
northern boundary of the section consecrated to the operations of the A.B. Br. Brooks had received similar
advice (though given in rather a rude manner) from Mr.
Stewart. It happened however that he soon became stationed at Collinsville & Belville (sic) Brother Hale so
far acted in accordance with the friendly advice given
as to proceed as high up in the State as Vandalia,
preached there and in the surrounding region till my arrival. Among other places he preached at Greensville
Bond Co which church is in part formed into an Auxiliary
to the A.B. The news of his appointment reached some
members of the Bethel Church in the same Co. and they
traveled 8 miles on the Sabbath to hear him preach. After services they asked him whether he had come from the
A.B. & then invited him very warmly to come and preach
among them on the following Sabbath. He did so last
Sabbath and has received a unanimous & pressing invitation to preach for them, which he has concluded to do
for the Winter. A wide and effectual door has thus unexpectedly opened for him. This is the largest church
in the State and one which we had not regarded as H
Missionary ground. The circumstances which preceded and
attended Br Hale's invitation to this place are of a
character peculiarly interesting considered in reference
to the bearing upon the operation of the two Boards in
Illinois. The Kaskaskia Presbytery had sent up to the
Convention resolutions exclusively in favor of the A.B.
and it was the evident intention to cleanse that Pres
of all heresy by keeping out all H M men. This was considered an important church and the Agents and friends
[footnote continued on next page]

Then, too, there were frequent clashes with Universalists. The preaching of universal salvation for all was looked upon as a doctrine of Satan, and it was the duty of all Presbyterians to oppose it vehemently. There was also a fear of Catholicism. The Catholic influence was strong around Saint Louis, and always threatened to permeate Illinois. "Batteries of light" had to be erected to beat back the invader.[23]

[footnote continued from previous page] of the A B had left no artifice untried to promote its purity. Hamilton, Fraser Spellman & Bouton done (sic) their utmost to bring it over to the faith, Mr. Stewart preached there once on the subject, made an attempt and failed, then a second time and failed, and has another appointment there for next Sabbath. The friends of the A.B. had urged the thing with so much pertinacity and handled the subject in such a manner as to disgust many members of the church, and when br Hale arrived were so full that they were ready to burst out. Their first vote on the subject stood 9 for A H M S & 5 for the A.B. but at his second visit Mr. Stewart urged them to rescind it & form an association & assured them if they would he would agree to supply their pulpit gratuitously one sabbath in four till they should get a minister from the A.B! He pressed the matter till they agreed to carry the vote through the entire church. When Br Hale arrived this was going on & had already produced much excitement, and a serious division of the church was feared. A proposition was now made to stop the voting and be auxiliary to neither Board, which carried at once as br Hale had corrected some false statements which had been made there respecting the A H M S (such as that it may send out Baptists Methodists infidels Roman Catholics &c) and urged them to go the whole for the A B rather than have a division. They were in such distress that they thought of sending a special message to Vandalia for me to go and visit them & they have sent an express invitation (which I have complied with) to me to be present next Sabbath with Mr Stewart who I suppose will go with the expectations of finding them all loyal subjects of the A B. This seasonable arrival of br Hale has powerfully reminded us of the following passage in Isaiah: And the hail shall sweep away the refuge of lies."

[23]Baldwin to Peters, December 24, 1834 from Jacksonville, Illinois.

The rigors of frontier life did not leave much time for schooling and higher education. "There is yet every thing to be done here on the subject of education," he wrote in 1830. In one part of Illinois he went to carry the Word of Life, but a Bible was of no use to the people because they could not read.[24] Frequently, the Home Missionary Society would put an appeal in its journal for young teachers to go west and start schools.[25] Sometimes the educated minister was looked upon with distrust. This prejudice against education is curiously reflected in the opposition which Baldwin met in his attempt to secure a charter for Illinois College.

> Col. Mather . . . is warm in the College cause. He applied to me to write a Report for the Com to present. So I spent two days of severe labor in making out one. I think it will either bring the charter or produce an explosion among the Honorables one of whom declared on the floor of the House last week that we has "almost literally born in a brier thicket, cradled in a hay-trough & reared in the Western wilds where the harmful seeds of a liberal education had never been permitted to intrude & check the youth of true born natural liberty."[26]

A voluminous correspondence exists between Theron Baldwin and Absalom Peters, secretary of the American Home Missionary Society. Nor was the Society unappreciative of the excellent work of their Agent. In 1834, when Baldwin was considering a call from the Presbyterian Church at Jacksonville, Peters wrote urgent letters, begging him not to resign from the Agency. "If you leave it, we know of no man to take your place," he wrote.[27]

Baldwin's letters and reports were frequently published in the Home Missionary Journal, so that readers became quite familiar with his work in Illinois. In June, 1835, the first of a series of "Letters to Young Men" appeared. These were seven in number, one appearing each month until the end of the year. The object of these

---

[24] Baldwin to Peters, May 21, 1830, from Vandalia, Illinois.

[25] American Home Missionary Journal, Vol. III, p. 60, July 1830.

[26] Baldwin to Peters, from Jacksonville, January 29, 1835.

[27] Peters to Baldwin, March 17, 1834.

46

letters was to draw young missionaries to the state of
Illinois and to the West in general. The letters give
a good description of Baldwin's own work, and describe
the need of competent and consecrated young clergymen
on the frontier. No one was better qualified to speak
with authority than he. His travels throughout the state,
and his frequent trips to the East made him a well-known
figure in missionary circles.

> My travel during the year ending April 11 1837
> amounted to 3600 miles. Sermons & public ad-
> dresses delivered 86, letters written more than
> 200; subscriptions obtained say from $1800 to
> $2000, Money raised from two individuals to build
> meeting houses in destitute places $700 . . .[28]

During this period he was in frequent touch with
many members of the Yale Band and was tacitly acknowledged
as their leader. Baldwin's formal connection with the
American Home Missionary Society was relatively brief,
however, lasting only until April 1837. For the rest of
his life he was to be identified with education in the
new states, first as principal of the Monticello Female
Seminary, and later as the secretary of the Society for
the Promotion of Collegiate and Theological Education at
the West. His work as a missionary educator will be told
in a subsequent chapter.

His zeal for the missionary cause was unflagging.
He had a reputation for great vigor and almost tireless
energy. He was greatly admired by all who knew him, for
he was truly a man of self-sacrifice and devotion.
Nevertheless, he was very human and genial; his correspondence shows a penchant for making puns.[29] His service
as Agent for the Home Missionary Society can hardly be
overestimated, for his work was so good that the Society
drew on other members of the Band during the next thirty
years to carry on the work which he had begun.

Closely associated with Theron Baldwin, was another
member of the Yale Band, Albert Hale. Little is known
of his early life. He was born in 1799, in Glastonbury,
Connecticut. When he was fourteen years old he was clerk-
ing in a store at Wethersfield. Sometime between the
years 1819 and 1821 he had a conversion experience. "Up

---

[28]Baldwin to Peters, April 19, 1837, from Alton, Illinois.

[29]Baldwin to Peters, January 29, 1835, "They have had some
trouble there as I expected with Mr Lawry . . . their sky
seems to be a little lowry just at this time . . . ."

to this time," we are told, "he was very gay and worldly-minded, and read his Bible only to make fun of it."[30] As soon as he was converted, however, he decided to study for the ministry. He went to Yale, was graduated in the class of 1827, and soon after joined the Illinois Band.[31] He arrived in Illinois toward the end of 1830, and for the first eight years of his labor he spent half of his time at the Presbyterian Church of Bethel, Illinois, and the other half of his time with Theron Baldwin as a co-laborer. In the fall of 1839 he became pastor of the Second Presbyterian Church at Springfield, where he labored for a little more than twenty-seven years. He eventually "gave up this position at length for what he called his uncanonical congregation. 'The church could get a pastor,' he said, 'but those in the highways and hedges could not.'"[32] He became a city missionary. In spite of mediocre health all through his life, he lived to the age of ninety-one or two.[33]

Albert Hale was a man of deep piety and Christian humility. He also seems to have been a very convincing preacher. He had not been at Bethel long before a revival occurred in his church which attracted considerable attention from other missionaries in Illinois. In a letter to a friend, which was later published in the Home Missionary Journal, Hale gives an account of the revival:

> I must tell you what the Lord has been doing for my dear people. When I wrote you last, you recollect that a few had hopefully passed from death to life. The spring was then just coming on, and my health rapidly declined. For several weeks it seemed to me that I should preach but little more, and, what was still worse, I saw evident marks of decline in the work of grace which God had been carrying on among us. We had now a four days' meeting appointed, to commence on Thursday before the fourth Sabbath in May. I looked forward to

[30]Sketches of the class of 1827 in Yale Memorabilia.

[31]Rammelkamp, C.H., Illinois College, A Centennial History, p. 25. There is no correspondence extant from Hale until 1842.

[32]Biographical sketches of the class of 1827, Yale Memorabilia.

[33]Letter of A. Hale to J.E. Roy, May 2, 1876.

the meeting with trembling. For a few Sabbaths previous to the meeting, the Lord enabled me to preach on several topics, which
were much blessed to the awakening of my
people. Deep feeling often pervaded the congregation, and my hopes respecting the meeting
were strengthened. Brothers Lippincott, Brooks,
Messenger, and T.A. Spilman, assisted me through
the meeting; also, Brothers Watson and Ewing
were with me a part of the time, and took part
in the exercises. The brethren came to the
meeting in the spirit of their Master, and during its continuance, it may truly be said, that
they preached the gospel with the Holy Ghost
sent down from heaven. Scarcely had the meeting begun, when it was manifest that the Lord
was with us. The countenances of impenitent
sinners and the prayers and anxieties of Christians, indicated it. On Friday we separated the
inquirers from the rest of the congregation, by
calling them forward to particular seats. But
few came. It was an awful moment to both saints
and sinners. One young man, who was sitting on
the seat which we requested should be cleared
for inquirers, a son of one of my elders, after
waiting to hear the invitation, and while bur-
thened with deep feeling, arose and left the
house. Others occupied his seat, and, after a
short address, his father was called upon to pray.
He poured out his soul in prayer, and when he
mentioned the case of children with pious parents, it was overwhelming. He could not utter
his feelings, and it was the pouring forth of
groanings which could not be uttered. The son
stood without, weeping. Saturday our house could
not contain the congregation, and we arranged the
seats in a little sacred grove in front of the
house. During this day, the feeling was increased,
and from twenty to thirty took the seats of inquirers, most of whom were deeply burdened with
a sense of sin and ruin, and one or two thought
they found peace in believing. In the meantime,
an increasing spirit of prayer and faithfulness
was manifested on the part of Christians. Sabbath was a great day. Our communion was deeply
solemn and interesting. The disciples of our
Lord Jesus ate and drank in remembrance of Him.
Ten, most of whom were the fruits of the work of
grace the winter past, and generally members of
the Sabbath School, for the first time commemor-
ated the dying love of Christ. At the close of

49

the afternoon service, an inquiry meeting presented a scene of deep interest. The inquirers
were requested to go to the meeting house, while
Christians remained at the stand to pray. About
60 resorted to the house, all of whom were in
deep distress. Sighs, sobs, and groans, could
be heard from every part of the house. Some
hopefully passed from death unto life. Such
was the state of things, that it was deemed
imprudent to close the meeting that night; and
accordingly notice was given that the religious
exercises would be continued through another
day. This was the last, and truly the great day
of the feast. Our congregation this day (Monday)
was not so large as on the Sabbath, but our
seasons of worship were scarcely less solemn
than the scenes of the judgment. Christians
had felt and prayed before, but this day they
were in agony for sinners. When the invitation
was given for the inquirers to go to the meeting
house for conversation, nearly every impenitent
sinner on the ground rose, and seemed in haste to
reach the place. The few that stayed back were
persuaded by their friends to accept the invitation. And now commenced a scene which will not
soon be forgotten. Those who were hoping were
seated by themselves, the anxious all around them.
Soon one left her seat, and placed herself among
those who entertained a hope of pardon; then another and another. This awakened the deepest
distress among those who were left. Many were
unable to restrain their feelings. In the course
of about three hours, probably twenty, or more,
hopefully passed from death to life. But few
were left, and some of these thought they found
the Saviour that night after leaving the ground.
At sunset we repaired to the stand, and closed
the exercises of this meeting by prayer, and
singing "Bless'd be the tie," &c. I have seen
most of the converts since the meeting, and in
general they appear well.[34]

He then adds this amazing paragraph:

You know the state of my congregation before the
meeting -- that an unusually large proportion
were pious. The Lord now almost seems to have

---

[34]Home Missionary Journal, August 1832, pp. 55-57.

finished up his work of saving mercy here.
Only two individuals, among the members of
my congregation who are heads of families,
remain out of the ark of safety, and they
are inquiring! In some families, where
one, two, or three persons were unconverted,
the Lord has finished the work! Indeed,
when I go around among my people, I hardly
know where to look for the impenitent sinners; but few are found who are not indulg-
ing hope of pardoning mercy, through the
blood of Christ.[35]

The revival was such a success that it was reported
by other missionaries, and received considerable notice
in the Home Missionary Journal.[36]

By 1834, things had quieted down a bit. It was at
this time that the Presbyterian church at Jacksonville
issued an invitation to Theron Baldwin to become pastor.
If he accepted, this would mean that the agency for the
American Home Missionary Society would pass to Hale.
Hale was very reluctant to have this happen, and there
is no doubt that his influence added to that of others
prevented Baldwin from accepting the call. Hale realized
all too well the crying need for preaching and churches
in other parts of the state. Yet he was very reluctant
to leave good work which had been begun at Bethel. He
and Baldwin attempted to secure the aid of a Cumberland
Presbyterian in the work of missionary exploration, but
the plan fell through. But although Hale had to spend
a part of his time with Baldwin acting as agent for the
Society, visiting and fostering the numerous feeble
churches and destitute communities of Presbyterians and
Congregationalists, his own church continued to prosper
even in his absence.[37] But having the charge of a con-

---

[35] Home Missionary Journal, August 1832, pp. 55-57.

[36] Messenger, B.Y., to the Society; published July 1832,
pp. 39-40; also, Home Missionary Journal for February
1833, pp. 158-159.

[37] Hale to Peters, July 1, 1834 printed in the Home Missionary for September 1834, pp. 89-90.
   "Since my return to my own people, we have held a
sacramental meeting. I regretted that it was out of my
power to spend even a single Sabbath with them, before
the time of the meeting. But so it was. Owing to other
engagements I was absent for nine Sabbaths in succession,
[footnote continued on next page]

gregation one-half of the time and itinerating the other was too laborious for his constitution, and he began to sink under it. During the winter of 1834-5 he left Bethel, and accompanied Baldwin on a trip to Louisiana.

By the spring of 1835, Hale was back in Illinois again. An invitation came to take charge of the church at Springfield. He was undecided what course to follow: The Springfield church would support him so that he would no longer have to rely upon the Society. Nevertheless, he was very reluctant to leave Bethel, and his work as missionary agent. He therefore declined the offer.[38]

In the summer of 1836, Albert Hale made a trip to northern Illinois and into Wisconsin. Here he was impressed by the great possibilities for service in a new territory which was just being opened up. Wisconsin's population rose from 30,000 in 1840 to 300,000 in 1850.[39] With this ever-increasing tide of immigration, the American Home Missionary Society tried to keep pace. On September 27, 1836, Hale wrote from Jacksonville:

> I have recently returned from a tour to the northwestern part of the state, and to Wisconsin Territory.

[footnote continued from previous page] prior to that on which the sacrament was to be administered. It must, however, be remembered, that my people do not forsake the assembling of themselves together for religious worship, both on the Sabbath, and once statedly during the week, whether they have a preacher with them or not. Whenever I am absent preaching the Gospel to others, by express arrangement, they make mention of me in their prayers to God; and it ought to be particularly noticed and remembered with gratitude to the great Head of the Church, that when on my recent return I met my dear people in the prayer meeting, and related to them the wonders of God's grace which I had witnessed abroad; they in turn informed me, that, though they had always, on former occasions of my absence remembered me with interest, yet they had never before had such freedom of access to the throne of grace in my behalf as on this occasion. Surely it should be the heathen, if anybody, who ask "Where is thy God?"

[38] Hale to Peters, June 6, 1835.

[39] Turner, Frederick Jackson, The Frontier in American History, p. 227ff.

My journey was principally in the lead mine district, and East of the Mississippi River. Brother Kent, of Galena, and myself, visited the principal villages and settlements. We found no minister of our denomination, and very few of any other. Indeed, we have no missionaries northwest of Rock River, except Brother Kent and brother Watson at DuBuque.

In Wisconsin Territory, with a population of 25,000, there are not more than four or five ministers, that we could hear of, of all denominations. The population of the Territory is somewhat peculiar. A far greater portion of them are foreigners[40] (Germans) than of the people of Illinois. They are, as a body, more intelligent. There is more open wickedness -- such as intemperance and gambling -- more infidelity, or rather, it is more bold and open; and there is more money. We need, immediately, two missionaries, to plant within forty miles of Galena. But they must be men -- men of sound minds, and warm hearts -- men who can meet opposition, and bear insults, and who are willing to labour hard, and bear reproach, for Christ's sake.

It must not be forgotten, that churches in Wisconsin are as scarce as ministers. All is new. There are a few professors of religion, scattered over the field, panting for the bread and water of life, and a large number, who once were enrolled among the people of God, but are now twice dead, and among the most formidable obstacles to the progress of religion.[41]

To which was appendaged this comment by the Society:

We wish it were in our power to furnish, immediately, the men that are needed for the field which our brother has surveyed. But where shall we look for them? The cry comes to us, on almost every breeze, "men! men!" And what shall we say?

---

[40]Turner, Frederick Jackson, The Frontier in American History, p. 227ff.

[41]Hale to Peters, September 27, 1836, from Jacksonville, Illinois.

Shall we say to the perishing, your case is
indeed deplorable, but it is also irremediable?
You need help, but there is no help for you?
Dark as your prospects are without a preached
Gospel, you must go to your graves and to the
judgment-seat without it? And shall we say
this in the name of the churches of our Lord
Jesus Christ, and in the name of his ministering servants, and in the name of hundreds of
young men, who have within a few years been
brought into the kingdom, and but few of whom
have consecrecrated their energies to the ministry of reconciliation? Are our Christian
brethren prepared, to share with us the responsibility of such a reply? Or will they inquire
earnestly and prayerfully, what the Lord will
have them to do, in this critical condition of
Zion? What are the causes of the present alarm-
ing scarcity of religious teachers? Is the tone
of piety in the church what it ought to be?
Is the command of Christ obeyed, pray ye the
Lord of the harvest, that he will send forth
labourers into his harvest? Are there no more
of the sons of the church, that will come forward to minister at her altars? And must this
fearful disparity between our destitutions and
our means of supply continue to increase, and
the kingdom of heaven are long be taken from us,
and given unto those who will bring forth the
fruits of it?[42]

Not only was there a dearth of men, but some of the
clergymen who did come, came for other motives than
Christian service. Many others found it necessary to
work at other trades, or farm, in order to support themselves and their families. Baldwin and Hale were vigorously opposed to this dividing of one's time and interests.

A minister is much needed for Carthage, the
county seat in Hancock Co. the brother who
resides there having been so much engaged in
the business of setting up Wind Mills that
his religious influence is utterly blown away.[43]

Sometimes the Society accidentally gave commissions
to men who were unworthy. Then there was the strong

---

[42]Home Missionary Journal, December 1836, p. 139.

[43]Hale to Peters, Jacksonville, Illinois, February 7, 1837.

temptation to speculate in land. Since money was often
scarce and salaries slow in being paid, the temptation
to raise money by other means was a real one. The case
of the Reverend A. B. Church evoked severe condemnation:

Br Baldwin informs me that some months ago Rev.
A.B. Church was commissioned by the A.H.M.S. to
come to this state & as he has been here & returned
& as we understand is on his way hither again we
have deemed it our duty (& certainly a most painful duty) to state a few facts in relation to him
that the Ex. Com of your Socy. (if they have given
him a Comn.) may not be in the dark. His business letters which he wrote to several of the
brethren before his coming were offensive by their
worldly spirit & in one instance at least drew on
him a severe reproof. On my recent tour I scarcely
visited a village between this & Galena where I
did not hear of him & that in a most unpleasant way.
The universal account of him being that he was the
keenest speculator in Illinois. On my arrival at
Galena, I inquired as to the truth of a report that
he (Mr. Church) had entered land on the sabbath &
was informed by Br Kent as follows, vz. That he
arrived at Galena in the stage on the sab. about
10 A.M. and went to the sabbath school & made himself known to Mrs. Kent (Br. K. being absent) &
offered to preach but as no appointment was out he
was put off. He returned to the public house & at
the tea table got a gentleman (professor of religion) to point out to him the clerk in the Land
Office. This was done & as soon as supper was
over he went to the clerk & giving him $2 asked
permission to go into the Land Office. The privilege was granted & tho' he could not lawfully
enter land that day still he managed by taking
preliminary measures to get what he wanted when
the Office was opened the next day. The clerk
had no regard to religion & soon set the report
in circulation that a minister had by bribing him
&c got into the Land Office & secured him land on
the sab. & the infidels & scoffers & opposers of
every name filled the village with the report.
Mr. C. however did not wait to hear the report
but was off on another tour for land. On his
return to the Land Office at Galena he spent another sab. & offered to preach. B. Kent told
him of the reports in circulation & that under
the circumstances he could not invite him to
preach as his conduct had given offence to the
friends of Cht. & opened wide the mouths of

opposers. In short he told him he could not
preach unless he would make a public confession
of his faults. This he consented to do & on
the sab. morng before the congn. he rose &
rather explained than confessed what had happened. He said he offered the stage driver
$20 to get him in to Galena on SatY before
the Land Office closed, as he was afraid some
one would enter the land he wanted but as he
would not he came in on sab. & his excuse for
doing business at the L. Office on the Sab.
was that he was brot up in N. Eng. where he was
accustomed to keep SatY night & that he did not
go to the office till after sunset but the man
who pointed out to him the clerk of the L. Office says it was before sunset. The explanation
was not satisfactory to Br Kent who preached in
the morning & at the close of the services he
stopt the male members of the church & referred
the case to them as Mr. Church was expecting in
the P.M. The members of the church decided that
Mr. Kent should preach again in the P.M. & that
it was inexpedient for Mr. Church to preach there.
This Mr. C came to this state highly recommended
by Dr. Humphrey & Dr Wood & others & it is due to
such men that they know the conduct of such men
whom they recommend. It is with pain that we
make these statements but we feel compelled to
do it. The cause of God is bleeding at every
pore. Unless our ministers cease speculating
& ministers from abroad cease to come among us
to speculate & break the sabbath & promote the
spirit of worldliness & other ministers still
cease to send their money & employ their agents
to speculate in land I know not what we may not
expect. If Mr. C. is commissioned by your SocY
I trust he is not sent to us for advice about
location. I lack wisdom for such a work. May
the Lord give us all wisdom & grace to live
above the world.[44]

But such men were exceptions. The great majority of
men whom Hale recommended to the Society for financial
aid were devoted to the cause of Christ and the work of
the church in Illinois. One letter recommends "aid for
D. Nelson to labor in destitute places in Adams County."[45]

---

[44]Hale to Peters, September 27, 1836, from Jacksonville,
Illinois.

[45]Ibid., February 7, 1837, from Jacksonville, Illinois.

Two weeks later he recommends aid for Cyrus Watson preaching at Bloomington and Waynesville. A similar recommendation was made for Milton Kimball preaching at Augusta in Hancock Co. Another letter requests aid for Hugh Barr at Carrollton; "the population of that place & all the surrounding country is rapidly on the increase & Br. Barr is a useful & successful preacher & in our view should be commissioned according to his request."[46] Another letter tells of a recent visit to Peoria, where he talked with Rev. I.M. Gumbell, the German missionary who was commissioned for Illinois or Missouri. He had been preaching in Chicago, but since little or nothing could be raised for his support, he had applied to Baldwin for aid from the A.H.M.S. On talking with Hale at Jacksonville, he was advised to locate at or near Beardstown, since there were numerous Germans there, many of them wealthy and well-educated, some being graduates of German universities.[47] One is impressed by the numerous places which Hale visited, and the many applications which passed through his hands. In a very real sense the Agent of the Society was the co-ordinating link between the fields of service in the West, and the financial and ministerial resources in the East. The Home Missionary Journal did not fail to acknowledge his important work:

> The Rev. Theron Baldwin and the Rev. Albert Hale have divided the Agency of this state between them during the last year, each of them devoting about half of his time to the service of the Home Missionary Society. Their reports are highly encouraging. Their labors have been abundant, and have been attended with much success, not only in the collection of funds and the strengthening of feeble churches, but also in the promotion of revivals and the conversion of souls. Their receipts for the Society have been about $2000 . . . .[48]

A year later the Society reported:

> The Rev. Albert Hale has continued to prosecute his labors for the Society in Illinois.

---

[46] Hale to Peters, April 20, 1837, from Alton, Illinois.

[47] Ibid., June 23, 1837, from Fairfield, Illinois.

[48] Home Missionary Journal, June 1837, p. 24.

The amount of funds raised on this field has
been $1,500. But, encouraging as this may be
regarded, considering the circumstances of that
new country, the benefits of the agency, in
visiting and encouraging the feeble churches,
in teaching them the amount, and assisting them
in the development of their own resources, have
been still more valuable to the cause than the
mere amount of pecuniary collections. It is in
contemplation to organize a board of agency for
this state, and its immediate vicinity, similar
to those which operated with such happy results
on other parts of the great field.[49]

In 1837, the entire country underwent another of a
series of economic depressions. The years immediately
preceding the Panic of 1837 were marked by a great extension of credit, and a rage for speculation. When the
crash came, landowners could not collect rents nor could
they pay interest or taxes. Specie was so scarce that
every bank in the country had to use notes. Money almost ceased to exist on the frontier. President Van
Buren did little to try to alleviate the situation.
Although the panic came in 1837, it was not until 1842
that the country really recovered.[50]

A financial depression is always very severe on
educational and missionary institutions. The American
Home Missionary Society had its full share of problems.
The venerable Absalom Peters retired, and his place was
taken by Milton Badger, a pastor in Andover, Massachusetts. Charles Hall, treasurer of the Society confessed
that "we are embarrassed exceedingly, & how we are to
get along we can't tell. We pray, work & trust, but
see we cannot . . . ."[51] "On examination of my affairs,"
wrote Hale, "I find myself falling into debt."

It is painful to me to ask the SocY to add a
farthing to my salary. I know & deeply feel
that every dollar committed to your hand is
consecrated to God, but it will do no good

[49] Home Missionary Society Journal, June 1838, p. 37.

[50] Harlow, Ralph Volney, A History of the United States,
pp. 315-6.

[51] Charles Hall to Albert Hale, September 21, 1837.

for me to go on in this way & at a year's
end be bankrupt. Nor will it benefit the
SocY to have an agent in trouble with his
pecuniary matters. I am not about to ask
the SocY to pay off my debts which amount
to some $300 but to ask that my salary be
raised to $500 . . . . the carriage in
which I ride is about worn out in the service, it needs very thorough repairs or a
new one.   Repairing will be likely to cost
$20 or $30, a new one of the most ordinary
sort $70 to $90. . . . It is painful for
me to ask the SocY to do these things for
me, but when I remember that within the last
5 months I have rejected one place where my
salary would have been $800 and another of
$900 & also that I have just sent back a re-
fusal to an invitation to a church where,
tho' no salary is named it would doubtless
have been about the same, & also that one
of the causes of my present embarrassment
is the loss of my horse which I was obliged
to replace at an expense of $100, I feel
that justice to myself & the cause too requires that the burden be in part removed.[52]
. . .

The Society granted his requests, but someone else
offered to take care of the repairs on his carriage, so
he sent the Society a bill for $2.75.[53] The work of the
Agency was becoming too much for Hale, and for some time
he had been looking around for a helper. It was only
natural that he would try to secure the aid of another
member of the Illinois Band. In its June 1839 issue,
the Society announced

that the Rev. Flavel Bascom -- well known
in the state as a devoted minister, has
been associated with Mr. Hale in the agency,
and from their united efforts, in connection
with those of the churches which have already
become our efficient co-workers, we anticipate

---

[52]Hale to Badger, from Alton, February 20, 1839.
[53]Hale to Badger, from Alton, February 23, 1839.

                    a large increase of good fruits in the field
                    of their culture.[54]

        Hale and Bascom planned to divide the field between
them, Hale taking the west and north, including Iowa and
the Lead Mines in the Galena area. Bascom was to take
the east and north, or the area around Chicago.[55] Then
the two would meet in Tazewell County about the first of
September. A letter of Hale's from Galena, Illinois
tells of the formation of a church at Bloomington. At
Davenport, twelve members were united in formation of a
church, and Hale expected several more to join very soon.
"The Iowa TerY is now altogether the most interesting
field for Home MissY. effort that comes within my lim-
its," he wrote. "The population is superior to that of
Illinois, there being a much larger proportion of it
from the middle & eastern states. It is of vast importance that the field be occupied with efficient men."[56]
Two evils existed in Iowa according to Hale. One was
infidelity; the other was the claiming of public lands.
The tenure by which claims were held were various and
doubtful, and "the quarrells & disputes arising from
them are endless."[57]

        Late in 1839, he accepted a call to become the pas-
tor of the Second Presbyterian Church in Springfield,
Illinois. For some time, Hale's health had been getting
worse, making it increasingly difficult for him to pro-
secute the work of the agency. Furthermore, Bascom
could carry on the work where he left off.

                Eight years spent in scouring a new country
                is enough for one man. It is a very differ-
                ent thing to do the work of an Agent here from
                what it is to do it in the older parts of the
                country. But the Lord has preserved me.[58]

        The Society accordingly announced his resignation,
but added that they still hoped "to avail ourselves of
his counsel and occasional labors, in prosecuting our
work in the southern section of the state."[59] Summarizing the work of Hale and other agents, the Home
Missionary Journal declared:

_____

[54]Home Missionary, June 1839, pp. 36-37.

[55]Hale to the Society, June 3, 1839.

[56]Hale to Badger, August 5, 1839 from Galena, Illinois.

[57]Ibid.

[58]Hale to Badger, December 4, 1839 from Springfield, Ill.

[59]Home Missionary Journal, July 1840, p. 61.

The work accomplished by these brethren, and by other Agents in similar circumstances, is not chiefly the collection of funds. It is, in the strictest sense, a missionary work on a large scale. They visit the churches where aid is needed, or settlements where churches are to be gathered, and the counsel and encouragement they give, often lead to the permanent establishment of the institutions of the Gospel, while their preaching of the unsearchable riches of Christ and their administration of the ordinances which he has appointed, become the wisdom of God and the power of God to the salvation of souls. It has been the privilege of these brethren, to labor in many most interesting revivals of religion, where the Spirit of God has borne witness with their spirits, that they were fulfilling, in the best sense, their high commission as ambassadors of Christ. Few ministers of the Gospel are more useful, as ministers, than those who go forth deeply imbued with the spirit of their Lord and Master to lay the foundations of christian society in our new settlements. Those States and Territories have been greatly favored of God, whose earliest history has been associated with the labors of devoted men, expended in planting over their length and breadth churches of Christ, and commending these churches to the care of those, whom he has chosen as messengers of his grace.[60]

Although Hale settled in Springfield, he still continued to act as a sort of medium between the Society and the brethren on the field. He was frequently called upon to recommend various men for financial aid. He was in constant touch with other members of the Illinois Band, particularly Baldwin, Brooks, Bascom and Foster. He was constantly in bad health, and in 1843 he stopped preaching for awhile and went East. He resumed his work in Springfield late in the fall, however. Since he was strategically located in the center of the state, the Society often sent him boxes of books, tracts, and reports which he could distribute to brethren in more remote parts of the state.

---

[60] Home Missionary Journal, July 1840, p. 61.

The second quarter of the nineteenth century saw the rapid growth of the Mormons. By 1844, when Joseph Smith was murdered, his converts numbered around fifteen thousand.[61] In 1845, many of the Mormons were ejected from Illinois. Though possibly biased (for Hale was opposed to war and violence), he has left us an interesting eye-witness account of the times:

We are in the midst of another "Mormon War." The Anti-Mormons burning & destroying all before them, at least so say reports. Our Governor issued his Proclamation on Saturday last calling for 500 men to go as Volunteers to the "infected district" & restore peace. But "Mormon Wars" are somewhat unpopular since the first experiment & the Proclamation failed to stir the elements. On Sunday a report was put in circulation that a pitched battle had taken place in which some 20 or more had been slain. This report was followed by another Proclamation & appeal & the issuing of an extra of the State Register, the state gov't. organ. This proclamation called for an instant assembling of the people to arrange matters & set off for Nauvoo. The people, & especially the loafers assembled in squads about the square, & I believe the govr. & his (men?) did effect an organization of a meeting but as no interest seemed to be felt, the few who were at the meeting adjourned to meet again on yesterday (Monday). Promptly on Monday morning a third proclamation, of a more hortatory character than the preceding made its appearance, but as I am informed, it was found impossible even to reassemble the adjourned meeting. Now "Caesar" is verily in a sad predicament. He can't make the people go to war. And if he could it is quite doubtful in some minds who should be considered the enemy, and the chances of life & death, peace or insurrection, it may be don't depend so much on the agency or an organized mob under the Governor as under Joe Smith's successor as has been supposed.

But verily we are in danger of becoming "no government" men, the government having been

[61]Harlow, R.V., A History of the United States, p. 325.

rendered too-contemptible by maladministra-
tion to retain the respect even of their own
peculiar friends. But the cause of morals &
religion in these days suffers. By these
movements & this public desecration of the
sabbath day men have a very plausible excuse
for sabbath desecration & vice & irreligion
thrive. May the Lord appear for us.[62]

Late in 1845 he went to Beardstown to organize a
church and to ordain "Br. Smith." The church was organized with fourteen members, "in the prime of life, intelligent, active, energetic, and pious."[63]

A year later, the United States went to war with
Mexico. Hale denounced the war vigorously, and preached
two sermons on the subject in 1847, taking for one of
his texts the words of the disciples at Jesus' anoint-
ing: "To what purpose is this waste?" In scathing terms
he denounced the war as wasteful, unnecessary and unchristian.[64] His language was very vigorous and straight-
forward, and caused such a stir that his sermons were
published by request, and circulated in pamphlet form.

We shall have occasion to see later how he dealt
with the slavery controversy which was to come to a cli-
max a few years later.

In 1854, the agency of the Home Missionary Society
was again offered him, and a good many people urged him
to return to his former job. But once again his health,
and particularly the health of his wife, prevented him
from accepting. Knowing the importance of the work to
which he was called, he declined with great reluctance.[65]
He continued as pastor in Springfield until 1866, when
he resigned and became city missionary, laboring "both
in the streets & lanes & on the highways & hedges."[66]
He died in 1891.

---

[62]Hale to Badger, Springfield, Illinois, September 23, 1845.

[63]Ibid., December 1, 1845.

[64]Hale, Albert, Two discourses on the subject of the war
between the United States and Mexico; preached in the
Second Presbyterian Church in Springfield, 1847, Illinois
State Historical Library.

[65]Hale to Badger, December 28, 1854; January 25, 1855.

[66]Hale to J.E. Roy, May 2, 1876, from Springfield, Illinois.

One of the most important members of the Yale Band was Flavel Bascom, who was Agent for the Home Missionary Society for a short time, and who was closely associated with Albert Hale for a good many years. In his Auto-biography, Bascom gives us a good insight into his life and work in Illinois.[67] His correspondence with the Home Missionary Society was voluminous, and his reports and observations were frequently printed in the Journal. Born in Lebanon, Connecticut, on June 8, 1804, he attended school for three summers between the ages of eight and ten. He says that at first he was very averse to attending school, "but a little of that kind of suasion which Solomon recommends for wayward children, removed my reluctance."[68] He attended Miss Wright's school, where he was impressed by the personality and character of Miss Wright herself, who made the pupils of her school recite portions of scripture to her on Monday morning which they had learned the day before.[68] Very much to his regret, she sickened and died, and the next six years were spent under farmers or farmers' sons who tutored him on the average of four months each winter. In 1821, he "attended upon the ministry" of Rev. J.H. Fowler,

> [E]ven in winter, where with no artificial
> warmth in the house, he would preach in over-
> coat and gloves, and my feet would come near
> freezing during the sermon. His ministry
> was not an efficient one. But at its close,
> or immediately after his dismission, a very
> extensive revival of religion prevailed for
> months. With very little assistance from
> neighboring ministers, the meetings, which
> were quite frequent, were conducted by the
> members of the church, assisted by the young
> converts. As the fruit of this revival 67
> were added to the church, the summer follow-
> ing, of whom I was one. And thus commenced
> my christian life at the age of 17. I had
> not before been a stranger to serious thoughts.
> I had felt the need of religion, and had in-
> tended, at some time, to become a christian.

---

[67]Ms. in Hammond Library Rare Book Room, Chicago, Illinois.

[68]Bascom, Flavel, Autobiography, pp. 4-5.

[69]Ibid., pp. 8-9.

But my ideas of what was implied in becoming
a Christian were vague, & I knew not how to
begin. And after I was numbered among the
young converts and was enrolled as a dis-
ciple, my views of spiritual things were comparatively dim & confused and my christian
experience was very superficial. I was far
from being satisfied with the evidences of
my conversion. But in all my doubts and dark-
ness I stedfastly kept my face heavenward.
My purpose to "follow on to know the Lord"
never wavered and in due time the day dawned
and the day star arose. "It was the star of
Bethlehem." And as the blessed Savior began
to draw my thoughts away from myself to himself, I gradually learned that "in him was
life, & the life is the light of men."[70]

In September, 1821, he walked twenty miles to Willington, Connecticut, where he boarded with Rev. Hubbel
Loomis for a few weeks prior to teaching school. After
brushing up on his primary studies, he secured a school
in the adjacent part of Monson, Massachusetts. Here he
taught for four months for nine dollars and fifty cents
a month and boarded among his employers. Being only
seventeen, he lacked self-confidence and the benefit of
prestige, nor was he happy boarding among strangers.
"At length the end came. With a thankful heart I gave
my farewell address, received by $38 and turned my face
homeward."[71]

After a short vacation at home he returned to Willington and entered upon the study of Latin. He boarded
with the Crockers, recited to son Zebulon (who was himself pursuing studies preparatory to college and recit-
ing to Mr. Loomis) and paid one dollar per week for
board, room, and laundry. He studied until July, and
then by labor at haying for one dollar a day he paid
for three months board. The next winter he taught the
school in Willington Village at ten dollars per month.
At the close of his school in the spring of 1823, he
began the study of Latin and Greek preparatory to enter-
ing Yale College.[72]

---

[70]Bascom, Flavel, _Autobiography_, pp. 22-24.

[71]_Ibid._, p. 29.

[72]_Ibid._, p. 30ff.

The fall of 1824 found him at New Haven. Although
feeling that his preparation had been very faulty, he
nevertheless passed the entrance examinations and entered into the full swing of college life.[73]

The first three years of the college course were
almost wholly given by the respective tutors. Declama-
tion was taught by Professor Chauncey Goodrich, Natural
Philosophy and Astronomy by Professor Olmsted, and Chemistry and Mineralogy by Professor Silliman. Bascom
found college very stimulating, and although he regretted
the absence of contacts with the townspeople of New Haven,
college society compensated.

> The tone of piety, and the religious influence
> that pervaded the College during my connection
> with it, were on the whole very healthful. Meet-
> ings for christian conference and prayer, in which
> all the classes mingled were held weekly and a
> weekly meeting in which each class met separately
> were kept up with a good degree of interest. Sev-
> eral seasons of special religious interest were
> enjoyed, in which Professor Goodrich & Dr. Taylor
> were very earnest & very useful in conducting
> evening meetings, in conversing with inquirers
> and in counseling with the pious students in
> reference to their active efforts.[74]

College expenses were light in those times. Term
bills including room rent and tuition were not more than
forty dollars a year, and good board in the Commons from
sixty to seventy-five dollars a year. If a student were
economical, he could go through four years at Yale on

---

[73]"For a time our location exempted us from hazing. But
when the Sophomores learned that two Freshmen were oc-
cupying a room better than theirs, a room which Juniors
usually occupied, they took extra pains to annoy us.
We were too high to be reached by squirt Guns. But two
or three stones, through as many panes of glass, were almost every night our salutation. Occasionally, after re-
tiring, we would be well nigh suffocated with Tobacco
smoke made by filling the keyhole of our door with fine-
cut tobacco & setting fire to it." Bascom, Flavel,
Autobiography, p. 40.

[74]Ibid., pp. 49-50.

six to eight hundred dollars. Bascom secured four hundred dollars from the Education Society and paid his own way through except for two hundred and fifty dollars which he had to borrow.[75] His academic record was very good, and he ranked as an Orator both his Junior and Senior years.

In the spring vacation of his Senior year, while only six weeks of study remained to be accomplished, he obtained a leave of absence in order to become Principal in the New Canaan Academy, a flourishing institution sustained by local patronage and by pupils from New York City. He continued in the Academy for a year and a half on five hundred dollars salary. In the autumn of 1829 he returned to New Haven and joined the Junior Class in the Theological Seminary. Here he studied under the great Nathaniel Taylor, who "so presented (his) doctrines, that each by itself seemed reasonable and right, and in their relations to each other all seemed consistent, and the whole system grand and glorious."[76] For "field work" he "was induced by Miss Peters, Principal of the Grove Seminary for young ladies, to take a Bible Class of young ladies in the Center Church School of which she was Assistant SupT."

In the summer of 1831 Bascom was licensed to preach by the New Haven East Association. A few days later he was invited to a Tutorship in Yale College, which he accepted. His pupils were the class of 1834; he instructed three divisions in Latin. He also preached frequently on the Sabbath, both in the city and in the surrounding country, and remarks that "the scale of compensation for such services in those days was very low in the vacant churches, and aid rendered to Pastors, was expected to be gratuitous."[77]

In the spring of 1833 Bascom resigned his tutorship, and received a commission from the American Home Missionary Society, to preach the Gospel in Illinois, his location to be determined after reaching the state. On the thirtieth of April he was married to Ellen P. Cleaveland, the daughter of Judge William P. Cleaveland of New London, Connecticut. After a short wedding trip, and some farewell visits among relatives they left on the third of June, for what was then regarded as the far West.[78] They went overland to Buffalo,

[75]Bascom, Flavel, _Autobiography_, p. 54.

[76]_Ibid._, pp. 57-58.

[77]_Ibid._, p. 65.

[78]_Ibid._, p. 68.

and then took a steamer to Detroit, where they purchased
a horse, and drove their buggy to Chicago. Since the
question of Bascom's location was to be decided by Hale
and Baldwin, they resumed their journey toward the central part of the state. They stopped for two weeks at
Union Grove, where they were entertained by William
Kirby and his wife. At length Hale and Baldwin arrived
at Union Grove, and these four members of the Illinois
Band decided that Bascom should locate at Pleasant Grove,
in Tazewell County. Summarizing the first four years of
his work, Bascom wrote to Peters early in 1838:

I came to this country in 1833 and selected a
field of labor because of (its) natural advantages. I located in Pleasant Grove a sparse
country settlement about the center of the
county. Methodists, Baptists, Campbellites,
Quakers, Mormons, and Cumberland Presbyterians
had the ground before me. Throughout the whole
region I was told by an old settler who was a
Methodist Father that there were preachers
enough here already, no openings, etc. . . .
but relying on your society for temporal supplies and the grace of God to give efficacy
for his work I pitched my tent and began to
labor as a missionary in Tazewell County . . . .
Thus I labored a year always collecting a
cabin full wherever I preached and accumulated
something in the way of S.S., Temperance Society, etc. During the year there were only
2 or 3 hopeful conversations . . . 7/8 of my
support was from your society.

The second year a church was formed at Washington
of ten members which I supplied once a month.
My labors were also extended to Peoria and a
church was formed there during that year. In
Pleasant Grove and Sand Prairie our numbers and
strength were gradually increasing. About the
close of that year, brother R. Barnes came to
my aid at Washington and Brother Porter at Peoria.
Tremont had by that time grown up requiring my
attention and next year was given to Tremont
and Pleasant Grove; Pekin and Sand Prairie
(still deriving half my support from your Society). The next year Pekin and Sand Prairie
were left destitute and my whole time was given
to Tremont and Pleasant Grove . . . . At the
close of that year my church was divided, the
part over which I am now placed claims my whole
time and raising my whole salary. The other

part has obtained the services of Brother
Huntington. The little church which existed
in this country in 1833 has increased from 6
members to 3 churches with an aggregate of
100 members . . . .[79]

In 1839, Bascom became an Agent of the American Home
Missionary Society, and aided Hale in his work in Northern Illinois. In accepting the agency of the A.H.M.S.
he stipulated for the privilege of locating at some
place, during the winter months, to supply some vacant
church, and thus relieve the society from paying his
salary for that period.[80]

To superintend the work of Home Missions in
Illinois, in 1839, was a very different thing
from such a superintendency in 1895. Then
there were no Rail Roads in the State. The
settlements in the Northern half of the state
were new, and wide intervals were between them
without any population. Roads had not been
constructed few Bridges had been built. Public buildings had not been erected except in
a few instances, and these were rude & incom-
modious. Travelling was slow, wearisome, and
in summer exposed one to those malarious influences, which were productive of fevers &
ague, and in winter to the bleak Prairie winds
and driving storms, which endangered life as
well as health. It was not uncommon in those
times, for persons to lose their lives by the
cold in passing from one settlement to another,
or to become bewildered in a storm on the
Prairie's, and perish before they could find
shelter . . . .

. . . My salary was at the rate of $500 a year.
I furnished my own horse & Buggy, and charged
my necessary travelling expenses to the Society. So hospitable were those pioneer settlers to ministers, and so low were the charges
at Hotels, that my expenses all the summer and
fall of that year 1839, were only $30, and by
donating that amount to the Home Miss. Society
I made myself a life member. This expense ac-

[79]Bascom to Peters, January 19, 1838. Cf. Home Missionary Journal, Vol. X, April 1838, pp. 202-3.
[80]Bascom, Flavel, Autobiography, p. 129.

count covered the whole time from Ap 1st to
Dec. 1st. and included Postage, which ranged
from 6-1/2 cents to 25 cents each letter[81]
Hotel Bills, Ferriage and horse shoeing.

I had different objects in view in visiting
the different parts of my field. In the larger churches I preached on the subject of
Home Missions and took collections for the
Society. In the missionary churches which
were supplied with ministers, I endeavored
to ascertain whether the respective congregations were contributing toward this support of their ministers as much as they
ought, and whether they were aiming at self
support at as early a day as practicable.
I sought also, to heal divisions and alien-
ations that might be threatening to unsettle
ministers in those churches, and to strengthen
their influence with their people, I coun-
selled with vacant churches in regard to pro-
curing Pastors and corresponded with ministers
in reference to destitute places. I visited
new settlements for the purpose of preparing
the way for organizing churches, where materials were found. In many destitute churches
I administered the ordinances of the Gospel.
I addressed County Bible Societies, delivered
Temperance addresses, and aided in protracted
meetings when requested, preaching usually
three times on the Sabbath, and as many times
during the week as I could find audiences.
I also attended ecclesiastical meetings, or-
dinations, Installations and dedications of
church edifices whenever it was practicable.
In performing such a work on such a territory,
I had not much time for rest or idleness. I
began the labors of my Agency in Tazewell
County where I had been laboring, and extended
them to adjacent Counties, including Peoria,
Marshall, McLean, Dewit, Sangamon, Morgan,
Fulton &c. Before the first of December following, I had traveled as far North as Milwau-
kee, on the N. West to Galena, on the West to
Galesburg, South as far as Alton & East as far
as Bloomington. To have made a thorough exploration of this vast territory in one season,

[81]Bascom, Flavel, Autobiography, pp. 128-9; 129-30.

with such facilities of travelling as then
existed was of course impossible. But the
places which most needed counsel and supervision were visited and some of them repeatedly. My visits were every where thank-
fully received, and they afforded constant
opportunities of aiding those early settlers
in devising and excuting (sic) plans for
promoting the interests of education, morality and religion in their respective communities.[82]

Because of the impossibility of prosecuting the
work of the Agency during the winter months, on November 22, 1839 Bascom left Pekin, Illinois to preach at
the First Presbyterian Church in Chicago. Chicago at
this time, had 4,000 inhabitants, and was an incorpor-
ated city. There was one Episcopal Church, one Methodist Episcopal, one Baptist and one Presbyterian.
The increase of business and the growth of the city
was already making it necessary for the churches to
move uptown. The membership of the Presbyterian Church
was two hundred, and the church building was thirty by
eighty feet. Among the congregation, he "found a good
degree of unity, but a very great diversity. There
were representatives from all of the New England and
Middle States, from several of the Western and Southern, as well as from England, Ireland, Scotland and
Wales. In church polity some had been life-long Presbyterians and others Congregationalists. In Theology
some were extreme Old School and some ultra New School."[83]

When the question of accepting the Pastorate
in Chicago was thus presented, requiring a
decisive answer, I found it more perplexing
than I had anticipated. The various elements
and diverse sentiments in the church, I was
aware would tax the personal influence and
prudence of the Pastor, in preserving harmony.
The peculiar condition of the city, yet in its
infancy, but rapidly developing, with its
institutions in process of organization, and
its vital connection with a vast interior
country which was rapidly emerging from its
primitive communities, I knew would require
of a Pastor in Chicago many onerous duties,
outside of the ordinary labors of a city

---

[82] Bascom, Flavel, _Autobiography_, pp. 128-33.
[83] _Ibid._, p. 141.

ministry. Then my relations to the A.H.M.
Society, in whose service I had spent the
preceding summer, was an argument against
accepting the Pastorate. The labors of a
Home Missionary Agent were growing continually in importance. My last summers experience had prepared me to do that work
in the future more effectively. I had a
liking for the work & the Society desired
my continuance in it. On the other hand,
it was urged that I had united the church,
and that there was reason to fear their
refusal to unite on another, if I declined
their call. I finally decided to compromise these conflicting claims, by accepting
the call on condition that I might prose-
cute my Agency the next summer and be installed as their Pastor the next Autumn,
and in the meantime procure a temporary
supply for their pulpit.[84]

On the fifteenth of May, Bascom resumed the work of
the Home Missionary Agency which he had suspended during
the winter. The funds of the A.H.M.S. had been considerably reduced because of the critical financial situation in the East. Bascom was told to reduce expenses
in every way possible and to raise as much money in
Illinois as possible.[85] He spent a vigorous summer
preaching, administering the ordinances, "counselling
in regard to agitating questions," "confirming the
little churches," and encouraging the scattered disciples wherever he found them. A typical trip is described in the Autobiography:

On the 24th I was so far recovered as to proceed on Savannah, where I found a few Christians, but no church & no preaching, but some
desire for Gospel Institutions, which I endeavored to strengthen. Thence I went to Fulton City, where I found a feeble church and a
minister in the midst of a day of small things.
I next visited Lyndon & spent a Sabbath with
Bro. Hazard & his people, pleasantly & I
trust profitably. Thence I passed on to
Sharon, Geneseo, Andover, Galesburg, Knox-

---

[84]Bascom, Flavel, Autobiography, pp. 150-152.
[85]Badger to Bascom, April 21, 1840.

ville, Peoria, & to my first Missionary field,
Pleasant Grove, in Tazewell County. In each
of the places just named I tarried a little,
and endeavored to gather the facts in regard
the circumstances and needs & wishes of those
who were Pioneers in laying foundations for
christian Society, so that the friends of Home
Missions might be enabled to contribute in-
telligently. . . .[86]

The first few months of Bascom's renewed ministry
in Chicago were much embarrassed by impaired health.
This necessitated a three-month's vacation the follow-
ing summer in Connecticut and New York. At Saratoga
Springs, he met Miss Elizabeth Sparhawk of Warehouse
Point, to whom he was married August 19, 1841.[87]

I now entered upon the labors of my ministry
in that important church, with health invig-
orated, and reinforced with a help-meet like
minded with myself, with renewed energy and
hopefulness. And in a good measure, the Divine
favor seemed to rest upon my labors. Acces-
sions to the church were received at nearly
every communion. Our prayer meetings were
well attended and were edifying, our S. School
flourished, and the benevolent activities of
the church were commendable. But the Anti-
Slavery agitation which grew more intense
throughout the country, interested my people
more and more as time passed, and the conser-
vatives and radicals were separated more widely
in sentiment and action. In the mean time,
the growth of the congregation, and the prospect of rapid growth in the city's population
suggested the expediency of organizing a second Pres. Church. Our old house of worship
which had been enlarged by one half during my
absence as Home Mission Agent, would hold no
more, and we must colonize or build. The
former plan was thought more expedient. In
the Spring of 1842 by appointment of Presbytery a colony of about 30 members was organized into the Second Church. On the principle

---

[86]Bascom, Flavel, _Autobiography_, pp. 164-5.
[87]_Ibid_., pp. 170-1.

of elective affinity, it so happened that the
more conservative members went into the new
organization, and chose R.W. Patterson for
their Pastor . . . .

Some of my people were a good deal disturbed
by this separation, imputing unworthy motives
to those who left, and inclining to make our
relation to each other, as churches antagon-
istic and unfriendly. But their Pastor did
not partake of that feeling. He favored the
separation, as likely to promote the growth
of our denomination in the city, and to promote concord, by making each church more homogeneous than one could be embracing all the
membership. The subsequent history of both
churches has abundantly justified the division.

Scarcely had the church become reconciled (to)
this first colonization, before other colonies
went out in quick succession, forming an old
school Presbyterian church on the North Side,
and the 3rd Church on the West Side.

After parting with these several colonies, the
membership remaining in the 1st church was made
up largely of persons who were formerly Congregationalists, and still had preference for that
polity. But the liberal policy of our New
School organization, adapted itself to their
ideas of Christian liberty and of church auto-
nomy to such an extent that they felt very little irksome restraint. But their orgainic (sic)
connection with slave holding churches in the
South, through the General Assembly, became a
source of growing dissatisfaction, and after
patience had had its perfect work, the 1st Cong.
Church on the West Side, colonized from the 3rd
Presbyterian, in 1851, and the Plymouth Congregational, from the 1st Presbyterian in 1852.
Both colonies have had a vigorous life and a
fruitful mission.[88]

In 1848, my church earnestly undertook what was
to them a very onerous task, the building of a
large Brick house of worship, on the corner of
Clark and Washington Streets. Nearly every dollar of the amount subscribed for this purpose,

---

[88]Bascom, Flavel, Autobiography, pp. 171-174.

was obtained by my personal solicitation.
It was a wearisome task, which ought never
to have been laid upon a Pastor. It used
up the time and strength which ought ever
to have been sacred to the upbuilding of
the spiritual Temple, rather than the material.

We entered the basement of the new church
late in 1848, and occupied it till October
1849, when the whole building was completed
and dedicated. The audience room was not
far from 60 x 90 feet, and the building itself was the best in all the North Western
States. It cost about $18,000. The dedi-
cation sermon by the Pastor, was from the
text in Haggai 2:9, "The glory of this latter house shall be greater than of the former." But history did not fulfill the prophecy in my application of it. Scarcely
half a dozen years passed, before property
became so valuable at that part of the city
that the congregation were induced to sell
their house & lot for $65,000, and build
on Wabash Avenue half a mile or more further
South. The house erected by such a struggle
and dedicated so hopefully was soon occupied
for business purposes -- first as a Music
Store, and then as a Billiard Hall. Having
by ten years of toil, brought my congregation
to such a point of growth and prosperity, I
was satisfied that some other man could take
them through another stage of progress more
successfully than I could hope to do. Receiving at the same time a unanimous call to
the Pastorate of the 1st Pres. Church of
Galesburg, Ill I was predisposed to regard
it as the call of the Master to a new field.
I tendered my resignation, therefore, to my
church, but only a small minority voted in
favor of accepting it. Again I asked the
church to unite with me in a request to Presbytery to dissolve my Pastoral relation, to
which they assented, and I was accordingly
dismissed.[89]

Bascom's next pastorate was to be at Galesburg, Illinois, and late in December, 1849, he made a four days'

[89]Bascom, Flavel, Autobiography, pp. 178-181.

journey there by horse and buggy. The village and township of Galesburg had been settled by a Christian colony from Central New York in 1836 and 1837 with a design of promoting evangelical religion and Christian education in the new state. The project had originated with Rev. George W. Gale.

The plan was admirable. It allowed subscribers to pay into a common fund such a sum as they pleased. When sufficient was subscribed, the subscribers were to select a Committee of their own number who should explore the Western States and select a location, where they could enter a considerable body of land -- a township if practicable -- at Congress price $1.25/100 per acre. A village was to be located in the central part of this tract, and outside the village lots, were to be 10 acre lots, and outside of these, the land was to be divided into farms of 40, 80 & 160 acres, and each lot and farm was to be apprized by the Committee according to the quality of the land, and the eligibility of its location -- the apprizal to recognize five Dollars as the average value of the farm lands per acre. On this scale of valuation, each subscriber might select his lands in return for the money he had invested. On this principle one fourth of the land purchased by the colony's money would repay the subscribers, and the other three fourths, was appropriated to the endowment of an Academy & College. The village in which these institutions were to be located was to be laid out on lands accruing to the College, and the College funds were thus to be largely increased. The compact, simultaneous settlement of such a homogeneous community, and the building of such a village & such Institutions in their midst, immediately gave a fourfold value to their lands, the endowment could well afford the generous provision for the endowment of their College.[90]

---

[90]Bascom, Flavel, _Autobiography_, pp. 184-186. Cf. also "Semi-Centennial Celebration of the First Church of Christ, 1837-1887," Galesburg, Ill., pp. 44-47, and p. 61; also "Pastoral Reminiscences," pp. 89-92 in the files on Illinois Congregational Churches in the archives of the Hammond Library, Chicago Theological Seminary, Chicago, Ill., with respect to Bascom's pastorate at Galesburg.

In 1850, the town of Galesburg contained about a thousand inhabitants. The Academy and Female Seminary had been in operation about ten years; four classes had been graduated from the College. The College "enjoyed the confidence of the community, especially by the Presbyterians and Congregationalists in an unusual degree."[91] But "the new Pastor found the College and the whole community in a ferment as well as the church"[92] because of the sensitiveness which existed between Congregationalists and Presbyterians as a result of the abrogation of the Plan of Union. Knox College was the scene of a fierce quarrel which had been inaugurated a few months before his settlement.[93] Bascom did much to act as peacemaker both in church, town, and college, but "though the volcano was capped, its fires were still smouldering & rumbling during the six years that followed."[94]

The winter of 1850-51 saw a revival in his church, and a number of college young people were converted under his preaching. During this same winter, however, his second wife died, leaving him four children to care for. A year later he married a third time, Ruth S. Pomeroy, "whose biography has not only run parallel with my own, but the two have blended into one."[95]

> It so happened that Mr. Lyman had a Lady Principal in his Academy, from Mass. I had heard of her as an excellent Teacher and a superior woman. Perhaps the thought had occurred to me, that she might be just such a Teacher as my children needed and just such a helpmeet as would fill a vacant place in my family & my parish work. Possibly such a thought had some influence in leading my steps in that direction. At any rate, I went, I saw, and I was conquered. That visit led to a second & that to a third, and the fourth time, I went by way of the County Seat, and took with

---

[91] Bascom, Flavel, _Autobiography_, pp. 186-187.

[92] Ibid., p. 195.

[93] Ibid., p. 196.

[94] Ibid., p. 197. A fuller discussion will be found in the chapter on the abrogation of the Plan of Union.

[95] Ibid., p. 207.

me a Marriage Licence, and returned with
the Teacher a captive. The next morning,
at the Breakfast table, the youngest boy,
a little four year old, said "Father, I
am glad you have got married." "Why so,
Johnnie?" I asked. "Because now I have
got a Mother," was his reply.[96]

Bascom's pastorate at Galesburg closed the first
of May, 1856. Summarizing his work there, he says,

There are some peculiarities in the social
and church life of a colony like that of
Galesburg. There are some decided advantages,
and some incidental evils, connected with the
forming of settlements by organized colonies.
A more homogeneous population and greater
strength for sustaining religious & educational
institutions at an early day, are secured. And
this is a matter of very great importance. But
on the other hand, this homogeneousness implies
an equality in standing, which is very apt to
beget a jealousy of each other's influence, in
the management of affairs. Leaders, Agents,
Committees, and all who are intrusted with any
official responsibility, are almost sure to be
accused of wrong doing, and discord and strife
are almost inevitable. Several Colonies locating in the in the (sic) West not far from
the time of the settlement of Galesburg, were
rent and crippled by internal strife. All
suffered more or less from the same cause.
Galesburg, having larger interests at stake,
and having a larger number of substantial families than most other colonies, was able to
endure the strain from this cause. But it
was a fearful strain, notwithstanding, which
destroyed her peace, marred her prosperity,
and put in jeopardy the very object of her
founders. The period of my ministry in Galesburg, was in the midst of the troublous times
growing out of the causes referred to above.
That my Pastorate was only six and a half years
in duration, in these circumstances is not
wonderful, especially since it was longer than
any which has followed it, and three times
longer than those preceding it. And when it
terminated it was on my own motion.[97]

---

[96]Bascom, Flavel, *Autobiography*, p. 200.

[97]Ibid., pp. 207-209.

In the Spring of 1857, Bascom received an urgent call to the pastorate of the Church in Dover, Bureau County. Dover is described as a retired and quiet village with a church which was united and enterprising; the community was just moving to establish a classical Academy.[98] His salary was one thousand dollars. "Serious and earnest attention to to (sic) the Gospel began to be manifest from the first of my labors in the place, and in the Autumn of 1857 and Winter of 1858, we enjoyed a season of deep & general religious interest, which added a large number to the church; and greatly strengthened the cause of religion in the place."[99] Bascom had much to do with the founding of the Academy at Dover, and he watched over it as one of its Trustees and Executive Committee. He remained at Dover until March 1864.

> Under his Pastoral care, the church was in-
> creased by the addition of ninety-nine mem-
> bers, 36 by letter and 63 by profession of
> faith. Much attention was given to the
> maintenance of church order and discipline,
> and Mr. B's wise judgment and painstaking
> care contributed largely to the prosperity
> of the church, while his active public
> spirit made his influence felt through all
> the community. The Council called to ad-
> vise in regard to his dismission testified
> that the church had been fully united in
> their affectionate regard and support of
> their Pastor.[100]

Bascom's next pastorate was to be at Princeton, Illinois, a village of four thousand inhabitants, and the County Seat of Bureau County. This famous church was organized in Northampton, Massachusetts on March 23, 1831, and was then transplanted in Illinois in the same year, being at that time the only Congregational Church in the state.[101] Most of its members were

---

[98]Bascom, Flavel, _Autobiography_, p. 211.

[99]_Ibid._, pp. 212-213.

[100]_Ibid._, p. 217.

[101]Cf. Sweet, Wm. W., _Religion on the American Frontier_, Vol. III, _The Congregationalists_, p. 246; footnote 20:
"The Hampshire Colony Church has recently published the early documents of their church in a book entitled _The Hampshire Church: Its First Hundred Years 1831-1931_
[footnote continued on next page]

scattered by an Indian War in the following year. There was no regular minister until the fall of 1833, when Lucien Farnham became pastor for five years. He was followed by Owen Lovejoy, brother of the famous Elijah Lovejoy, and his pastorate covered a stormy period of anti-slavery agitation in church and state. A number of factions were stirred up, with the natural consequence that the next five pastorates were short and unsuccessful. Bascom occupied his new pulpit on the first of May, 1864. During the five years of his ministry in Princeton, eighty-one were added to the membership of the church, thirty-nine by profession, and forty-two by letter.[102]

[footnote continued from previous page] (Princeton, Illinois, 1931) by members of the church. In 1831 a meeting was held at Northampton, Mass., to organize a church from those who anticipated migrating to Illinois. The preamble to the constitution states their purpose as 'better providing for themselves and their families, provided the privileges of a social, moral and religious character which they now have and which they highly value, can be made secure to them in their future home.' There were members from several churches, including a doctor and his wife. No minister accompanied them. A scout had been sent out the previous year, and he selected a place at Bailey's Point on the Vermillion River and had a cabin ready for the group which arrived later in 1831. The entire group did not come at once, but eventually most of them managed to reach the Illinois settlement. The first entry in the old church record-book reads as follows: 'the Hampshire Colony Church of Christ founded at Northampton, Mass., March 23, 1831, settled on the Bureau River, County of Putnam, . . . and named the town Greenfield' (pp. 10-11). Rev. T. Baldwin visited the settlement in February 1834, and a little later Lucius Farnham and William Kirby met here to hold a communion service. A church building was erected in 1835, and Lucius Farnham became the first pastor. At this time the settlement was called Princeton. L. Farnham, in a letter to A. Peters, July 1, 1835, states that he arrived the previous October and found the little church awaiting him. He says: 'The Bible Class embraces nearly all the Congregation.' Prayer meeting was held every Wednesday evening, with a female prayer meeting every Saturday afternoon, besides the monthly concert. In April of this year he notes that the land is being entered in order to obtain proper titles, and much hardship is resulting."

[102]Bascom, Flavel, Autobiography, p. 226.

The conversion of men to Christ and the ad-
vancement of his kingdom encounters obstacles
in every community. The natural heart is not
loyal to God, and does not yield to his claims
readily. The current of human affection, desire & interest is away from him. It is not
easy therefore to awaken deep interest, and
hold attention to the subject of religion any-
where. But in some places there are peculiar
difficulties. In Princeton, a number of prominent and influential families, did not accept
the doctrines of the Congregational church,
but adopted the Unitarian or liberal views of
christianity. At different times they had
employed Preachers of their own, and had attempted to maintain an organization that would
represent their views. They had no permanent
success in that direction, and yet their personal and social influence, was not helpful to
evangelical effort in the community. It was
rather a chilling soporific element in the spiritual atmosphere of the place. It is very difficult, in such an atmosphere, to produce such a
conviction of personal guilt, as leads one to
cry out "What shall I do to be saved?" If men
of known or supposed rationalistic tendencies
occasionally attend church and aid in paying
the Salary or an orthodox Preacher, the church
is tempted to accommodate itself in some measure to their views and feelings. They even
wish their Pastor to avoid in the Pulpit those
subjects, which would be unwelcome to those who
prefer smooth things.

I did not consciously tone down the doctrines
which I preached to accommodate a state of feeling above indicated. But I was often painfully
conscious of preaching to minds unreceptive,
and hearts insusceptible to impression. Yet I
had evidence that my ministry was helpfull (sic)
to a goodly number of our members who evidently
grew in grace and divine knowledge, becoming
more stedfast in faith and efficient in duty.[103]

After he had preached at Princeton for five years,
he decided that the church needed a change of pastors.
During the summer of 1860, while the house of worship
was being rebuilt and enlarged, he had ample time for

---

[103]Bascom, Flavel, Autobiography, pp. 227-229.

reflection. During the summer he supplied the church
in Altona, and then accepted an invitation to Hinsdale,
and took charge of that church on the first of October,
the same year.[104] Hinsdale was a suburban village
eighteen miles from Chicago. Between 1864 and 1869 a
population of several hundred people had located there.
A Congregational Church had been organized and a large
school house built by private enterprise. The school
contained a hall used for public worship. The first
pastor of the congregation was Reverend Clarendon Sandey,
who was ordained in the spring of 1867, and remained
about two years. Through the summer of 1869 there was
no regular supply. When Bascom began his ministry in
October, there were few church members, they were feeble[105]
in resources, and they had very little courage or hope.
On the same Sunday that Bascom began his ministry, a
Baptist minister attempted to organize a Baptist congregation in the Depot building, and a Methodist preacher
a Methodist society. The latter soon petered out, but
the Baptists "with more zeal than prudence" began to
build a church without sitting down first to count the
cost. The building ultimately was forfeited by fore-
closure of a mortgage, but the Baptists had the use of
it for several years. Since they had a church with no
preacher, and the Congregationalists a preacher but no
church, the two groups joined hands for awhile. But
because of financial misunderstandings, and a desire on
the part of the Baptists to choose their own pastor,
the Congregationalists later returned to the hall in
the school house in the spring of 1872. Of Hinsdale,
Bascom says:

> An attempt to build up an evangelical church
> in Hinsdale encountered some peculiar obstac-
> eles (sic). The business interests of so many
> families centering in Chicago, and the absence
> from home during every week day of so many men
> while pursuing their business in the city, al-
> most forbid any cooperation of the male mem-
> bers of the church with the Pastor in looking
> after its interests. In fact their business
> relations to the city and their absence from
> home so large a portion of the time seemed to
> prevent their becoming fully identified with
> the place in their feelings of interest or re-

---

[104]Bascom, Flavel, _Autobiography_, pp. 233-234.

[105]_Ibid._, pp. 235-236.

sponsibility. The proximity of the city also
affords to our young people the temptations
and facilities, to indulge in those amusements
and recreations, which do not aid them to think
on their ways and turn their feet to God's testi-
monies. Our whole population are more or less
under the "influence of that spirit of intense
worldliness," so prevalent in a large and growing city. A suburban congregation are perhaps
peculiarly inclined to appreciate eloquence in
a Pastor more than orthodoxy, and smartness
more than fidelity & zeal. And in this community an influential portion of the early citizens
were not in sympathy with evangelical truth,
and their influence has been like an incubus
upon the spirituality of the churches, and a
serious obstacle to the growth of evangelical
religion.[106]

Although he had built his own house there, he asked
soon after to be released from the church. From June
until December 1872, he supplied his former church in
Galesburg, "being kindly furnished with a free pass on
the Rail Road for that purpose."[107] With the settlement
of the new Pastor, Reverend H.S. Huntington, his work
at Galesburg ended, and he was asked by the church at
Aurora, Illinois to supply their pulpit until they
should obtain another minister. His stay at Aurora
lasted six months where his "ministrations were well
attended and apparently appreciated."[108] In the early
part of the summer of 1873, he arranged an exchange of
pulpits with Reverend N.A. Prentiss of La Salle. The
impression was so favorable that the church at Aurora
called Prentiss, and Bascom was invited to supply the
church at La Salle. So the two men exchanged pulpits.

Pending the motion to invite me to supply
their pulpit for a year, some one raised
the query, whether a younger man would not
be more suitable for their minister. A
leading member of the church replied that
it would be difficult to find a younger man
than Dr. Bascom. The motion therefore pre-
vaild (sic) & I was invited accordingly.[109]

---

[106]Bascom, Flavel, _Autobiography_, pp. 239-241.

[107]_Ibid._, p. 244.

[108]_Ibid._, p. 248

[109]_Ibid._, p. 250.

The town of La Salle numbered about six thousand people. Located on the Illinois River at the junction of the Illinois and Michigan Canal, about one hundred miles from Chicago, it seemed to be ideally situated for commerce and business. A certain amount of commercial prosperity was enjoyed for awhile, but time soon proved that Chicago was the city to benefit from this canal trade. Furthermore, the multiplication of railroad lines diverted the traffic of the canal towns to other depots. La Salle had been fortunate, however, in discovering deposits of bituminous coal underlying her bluffs. It was being mined by several companies, and two large rolling and smelting companies were employing a large number of men.[110] "But," says Bascom, "the employees in the mines & zinc factories were almost all foreigners. The population was largely Irish Catholic, while Germany & Poland did not lack representatives."[111] A Congregational Church had been in existence for twenty years. A comfortable but temporary house of worship had been erected, but the population of the town had fluctuated a good deal, and the church could do little more than maintain its number from year to year, and its influence was not very great. In the spring of 1874, he terminated his connection at La Salle, and moved to Ottawa, Illinois. The First Congregational Church had a flourishing existence. Bascom had been one of its co-founders, and M.K. Whittlesey had been pastor there for more than twenty years. For awhile there were two churches, but later they were forced to reunite, and for three or four years enjoyed the ministry of Julian M. Sturtevant, Jr. Sturtevant then went to Denver, and Bascom supplied the church at Ottawa for awhile.[112]

In the spring of 1876, the family moved to Peru, Illinois for the sake of being near George Bascom, who was pastor of the Congregational Church there. Son George went East for the summer to attend the centennial exhibition, while his father supplied the pulpit. In the spring of 1877, the elder Bascoms were back in Hinsdale, where they met a cordial reception from their old neighbors. Hearing that the Congregational Church at Bristol had been destitute he paid them a visit and proposed to preach for them,

---

[110]Bascom, Flavel, _Autobiography_, pp. 251-254.

[111]_Ibid._, p. 254.

[112]_Ibid._, pp. 258-263.

taking only such collections, as were made
each Sabbath for my compensation. Thus they
could not get in debt to me, and when I left
them there would be no arrearage to make up.
In that way I supplied them till late in the
next Autumn. Though their numbers and pecuniary ability were not increased, yet their
courage and hopefulness were revived, and
with such Home Missionary aid as I led them
to expect, they determined to take a new
lease of life, and up to the present time
(1881) they are enjoying the Ministrations
of a good Pastor.[113]

By 1881, Hinsdale had increased considerably in
size and population, and a new house of worship was
built.[114] During the same summer Bascom supplied the
church at Western Springs, Illinois. Early in 1883 a
Congregational Club was organized for the Chicago area.
Having as its object a more intimate acquaintance among
Congregational ministers and laymen, it met every month
to sponsor a closer union for cooperation and efficiency
in Christian work. At its second meeting Bascom read
a paper on the origin and progress of Congregationalism
in Illinois.[115]

The Autobiography breaks off at the year 1885. Two
years later Bascom returned to Princeton, Illinois, to
be with his former congregation and eldest son. During the same year (1887) he made a trip to Florida. On
his way home he contracted bronchial catarrh, and on
August 8, 1890, he died of bronchitis and heart failure.[116]

Another member of the Yale Band who became an Agent
of the American Home Missionary Society was William
Kirby. Born in Guilford, Connecticut on July 10, 1805,
he prepared for college under the Reverend Mr. Dutton
and entered Yale College about 1823.[117]

---

[113]Bascom, Flavel, Autobiography, p. 268.

[114]Because of building difficulties it was not completed until August, 1882.

[115]Bascom, Flavel, Autobiography, pp. 275-276.

[116]Sketches of the Class of 1828 in Yale Memorabilia.

[117]Stillwell, Frederick E., History of the Mendon Congregational Church. A Brief Sketch Delivered at the Mid-West
Congregational Historical Society Meeting held Dec. 27, 1928
at the Theological Seminary, in the Church File of the
Hammond Library.

. . . (He) . . . had already chosen, with Moses,
to suffer afflication with the people of God,
rather than enjoy the pleasure of sin for a season. Nor could it have been many months after,
if it was not previous to this time, that he
settled another great question of his life, by
devoting himself to the Christian ministry.
Long before his college course was ended, it was
well understood that Kirby was to be found on
the side of Jesus Christ, and that his life was
to be devoted to the work of the ministry.[118]

It was during his college residence that he became acquainted with several men of kindred
spirit, who have been the associates of his
life; and the bond of union which first drew
them together, was the tie of Christian sympathy, tried and proved amid the temptations
and dangers of college. There were, in those
days, times in Yale College which tried men's
souls; and those who, as Christians, had experienced those trials and resisted those
temptations together, were not likely soon to
forget and to cease to trust one another.
Amidst those college trials, was formed a
circle of friendship and confidence, which I
trust not even death can break. Among the
names which composed that circle, were several long familiar as household words to most
of my audience; and among them was that of[119]
William Kirby.

As a scholar, Kirby ranked high in his class, being
graduated in 1827 with high honors. Shortly after his
graduation he began his theological training in the
Theological Department of Yale College. He was "an
earnest, laborious and successful student, equipping
himself, with all diligence and seriousness, for the
great conflict of life to which he was looking forward."[120]
In 1828 he became interested in Home Missions, and
joined the Society of Inquiry Respecting Missions. He
was one of the original seven members who formed the
Illinois Association. On March 15, 1831, he wrote to
Absalom Peters that he was

---

[118]Sturtevant, J.M., The Memory of the Just Funeral
Oration for William Kirby, Yale Memorabilia, Class of
1827, p. 5.
[119]Ibid.
[120]Ibid., p. 6.

. . . expecting soon to leave New Haven for
the West. It is my wish to go out in the
employment of the A.H.M.S. Can I obtain an
appointment from your SocY to the State of
Ill.? If so can it be furnished me before
the second week in April? Whatever may be
the fact will you be so kind as to inform
me, seasonably. It is unnecessary to <u>send</u>
the <u>commission</u> as I shall be in N.Y. the
forepart of next month.[121]

According to Sturtevant, going west entailed a good
deal of sacrifice for William Kirby.

He felt strongly the claims of a mother, who
stood in peculiar need of the assistance of
her children, and especially of this, her
oldest son. But he felt that he should find
means of being dutiful to his mother, without
turning a deaf ear to his Master's call, and
with an unfaltering hand subscribed his name
to a promise which he most religiously fulfilled to his dying day. It is also interesting to add that he did find means, in the
midst of all the difficulties of missionary
labor in a settlement so new, of abundantly
discharging filial duty.[122]

As he was completing his theological training, he
wrote to Captain Elisha Kirby at Guilford, Connecticut,

. . . whatever may be my lot -- I feel happy in the prospect of speedily executing my
plans of usefulness. I can be happy only
when I feel that I am useful. And I can be
useful only when I can be instrumental of
reclaiming souls from the dominion of sin,
to the service and favor of God. With the
blessing of God upon my efforts I feel that
I shall be able to accomplish this object
more extensively by going to the west than
I could by remaining here. . . .[123]

---

[121]Kirby to Peters, New Haven, March 15, 1831.

[122]Sturtevant, J.M., <u>The Memory of the Just Funeral
Oration for William Kirby</u>, <u>Yale Memorabilia</u>, Class of
1827, p. 7.

[123]William Kirby to Elisha Kirby, Guilford, Connecticut, April 7, 1831.

Soon after, he emigrated to Illinois and engaged, temporarily, as an instructor in Illinois College.

In this situation he continued two years, during which time his constitution experienced, from the constant confinement and exhausting labors of the schoolroom, (for such was then the life of an instructor in our college) and from obstinate and protracted attacks of intermittent fever, a shock, from which it never entirely recovered. He has seen hard labor since, but I suspect the two years he spent as an instructor, were the most exhausting of his life. His constitution sank under it; and this circumstance, as well as his constantly cherished intention led him to seek[124] a more active and stirring field of labor.

In the fall of 1832, he was married to Miss Hannah Wolcott, who had come to Jacksonville, Illinois, from East Windsor, Connecticut. In the spring of 1833, he commenced his labors as a preacher and pastor, with the church at Union Grove in Putnam County. Some of his early impressions of the West were printed in the Home Missionary for March, 1834:

. . . Permit me to notice a fact, which finds a parallel only in the history of the early settlement of New England -- that Christians seem to be roused to the importance of laying well the foundations of society in the new but rapidly rising communities of the West. They begin to feel that they sustain responsibilities in this matter, which they cannot throw off with a clear conscience. They have an interest, not only to know, but to decide, what shall be the moral and religious tone of feeling that shall pervade the immense masses of population that shall fill these boundless prairies and fertile plains. The pilgrim fathers were driven from their native shores by the cruel hand of persecution; but Christians at this day, stimulated by a sense of duty and a regard for Christ's kingdom, cheerfully leave the favoured scenes of older states, to exert their influence in forming

---

[124]Sturtevant, J.M., The Memory of the Just Funeral Oration for William Kirby, Yale Memorabilia, Class of 1827, pp. 7-8.

the character of the infant portions of our country. . . .[125]

He testifies to the usefulness of the Society's Agents:

> In riding through the country, I have repeated occasion to notice the influence of your agents upon the feelings of the community. Where they have once been, they are seldom forgotten. No Christians that became acquainted with them, forgot their labours of love, or the interest they manifested for souls. One individual, adopting the language of Paul to the Galatians, could think of their visit only as "Angels of God." Their praise is on the lips of the good people throughout all this region. Through their instrumentality, your Society cannot but feel an assurance that they are doing good; and in this assurance, find a rich reward for their labours and self-denial.[126]

Union Grove did not prove to be a good place in which to work. There were "elements of discord at work" (probably between Congregationalists and Presbyterians) and, at the end of a year, he judged it to be his duty to seek another field of labor.[127] In 1834, he moved to Blackstone's Grove, near Chicago.

> Here Mr. Kirby and his family had an experience of the hardships of frontier missionary life, such as has fallen to the lot of few even of the pioneers in the Home Missionary enterprise. His people were a community of farmers, the most prosperous of whom had hardly been a year and a half upon their farms. Their supplies of provisions were still mainly from abroad. To supply a family regularly with such a necessary as wheat flour was out of the question. A bushel of corn meal made a family feel rich. Mr. Kirby had the privilege of buying corn, at a distance of eight miles from his residence, for a dollar and a half a bushel, pro-

___

[125] _Home Missionary Journal_, March 1834, p. 198.

[126] _Ibid._

[127] Sturtevant, J.M., _The Memory of the Just Funeral Oration for William Kirby_, _Yale Memorabilia_, Class of 1827, p. 8.

vided he would be at the trouble to shell it
for himself. In the circumstances it was considered a privilege to be thus supplied. He
might then carry his corn eight miles in another direction to mill. Unable to get it
ground on the day on which he carried it, he
might return to his home, eight miles distant, and go again a journey of eight miles
and back for his meal, and when he reached
home, rejoice with his family in the possession of so rich a treasure. His nearest
post-office was Chicago, at a distance of
twenty-eight miles. These difficulties were
to be encountered, while he endeavoured to
accomplish the labors and the studies of the
ministry, and when he had no other income
than the meagre stipend of the Home Missionary.[128]

On April 1, 1836, his report to the A.H.M.S. included fifteen additions by letter to his church, and
two by confession, three hopeful conversions, two Sabbath schools, sixty pupils, two Temperance Societies,
with two hundred subscribing, two stations of monthly
concert, and fifteen dollars pledged to foreign missions. At the same time he added,

My ministerial labors have been greatly affected by ill health. I have suffered severely from the ophthalmia. I have some of
the time been neither able to read or write.
Such an impediment to my usefulness I have
felt severely. The interests of religion
have suffered notwithstanding that I have
preached every Sabbath & with two or three
exceptions most generally, more or less
during the week. There has likewise been
much excitement on the subject of lands,
difficulties in the church govt. (?) of it
to nullify the influence of the truth.[129]

Land disputes were frequent in a territory which
had recently been opened to the public, and until conflicting claims were settled, religion often had to
take a back seat. Hence, it was with a sigh of relief,

---

[128]Sturtevant, J.M., The Memory of the Just Funeral
Oration for William Kirby, Yale Memorabilia, Class of
1827, p. 8.
[129]Kirby to Peters, April 1, 1836.

when Kirby wrote that the land sales were past, and
that he hoped to be able to preach with the conviction
that brighter days were before him.[130]   In this, however, he was soon disappointed, for

> . . . the field had no sooner begun to look
> inviting, than a dark cloud arose & overspread
> it with gloom. While standing ready to thrust
> in the sickle & reap a harvest of souls as I
> hoped, an unexpected question arose, which for
> a time threatened a division in our church.
> That question was simply this: "where shall
> we meet for worship." Until this period by
> common consent we had held our sacred assem-
> blies at my house. It was deemed the most
> central & commodious (though small) of any
> that could be had. Our meetings were usually
> well attended, & our prospects with the
> blessing of God were fair for the building
> up of the cause of Christ. But the question,
> shall we not remove to some other place?
> came up.
>
> In order to understand the case it should be
> remarked that the church is made up (of) four
> different neighborhoods. In one direction,
> the extremes are 20 miles apart. In another
> 8 or 10. It was proposed to change the place
> of worship, so as to carry it into a neighbor-
> hood where there are several of our best &
> most efficient members residing, a place
> which will accommodate a large minority, but
> compel the majority to travel by far more
> than their proportion of the distance. Yet
> however all might have been well, if the
> church as a body had been consulted. But a
> few individuals attempted it, resolved to
> carry the measure at any rate. I saw that
> our little church was in danger of being
> rent asunder, unless the proposed measure
> could be speedily crushed. I attempted it,
> not by harsh speaking, . . . but by preaching
> in rotation in the different neighborhoods.
> And by so doing, I incurred the displeasure
> of those whose wishes I opposed.

---

[130]Kirby to Peters, July 4, 1835; in the Home Missionary, September 1835, pp. 81-82. The unsigned article
"Difficulties in a New Country" is by Kirby.

In these circumstances, in confirmity with a
resolution of Gen. Ass. & PresY the church &
congregation were called upon to say whether
the pastoral relation should be instituted
between them & their minister. They met, but
decided nothing. Many objections were however
brought forward. This was done, in my absence in discharge of my duty as trustee of
"Illinois College." On my return I thought
it was my duty to say to the people that my
continuance among them would depend upon
their doing sufficient for my support. My
reasons for this step were as follows:

1st They are as a church abundantly able to
do it, without making any real sacrifice.

2 The dissatisfaction manifested made it my
duty to insist on something that would be
proof of a strong desire for the continuance
of my labors among them.

3 With their ability (for God has greatly
prospered them) I felt that they could not
plead the promises of God, for a blessing
upon my labors, while they were greatly deficient in fulfilling their vows.

They have made an effort to raise something
but I think it will not be sufficient to
sustain me. And I have made up my mind to
leave. I have been thus particular, that
your Society may be able to judge of the
motives & circumstances which influence me
in this matter, & not think that I am too
much given to change . . . . [131]

Another factor induced him to make a change. Kirby
had been a Trustee of Illinois College from its organization, along with the other members of the Illinois
Association. But since he lived at a distance of more
than two hundred miles from the College, he found it
difficult to attend the annual meetings of the Board.
Furthermore, such trips were expensive. Desirous of
being nearer the College, he accordingly accepted the
call of the church and congregation at Mendon, Adams

---

[131]Kirby to Peters, October 28, 1835.

County, and began his work there in 1836.[132]

> Here he pursued his work for nine years, and
> his labors were attended with repeated and
> cheering manifestations of Divine approba-
> tion. Several -- it is not known to the
> speaker how many -- seasons of high religious
> interest were enjoyed, during which numbers
> were added to the Lord. The church was
> strengthened, and enabled to assume the en-
> tire support of its pastor. The life of a
> diligent and faithful pastor of such a church
> is almost too tranquil to have a history which
> can be written on earth. It is the history of
> Christians strengthened, guided, encouraged, --
> of sinners warned, convicted, saved, -- of com-
> fort carried to the house of sorrow and the
> chamber of death.

> Such a history, it is believed, Mr. Kirby's
> labors had at Mendon. He was not without his
> difficulties and his trials; but he exerted
> an important and permanent influence for good,
> and did much to prepare the church for lasting
> efficiency and usefulness.[133]

The church at Mendon was the first Congregational
church in Illinois, having been gathered in February,
1833. The church at Princeton, Illinois, is older as
a Congregational Church, but it was organized at Northampton, Massachusetts, March 23, 1831, and migrated to
Illinois, arriving June, 1831. William Kirby was the
second regular pastor at Mendon. Accepting a call to
preach in 1836, he was to give three-fourths of his
time to Mendon, with a salary of three hundred dollars
a year in semi-annual payments. By 1837 his popularity
had brought forth an increase of two hundred and fifty
dollars a year in salary. In 1837 two corner lots were
donated to the church, and there the pioneer members
built their first separate church edifice. It was a
frame building thirty by forty feet and did service
for about fifteen years.[134]

---

[132]Sturtevant, J.M., _The Memory of the Just Funeral Oration for William Kirby_, _Yale Memorabilia_, Class of 1827, p. 9.

[133]_Ibid_. Kirby was installed at Mendon in 1839.

[134]Stillwell, Frederick E., _History of the Mendon Congregational Church_. A Brief Sketch Delivered at the Mid-West Congregational Historical Society Meeting held Dec. 27, 1928 at the Chicago Theological Seminary.

There is no more extant correspondence from William Kirby until 1843. On November 10, 1843, apparently at the request of the A.H.M.S., he wrote a long article on the History of the Churches in Adams Co. This article was published in the Home Missionary for January, 1844, with the probable intention of following it up later with historical sketches of other counties in Illinois.

In 1845, Kirby entered upon the General Agency of the American Home Missionary Society, first for the whole state, and subsequently for the central and southern portions of it.[135] We have already seen how demanding was the work of a Missionary on the Illinois frontier.

Of the severe labors and hardships of these last years of his life, few have any adequate conception. Protracted and painful absences from his family, amid all his own liabilities and their's to sickness and death -- long and toilsome journeys, amid the rigors of winter, and the scorching heats of summer -- the scanty accommodations and hard fare of the traveller in frontier settlements, and a multitude of other circumstances combined to render it a service of great toil and hardship. It was performed with uncomplaining fortitude and cheerfulness, for the love he bore to the kingdom of Christ.

But there was another feature of this service, which I suspect he found a greater trial to his feelings, in some instances, than its toils and its hardships. The leading design of the Agency was not to raise money for the Society; that was entirely secondary. Its leading object was to advise, strengthen, and encourage feeble churches in their efforts to establish permanent Christian institutions. In the prosecution of this object, he was brought in contact with all those local sectional and partisan jealousies and passions, which, in all our new settlements, do more to

_____

[135]Sturtevant, J.M., The Memory of the Just Funeral Oration for William Kirby, Yale Memorabilia, Class of 1827, p. 9.

94

weaken churches than smallness of number or
poverty of resources. Especially was he
liable to be brought into collision with
those ecclesiastical questions which divide
the two great bodies of Christians, by whom
the American Home Missionary Society is mainly
sustained. That cool, deliberate, and impar-
tial judgment for which he was eminently distinguished, peculiarly qualified him for the
successful prosecution of his labors in such
circumstances. That he never erred in fulfilling his delicate trust, I do not assert.
But it seems to me, that amidst feelings so
intense as have been excited on that subject,
it was morally impossible that he should have
escaped censure, and severe censure, whether
he erred or not . . . . Mr. Kirby was no
ecclesiastical politician . . . .[136]

There are over seventy extant communications from
Kirby to the Society between the years 1845 and 1851,
when he died. A letter dated July 15, 1845, gives an
excellent glimpse into his work:

My labors have been expended in Hancock Co.
regularly since April 1st inst. I have
preached at R.P. (Round Prairie), Carthage,
Montebello, La Harp & Mills Grove, the last
two named places only once. Carthage has
need enough of the Gospel preached with
the Holy Ghost sent down from H-n. There
is a small Cong. Ch. yet in existence there,
but religion is in a woful (sic) state.
There are some few members of this & the
other chs, baptist & Methodist whose garments
are not defiled. But the greater part of all
the professors of the different denominations,
have suffered the Mormon excitement to absorb
their energies, & divert their interest from
the Kingdom of X. Gen. Dumming the Sheriff,
who shot, recently Dr. Marshall, was a member
of the Cong. Ch. I fear that he is one of
those whose religion will not bear transpor-
tation. The audience is good on the Sabbath,

[136]Sturtevant, J.M., The Memory of the Just Funeral
Oration for William Kirby, Yale Memorabilia, Class of
1827, pp. 9-10.

being generally about 150, most of them persons of intelligence, who know the value of
religious Institutions, to the welfare of a
community. Some 50 dols I think would have
been raised if I had continued to preach to
them, towards my support.[137]

As we have already seen, one of the tasks of the
Agent was to recommend various preachers to the Society.
Much of Kirby's correspondence consists of sketches of
various men and their work in different parts of Illinois.

Br. Nichols I have known for some years, in-
timately. He was for a while at Columbus,
commissioned by the A.H.M.S. His health
failed by an attack of Bronchitis, just before which the people came to the conclusion
that he could be no longer useful to them.
He then turned his attention to farming &
for about 2 yrs. was engaged in that or some
other manual labor. He then felt so much
restored that he wished to resume his work
of preaching the Gospel. Though there were
destitute chhs. in this vicinity none seemed
inclined to imploy (sic) him. The brethren
of PresY and others thought he might be most
useful in the tract cause & succeeded in pro-
curing for him an appointment in that service.

Br. N is a man of undoubted piety, and re-
spectable intellectual powers. His Theological Studies were prosecuted at Auburn under
D. Richard. But I think from various causes,
he has made but little progress since he has
been at the west. He is not a very acceptable pastor, although the churches listen to
him occasionally with interest. I will spe-
cify a few particulars as the probable reasons of this want of public favor.

1 His manner is very unpleasant. He has a
whining cant sufficiently natural, but made
intolerable by an affectation of compassion
(I shd think) for his hearers. His words
are drawn out & "drop their lazy length along"
to the no small annoyance of his hearers.

137 Kirby to Badger, July 15, 1845.

2. He often lacks all common sense, in untimely remarks about his own achievements
& speaks of them as remarkable when his wiser
brethren hang their heads with shame. He is
not careful to apply the maxim, Let another
man praise thee & not thine own mouth, a
stranger & not thine own lips.

3. His efforts though some times very good,
generally indicate a want of study & preparation. He has a strange confidence in his
own powers combined with a singular regard
for the good opinion of others.

Perhaps I ought not to have written all this.
It might have been enough to say that though
he might do good in some fields where the few
intelligent ones would hold him up & assist,
there is little to encourage the expectation
that he would succeed in building up very fast,
where intelligence is combined with opposition
to the truth. Could he find a field where the
people are united in him (like Hills Grove &
brother Williams) I should not hesitate to
recommend a small appropriation to sustain him,
as a feeble support of the ordinances of the
gospel is better than none . . . .[137]

It is interesting to note how often Kirby attempted
to unite two or more feeble struggling churches. The
little churches at Geneseo and Sharon are a case in point.[138]

Frequently, Kirby would be called upon to settle
complaints arising between pastors, churches and the
Society, or to settle arguments arising within a church.
The letter of March 17, 1849 is an answer to inquiries
concerning complaints of G.W. Eliot, the church at Meta-
more, and Reverend M.N. Miles. The letter is interesting as showing how loyalties may be divided between two
pastors, causing a split in the church. Then, too, he
had constantly to fight sickness and overcome travelling
difficulties:

---

[137] Kirby to Badger, September 30, 1845.

[138] Kirby to Badger, July 2, 1846; and September 24,
1848 regarding a union of the Manchester Church with
Winchester or Whitehall.

97

I have visited, though late the Co seat of
Woodford Co. & made the best of my time while
in that region a period of 3 weeks. I could
not reach the place immediately on the recT
of your letter. Much of the Winter long journeys
have been impracticable. And on my return I was
obliged to take my buggy into pieces & carry it
across streams on skiffs & swim my horse to get
back. And every day the stream and roads were
becoming worse. It took two days on my return
to perform the journey of one when I went up.
You will not be surprised therefore to learn that
I have been suffering for nearly 2 weeks with the
influenza so as to disable me from mailing my
annual report in due season . . . .[139]

. . . . our youngest child . . . we were called
to bury a week ago last sabbath. He was afflicted
for 3 weeks with the "cholera infantum" which was
at last checked, when the hooping (sic) cough
set in and after some 2 weeks carried him off.
He was among the loveliest of children, but the
Gospel leaves us no room to mourn his lot . . . .[140]

Kirby was by no means unmindful of his obligation to
Illinois College. On January 9, 1850, he wrote to Badger:

And when I add that the two Co^S of Adam and
Pike have raised 10,000 for Indowment (sic)
of a Professorship in Ill. Coll. you will
acknowledge that we have made some head way.
I hope you will not put this fact into print,
our work for the College is in progress, and
we do not intend to stop short of 30,000 dols.
The amT raised has by a vote of the Trustees
been pledged to a Professorship of Rhetoric
& Oratory, and the incumbent is to be Pres-
byterially connected, if we can find such &
yet Congregationalists have subscribed the
greater part of it.[141]

Sturtevant says that Kirby was very punctual in
attending the regular annual meetings of the Board

---

[139]Kirby to Badger, March 17, 1849.
[140]Kirby to Badger, August 15, 1849.
[141]Kirby to Badger, January 9, 1850.

from 1833 until the time of his death.

I find but two regular meetings of the Board at
which his name is not entered as present. One
of these was the meeting of 1833, which was held
out of time, on account of prevailing pestilence.
At the time when the other absence occurred, he
reached the Illinois River, on his way and found
it impassable. This punctuality has been maintained when, for a portion of the time his residence was more than two hundred miles, and for
the greater part of the time little short of one
hundred miles from Jacksonville, and when the
journey was to be accomplished in his own con-
veyance and entirely at his own charges, both
for his time and his expenses, and often over
muddy roads and across swollen streams. We
hear of the princely liberality of the rich to
the cause of learning; and may it be still more
honored that it may be more practiced. But
here, in the silent, unostentatious history of
a minister of the Gospel, whose nominal salary
was but four hundred a year, and that subject
to large discounts which Home Missionaries understand very well, is a noble liberality to the
cause of learning, which deserves to be remembered when the princely donations of the wealthy
are forgotten. And yet, in addition to all this,
he was a subscriber of $100 to the endowment
fund of Illinois College.[142]

Late in 1851, Kirby was overtaken by an attack of
pneumonia just as he was finishing a successful effort
to found a Presbyterian church at Naples. The disease
was so violent that he conversed little during his ill-
ness. "I am ready," he said, "to go or stay; I trust
I am prepared. I rely not upon the good opinion of
others, nor upon anything which I have done. I can
truly say I have no doubts."[143] Two days later he
died, on December 20, 1851.

Kirby invested his life in the church on the Illinois frontier. A paragraph which he wrote to Badger
a few years before his death very aptly describes his
own life-purpose:

---

[142]Sturtevant, J.M., The Memory of the Just Funeral
Oration for William Kirby, Yale Memorabilia, Class of
1827, pp. 11-12.
[143]Ibid., p. 11.

. . . This is one of the signs of promise respecting the future religious history of the
West. The young especially will go where they
are interested, where there is light & knowledge. Their fathers may die as they are, but
their children will listen to the preacher that
is able to make himself understood & to throw
around his subject the light & interest which
only a disciplined thinking mind can give it.
Hearers it is true may not be drawn together
at once in large numbers. But let a competent
educated minister, stay long enough, in a community to be known, let him by his own efforts
create a capital which he can not bring with
him, and he will have hearers and influence
too, if he deserved them. There is many a man
at the West, who when he first made his appearance, was looked down upon by ranting ignorance who now fills a sphere of influence &
usefulness, which those who dispised (sic)
him as a stripling, might well covet. Any
man who has a heart & qualifications to do
good, will find the opportunity to do it even
at the West.[144]

The fifth and last member of the Yale Band to become one of the agents of the American Home Missionary
Society was Elisha Jenney. Of his early life we know
little beyond the fact that he was born in Fairhaven,
Connecticut, in 1803, and was graduated from Dartmouth
College in 1827. He then came to Yale, and in the following year became a member of the Society for Christian Research. He received his degree in divinity from
Yale in 1831. On August 27, of the same year, he offered himself to the American Home Missionary Society,
and requested an outfit and commission.[145] The Society
would have to pay his travelling expenses, he said, because he was several hundred dollars in debt. He made
the arduous trip west, and reached Illinois late in
1831, or early in 1832, settling at Rushville, Illinois.
On March 31, 1832, he made out a lengthy report of his
work at Rushville, part of which was printed in the
Home Missionary Journal for July, 1832.[146] He says,

---

[144]Kirby to Badger, March 5, 1847. See Home Missionary,
June 1847, pp. 40-41.

[145]Jenney to Peters, New Haven, Conn., August 27, 1831.

[146]It is printed under the caption From a Missionary in
Illinois, p. 40; the original letter is addressed to Peters.

I came to this place unasked. For a long time
it seemed I was almost (undesired?). This was
very trying to my feelings; and though it may
be the duty of a missionary sometimes to impose
himself on a community, I shall not venture to
repeat the act. When you wish to send a man to
a particular place, would it not be best to make
this known to some pious persons there, and let
them incline the people to give him a call? They
will then regard him as their man, be more likely
to attend upon his preaching, & contribute to
his support . . . .

At first my congregations, on the sabbath, were
small, not exceeding 25-30 persons. Now they
are increased to 90 or 100, whenever the weather
is pleasant & the walking good. Our place of
worship is a little out of the village, a location very inconvenient, & a house very uncom-
fortable. Unless the walking be tolerably good,
it is almost inaccessible: and when there we
are incommoded with bad seats and with dirt.
But for these circumstances my hearers would probably be twice their present number. When I
came it seemed almost impossible to hold evening
meetings. The people had never been accustomed
to them, and would not attend. This was discouraging: for week after week, seeing only 10 or
15 present. I felt that my labors would be lost.
But the Lord has appeared for us, to a limited
extent, and we now have 3 such exercises. These
are not so well attended as they ought to be:
but they are interesting & profitable. Most
of the religious feeling which exists among
christians, originated at these meetings, and
having here met the Lord, they seem determined
to persevere in their attendance. When I commenced preaching here, the church was in a very
unfavorable state. There had been no public
exercises on the sabbath, for a long time, and
that day was, I fear even by professors of religion, worse than wasted. They, as a body, had
gone far into the region where God is unknown;
but they have since heard his voice, saying,
"arise & come up to my help against the mighty."
All have heard, & some have obeyed. Yes, there
are those among us, either members of our
church, or in communion with us, who are firmly
on the Lord's side, and are gradually rising to
still greater heights in christian excellence.
They mourn over the past, over their coldness,

their deadness, over their ingratitude, & the
reproach they have brought upon the cause of
religion. They mourn with the fixed purpose to
let their example shine for the future, & to
press on towards the perfection & happiness of
the righteous. With these facts in view, & the
promises of the Bible to rest upon, we have been
praying & laboring, & hoping that God will renew
his work in our village. Nor do we ever altogether despair of such a blessing. He has been
long calling upon us to come out & be separate;
and we have refused . . . . As grounds of encouragement, the following may be stated, a few
have lately become hopefully pious, more are in
some measure, anxious about the salvation of
their souls; and there is an increasing solemnity throughout our congregation on the sabbath.
But then this has been the state of things for
several weeks; and yet there are no very
marked results.

Our Bible Class consists of about 20 members,
mostly adults. It is the first exercise of
the kind ever held here. Some interest has
been taken in it, by those who regularly attend:
but as every evening of the week is occupied by
some meeting, religious, singing, or debating,
I shall discontinue it for the present. The
Sabbath School, I am sorry to say, has dwindled
away to -- nothing. This is not to be attrib-
uted to remissness on the part of teachers. They
have visited every family, & made efforts to get
out children. But there are obstacles to success.
One is, the inconvenient location of our school
house; and the severity of the weather for most
of the winter: another the want of comfortable
clothing. During the last summer the school
numbered 60 or 70 scholars. For four months
past, there have not been a dozen present. It
was suspended a few weeks since, but will be
resumed next sabbath . . . .

Jenney's stay at Rushville was brief, however. On
the twenty-fourth of May, he went to Carrollton, Illinois, and in July held a protracted meeting with Thomas
Lippincott at the church where Henry Herrick had been
the former pastor. The congregation experienced a revival, a description of which soon followed in the Home
Missionary Journal for October, 1832.[147] Then, after

147Home Missionary Journal, Vol. V, p. 85.

the enthusiasm of the revival had abated somewhat, Jenney again decided (for reasons we do not know) to change his field of labor. This called forth considerable protest from the Society.

. . . There are several things in our operations in the West which we would be glad to correct, one of which has occurred in relation to yourself. I refer to the frequent change of location. You are aware that our policy is, as far as practicable to make the aid we grant tell on the permanency of religious institutions in the place aided. Thence, we expect our Missionaries to remain as stationary as practicable. Two evils result from a contrary course: the change of ministers produces a fastidiousness in the people, & their interest in the preacher does not have time to accumulate & become mature enough for them to enter heartily into the work of supporting him. Hence, the great burden of his support comes on the Missionary Society, and instead of our missionaries being less expense to us the second year, they ask for the full pledge of $400. Thus, in your case, you request a renewal of our pledge at that rate per ann. and the reason you assign, is, that you are not settled, or permanently located. Now, Dr. Br. we do not say these things as judging your course & deciding that you ought not to have left Carrolton; for at this distance, & with the limited information we have on the subject we cannot say but that there were very good reasons for that course. But, you will readily perceive it increases the expense to us of sustaining you and on that account we regret it. We are wading through a sea of embarrassments arising from the comparative smallness of our resources & the number and urgency of the applications that come upon us.

Another thing concerning which our Committee directed me to correspond with you, is the intimation contained in your letter that you expect to leave the missionary service in a few months & engage in establishing a seminary. This object is doubtless a good one, but as our Society is sustained by a . . . public for the single object of preaching the gospel, we wish to make our grants bear on that. Now if brethren who are sent out by us, with outfits to a large amt. from the Miss. funds, and sustained in their

incipient labors at a heavy expense to the Soc[y]
desert us, & go to building up Colleges & seminaries, it is discouraging to us as a <u>Missionary</u>
<u>Society</u>; for though they are doing a good work,
& an indispensable work, it is not <u>the work</u> for
which we sent them, nor for which our patrons
furnish the means to pay them; and we are under
the necessity of paying outfits & heavy amounts
to sustain others to take their places as missionaries. Thus, the advantage gained by one
set is lost by introducing another. Our Committee
wish to know then, whether you expect to devote
your labors to preaching or whether you expect
to be employed in some other department. On the
answer will depend in some degree the renewal of
your commission. They feel as if it were comparatively a small object to procure your labors
for 6 months, if you must then leave the field
and their employ, especially when those 6 mos
labor are to cost at the full rate . . . . You
will at once perceive, Dr B. that the views of
the ComT on these points grow out of their duty
to the missionary cause, & their responsibilities
to the public who have set them to attend to this
work. None but the kindest feelings are entertained toward yourself; the ComE have every
reason to be satisfied that you have been a
laborious & faithful preacher & they would rejoice if your views of duty would allow you to
devote yourself hereafter in the same successful[148]
manner exclusively to the missionary works.

This letter caused Jenney some "unhappy hours" and
he hastened to supply the Society with additional information which "placed the whole matter in a light so
different from what it was before," that the committee
cordially renewed his commission with a guaranty of
four hundred dollars.[149]

On November 7, 1834 Jenney wrote to Peters from
Lower Alton, telling about his work there, but also
announcing that his engagement with the people would
terminate the following April.

When I came here, there were only 18 persons in
our communion. The number is 49, -- 10 of whom
here united with the church by profession. And

---

[148]Hall to Jenney, November 23, 1832. Letter Book F #318.
[149]Hall to Jenney, February 19, 1833. Letter Book F #439.

then, there have been 6 deaths among those who
intended to associate themselves with us. During my residence here, 19 hopeful conversions
have occurred, 6 of whom have not yet connected
themselves with any church, and 2 have removed
far beyond in bounds. The tone of religious
feeling is not high among our members; and yet
they have thriven out upon different benevolent
objects, not less than nine thousand dollars.
And then there is perfect harmony in our church.
No unkindness of feeling has ever been cherished
as far as I know, by one brother towards another.
. . .

After what I have said respecting the beneficence
of my church, you will b (sic) surprised to learn
that they contribute very little to my support.
It is now more than two years since I came here,
and they have not given me two hundred dollars.
This is to be regretted more particularly on account of its influence upon them. It cannot fail
to be very injurious, should they get the impression, that they can have the gospel without
paying for it. Would it not be best to leave them
to learn by experience the value of a stated ministry? In that case they might call some one to
labor with them, & of course make definite &
liberal proposals to him. Taking upon themselves
such obligations, they would not only b, (sic)
but also feel, bound to meet them. It has troubled me not a little, lest I become the occasion
of more evil than good. But what can be done?
The subject has been brought repeatedly before
the church. Subscription papers have been circulated through the village, & pledges to a considerable amount, have been given. But the business of collecting goes on very slowly. Some
time since I laid the subject before the church
by letter: & told them plainly that I must leave
then, because they furnished me with nothing better than subscription papers with which to feed
& clothe myself. But the only reply received was,
that a resolution had unanimously passed, to have
me continue, & that a committee was appointed to
take measures to secure my support. That looked
encouraging. But the result -- . It has not yet
thrown a dollar into my pocket; but the promise
is that considerable shall be done.

I state these facts, not in the way of complaint,
though I have much reason for that. My object is

to let you see that if I again draw upon your
society, it will b (sic) because stern necessity urges me to do it.[150]

Early in 1835 Jenney made a trip to Jacksonville to
confer with the brethren there relative to a Female
Seminary which a member of his church proposed to erect
at the expense of around ten thousand dollars. While
in Jacksonville, he was requested to preach during the
evenings.

The Spirit came down, & we were encouraged to
believe that much good would be done. I continued there for two weeks. It was a season
of great interest, & the work extended, beyond any similar work in the village. We
had, at least fifty, in the anxious list: &
the number of hopeful conversions was -- but
I prefer to leave that part to be told when it
should b (sic) found who of them have really
turned from sin to holiness.[151]

The Presbyterian Church at Jacksonville invited him
to preach there for an indefinite time, and Baldwin advised him to do so if he could not get a more liberal
support where he was. But he refused to go because it

. . . would be hazardous to my reputation,
perhaps distructive (sic) to my usefulness
to be brought so much in contrast with the
superior minds which are there. A far
humbler sphere would be better suited to
my disposition & talents.[152]

We hear no more of Elisha Jenney until the year 1848.
He says that during this interval he preached regularly
to destitute settlements without any pecuniary compensation.

. . . Yet not exactly so: for I have received $6.25 in money, besides 5 lbs of
cheese & 2 lbs of butter, for my services.
This course I have been unable to pursue,
yet not without practicing more rigid self-

---

[150]Jenney to Peters, November 7, 1834 from Lower Alton, Ill.
[151]Jenney to Peters, March 4, 1835 from Lower Alton, Ill.
[152]Ibid.

denial, than any one perhaps, ought volun-
tarily to subject himself to . . . .[153]

Twenty-two months of the time he was connected with
Monticello Female Academy, in Godfrey, Illinois, of
which Theron Baldwin was Principal. He also acted as
one of the trustees of Illinois College. In June,
1848, the church at Spring Creek, Illinois, sent the
following communication to the Executive Committee of
the American Home Missionary Society:

> We the Elders of the Spring Creek church, in
> connection with the Presbytery of Illinois,
> would represent,
>
> 1. That the number of members of this church
> now in good standing, is twenty-seven.
>
> 2. That the worshipping congregation on the
> sabbath, varies from fifty, to one hundred
> and fifty, according as there are, or are
> not, other meetings held, the same time, in
> the neighborhood.
>
> 3. That we are unable, without foreign aid,
> to sustain the regular preaching of the gos-
> pel among us, which, nevertheless, we think
> the interests of religion require should be
> done if possible.
>
> 4. That the utmost we can raise, in & out
> of the church, is about one hundred dollars
> per annum.
>
> 5. That we have engaged the services of
> Rev. E. Jenney, for the current year, com-
> mencing on the second (2d) sabbath of May.
>
> In view of these facts, we humbly request
> you, brethren, to appropriate, for the
> support of the gospel, in this neighbor-
> hood, the sum of two hundred dollars, ($200),
> thus securing to our present supply, three
> hundred dollars per annum, which is all he
> asks, or wishes to receive, as long as we
> are dependent on the friends of religion
> abroad . . . .[154]

---

[153]Jenney to Badger, August 1848, from Waverly, Illinois.
[154]Church at Spring Creek, Ill. to the A.H.M.S., June 1848.

The application is endorsed by both Hale and Kirby.
The Society granted the request for funds, and Jenney
labored at Spring Creek with a fair amount of success.
By the beginning of 1850, he was able to report over
sixty church members, forty-four on the ground and in
good standing; six hopeful conversions, fifty Sabbath
School scholars, one hundred and fifty volumes in the
library, and twenty-three dollars contributed to missions.[155]

In addition to his duties as pastor of the Spring
Creek Church, Jenney was also a Missionary of the Illinois Presbytery. He soon found himself in the somewhat embarrassing position of trying to serve two mas-
ters. The Presbytery was anxious for him to explore
the needy portions of the state. The American Home
Missionary Society complained that he was spreading
himself too thin, and should remain in the territory
designated by the terms of his commission. Finally,
the A.H.M.S. lost all patience, and wrote:

> Your commission states particularly, I believe,
> the points where you were expected to labor.
> You speak of them indeed as constituting the
> field assigned, so that I suppose there is no
> misunderstanding on this point. Such inci-
> dental labor, in the immediate vicinity of
> these places as would be compatible with your
> regular stated services which as pastor find
> it practicable to render in the vicinity of
> these congregations, it was not intended of
> course to exclude. But the commission does
> not extend the field over a larger territory
> than the one named in it, nor was it supposed
> your labors would be, nor can they be con-
> sistently. The arrangement was made, with
> the Com. . . . We have never given any such
> latitude of interpretation to our commissions,
> or any occasion as we are aware, for the re-
> presentations which you say have been made to
> you. We expect each missionary to abide
> strictly by the terms of his commission, to
> perform the kind of labor contemplated, &
> within the limits ascribed . . . .[156]

---

[155]Statistical report to the A.H.M.S., dated February
14, 1850.

[156]Badger to Jenney, December 10, 1855. Letter Book,
1854-5 #1632.

In defense of his action, which the Society had pronounced "irregular, even so much so as not to be tolerated any longer"[157] Jenney called upon Hale to support him,[158] and declared that he had "acted all along, in accordance with the principles laid down in my first report, Sep. '51 & published, in the 'Home Missionary,' without note or comment, & consequently, as I supposed, endorsed by the Secretaries of the Society."[159] The upshot of the whole controversy was for the American Home Missionary Society to employ Jenney as an Agent for the state.[160] For the next ten years he dispatched his work with fervor. The amount of correspondence between Jenney and the A.H.M.S. is tremendous. His tours were long and extensive, and his reports describe minutely the religious state of each town and village which he visited. A tour in the spring of 1858 included Upper Alton, Plymouth, Atlanta, Virden, Rosemond, Pana, Shelbyville, Neoga, Centralia, Deuquoine, Richview, Vandalia, and Shipman. At Upper Alton he assisted Professor Sanders of Illinois College in raising one thousand dollars or more for the College. At Plymouth, bitter feelings between Presbyterians and Congregationalists over slavery had to be soothed. At Shelbyville, he had to inquire into the conduct of the minister.

> The charges brought against him are not very serious. 1. He has been known to play a game of checkers with a non-professor. 2. He is not faithful in social intercourse, especially to the younger members of the families. 3. He is too bashful to render him as useful as he otherwise would be out of the pulpit. 4. He suffered his eyes to be bandaged by some ladies, in consequence whereof he stumbled & fell. . . .[161]

On the first of September, he reported to the Society a tour which included Chatham, Cumberland Precinct, Hickory Creek, Marshall, New Providence, Mattoon, Middleport, Rantoul and Pera, Tolono and Arro Gordo.[162]

---

[157] Jenney to Badger, May 1, 1856, from Waverly, Illinois.

[158] Cf. Badger to Hale, January 26, 1858. Letter Book 1857-58 #2073.

[159] Jenney to Badger, May 1, 1856 from Waverly, Illinois.

[160] Cf. Badger to Hale, March 4, 1858. Letter Book 1857-58 #2373 and Badger to Jenney, February 23, 1858. Letter Book 1857-58, #2277.

[161] Jenney to Badger, July 8, 1858 from Waverly, Illinois.

[162] Jenney to Badger, September 1, 1858 from Waverly, Ill.

By the middle of October, he had visited Winchester, Barry, Newtown, Liberty, Columbus, Camp Point, Versailes (Brown Co.), Manchester (Morgan Co.), Bunker Hill (Macoupin Co.), Woodbury (Macoupin Co.), Tavy (?)[163] (Madison Co.), Farmington, Concord, and Pontiac. At the end of the year, he wrote a twenty-eight page communication telling of the history of his labors. This report shows that many of the churches in Illinois were breaking away from the American Home Missionary Society. The communications may also show that Jenney was a none-too-popular figure upon the scene.

For the year 1859, there are thirty letters extant which were written to the Society. His travels frequently brought him in touch with other members of the Yale Band. In January, he consulted with Hale, Brooks, and wrote:

> My interview with brother Sturtevant has been in an eminent degree Pleasant (sic) & satisfactory. He acts as stated supply for the Congregational church while they are destitute of a pastor; & with his permission I yesterday presented the claims of the Society to his people. The result was not what we wished; but it exceeded our expectations. The fact is, the Congregationalists are building a large & expensive house of worship which costs $24,000 a quarter more than they supposed it would, when they commenced. This excess they have not yet provided for. Hence their present embarrassment. They cannot do what they would; but give you a small token of their goodwill.[164]

At Atlanta, he found that

> . . . the immediate prosperity of that church is very doubtful. Brother Lemuel Foster's residence there is an obstacle. True, he no longer preaches, but in public estimation, he is identified with that enterprise; & many so feel towards him, that they will not even go where they suppose he has any control, or influence. And, then, the members of the church

---

[163] Jenney to Badger, October 1858.

[164] Jenney to Badger, January 24, 1859.

are gradually falling off. Since I visited
the place, in June last, about one third of
them have moved away. Those who would have
come in & made their number good, but for
the prejudice alluded to, have united themselves with other denominations. Now that
people are destitute of ministerial aid, &
must continue so for the present. The room
in which they meet is very uninviting; &
it is impossible to gather a congregation
there. Hence, the conclusion to which they
came, while I was with them, a three days'
visit, was, that they ought not, during this
winter, to attempt to sustain preaching. So
you will receive no application from that
quarter until Spring, perhaps not even then,
for they will not need foreign aid, provided
success attends an effort now being made,
to unite OS Presbyterians & Congregationalists[165]
That, however, will not probably be effected.

During the same year he reported twelve churches
organized, eleven houses of worship built and three
repaired, revivals in seven churches ("but only to a
very limited extent"), eight churches had had "unusual religious interest" and that, while twenty-six
churches had regular preaching every alternate sabbath, or once in four weeks, not less than sixteen
were destitute of ministerial aid, ("all of whom, with
two exceptions, are unable to sustain preaching without help from abroad.")[166]

It is a matter of regret that I can do no
more for the Society. I am absent from home
most of the time, but less than I should be,
were not travelling attended with so great
expense. I have not yet seen reason to regret any outlay of the kind. But when railroad fare amounts to $15 a month, or there-
abouts, as it does sometimes, then I have
to pause & enquire whether your treasury will
justify that. My field is a large one, & it
is desirable I visit some portions of it of-
tener than once a year. But as things now are,

---

[165]Jenney to Badger, January 24, 1859.

[166]Jenney to D.P. Noyes, March 1, 1861 from Galesburg,
Illinois.

I cannot do that without experiencing a
pecuniary spasm. Is there no relief? What
would be the effect, if the Ex Com were to
appeal to the rail road companies of this
state, (the principal officers of some of
which reside in your city) to issue passes
to your agents? It could not make matters
any worse than they now are; and might furnish brother Kent & myself with the means of
doubling our usefulness.

Half fare tickets are no longer granted on
most of our roads; &, whether they will be
again, is somewhat doubtful. But I happen
to know of two instances in which clergymen
(Mess Osborne & Rankin) have received free
passes.[167]

Jenney's correspondence shows what a variety of
activity he was engaged in. It deals with several
destitute churches in Southern Illinois, among which
was that at Jacksonville; he also informs the Society
who is supplying what churches where; he informs the
home office of the various men on the field, and what
the churches think about the men who are serving them.
Then there are other matters such as the collection
of funds from various churches to be sent to the missionary society, the distribution of boxes to needy
ministerial families, reports on his travels. The
opening page of his annual Report dated March 1, 1863
will summarize the picture regarding the church on
his field:

Two churches have been organized. Nine are
now destitute of ministerial aid, for three
of which, however, arrangements have been made
that can hardly fail to secure them stated
supplies. Two young men have been licensed to
preach the gospel, both of whom are now laboring with flattering prospects of usefulness.
Eleven churches have dismissed & twelve received, pastors or stated supplies. Twenty-
seven ministers have, directly, or indirectly,

---

[167] Jenney to Badger, March 1, 1860, from Waverly, Illinois. Cf. also Badger to Jenney, July 17, 1858.
Letter Book 1857-58 #506.

applied for places, only three of whom are
now laboring on my field, though seven others,
at least, have found employment elsewhere.
Those churches aided by the Society a year
ago, are now self-sustaining, i.e. they themselves pay for all the preaching they have,
two of them every sabbath, one twice a month.
We have had an accession of six ministers, &
three have left the State, one of whom wishes
to return, & probably will. Several of the
churches have agitated the question relative
to the erection of houses of worship; only
one, however, has advanced far towards accom-
plishing that object.[168]

Twelve months later he wrote:

The year just closed has been to our churches
one at least of ordinary prosperity. True
there have been trials & embarrassments, such
as were unknown to them previous to the national strife in which we are engaged . . . .

. . . They are, without an exception, loyal to
the government, & ready for any sacrifices &
hardships in the cause of humanity & religion.
. . . And the more thoroughly their state has
been examined, the deeper is the conviction,
that they ought, all of them, to be sustained
& encouraged. . . . A portion of them, however, are not progressive. . . . Others of
these churches are aiming at, & gradually ap-
propriating self-reliance. Their present
state, compared with what it was in the beginning is such as to awaken gratitude & in-
spire hope. . . . Fourteen of our churches,
perhaps more, have been, or are now being
blessed with revivals, of greater or less
power . . . .[169]

And again, in March, 1865:

Another year has passed with all its events,
both sad & joyful. It has been a year of loss
& gain to our Home Missionary, as well as
other, churches. How many of their members

---

[168]Annual Report to the Society, March 8, 1863.
[169]Jenney (to Badger) Annual Report to the Home Missionary Society dated March 1863-1864.

have been absent in the service of our country! Of these some have fallen by disease or the missiles of foes. When we parted with them, to go forth to the work of blood and death, we did hope they would return again to perform another, if not a more christian, service. To a great extent they were the flower & strength of the churches to which they belonged, & bid fair, not only to succeed the aged & inform, but to more than make their places good. But their career has been cut short. Death has met them in the way; & we know that we shall see them no more.

Our churches, feble (sic) enough before, cannot well endure such depletions. Yet none of them have been rendered extinct thereby. Distressed are they, but not despairing; cast down, but not destroyed. Bearing these marks of the war, they have the life of Jesus made more manifest. The loss has been great, the gain, in some instances, greater. This consists not in increase of wealth, nor in additions to their membership; but in that which is above all price, the graces of the Spirit. That sense of dependence which diminished earthly strength has taught them, & that felt need of more fervent, agonizing prayer for spiritual blessings, which brings & binds them to the mercy seat, have assimilated them to Him whom they love & serve.

In this way a seen & felt evil has, not in all cases, however, worked for good. We have better christians in our churches, more devoted and active, in consequence of these very bereavements. Nor is this a strange result. It is just what might have been expected. Tribulation worketh patience, experience, hope & heaven. . . . [170]

In his Annual Report from March 1, 1865 to March 1, 1866 Jenney states that he travelled 5,511 miles during the year, not including two journeys to New England and back, and preached ninety sermons, spending more

---

[170]Annual Report to the American Home Missionary Society dated March, 1865 (introductory paragraphs).

time than usual, especially for the last quarter, with destitute congregations.

There are on this field, embracing seventy nine counties, eighty six Congregational churches, of which thirty one are self-sustai(ned) & fifty five dependent on foreign aid, or would be if they had a minister & preaching the whole time. Together they have a membership of nearly, if not quite, six thousand, in a population of one & a quarter million, or as one to every two hundred & ten souls.[171]

Hitherto we have been credited for a commendable degree of liberality in contributing to benevolent objects. Whether we deserved that or not may be a mootable question; but certain it is, we have gone farther in that direction, during the last year, than we ever did before, especially in reference to Home Evangelization.

Installation is still the exception, not the rule, with us. If the scriptures require that ceremony: if, too, it tends to bind pastors & churches more closely to each other, these things seem not to be very apparent to most. Hence the almost universal ignoring of a practice which obtains extensively & works happily in the eastern states.

During the year nine ministers of the gospel have entered this field, & ten have gone from it, at least closed their relations to the respective churches over which they were, & are now candidates for settlement elsewhere. Fourteen of our congregations are without pastors, or stated supplies; & six of these must continue to be unprovided for, no one can tell how long, because they cannot furnish houses in which ministers may reside, or else are so situated as not to be able to unite, two or more of them, in sustaining the institutions of the gospel.

---

[171]Annual Report to the American Home Missionary Society dated March, 1866.

This leads me to speak of parsonages. These are of immense importance, more so in numerous instances, than houses of worship. Substitutes for the latter may generally be had, in some form or other, an "upper" in a lower room. But many a community might be named, where churches of our order have no preaching because there are not dwellings in which ministers, with their families, can reside. Happy would it be for the great cause if this matter could have its proper place in the work of Home Evangelization. A few hundred dollars contributed here & there would secure the means of grace to many a village & settlement now destitute of them.

In respect to church erection, it gives me pleasure to state that five houses of worship have been dedicated, three are in a more or less advanced state towards completion, while four have been repaired, or rather greatly improved.

Our churches are being quickened & strengthened. We are, in fact, in the midst of a most blessed revival season. Works of grace are in progress throughout the state. These generally commenced later than usual. Most of them can be traced to "the week of prayer." To report fully in regard to them is not possible without delaying this communication till an extensive correspondence shall put me into possession of facts. You will, however, learn all that is necessary from other sources . . . .[172]

The intense strain of missionary itinerating began to have its effect on Elisha Jenney. In the fall of 1867, he fell into a melancholy state of mind, bordering on insanity.[173] His mind became seriously affected and his physical system much deranged. He bewailed his shortcomings as an Agent, and showed morbid conscientiousness in signing applications from the churches. On November 1, 1867, he officially resigned from the Agency, but the resignation was retained by his wife,

---

[172]Annual Report to the American Home Missionary Society dated March 1866.

[173]Sturtevant to Badger, Jacksonville, Illinois, December 7, 1867.

in the hopes that his health would improve.[174] His
resignation was accepted the following year, and for a
time he served the Society in an unofficial capacity.
He retired to Galesburg, Illinois, where he lived until 1882, dying of heart disease.[175]

---

[174]A.M. (Mrs.) Jenney to Badger, November 11, 1867 and
December 12, 1867.

[175]A letter to the Secretaries, dated December 27, 1867,
is of some interest:

"Having to a great extent recovered from the state
of mind in which I was awhile since, I feel in duty
bound to explain, or rather apologize for, conduct that
must seem to you very reprehensible.

"It was not right in me to resign so peremtorily
(sic) nor should I have assumed that my resignation
was accepted without due notice to that effect. But
at that time none who understood my case, deemed me
fully responsible for my doings.

"It is with a shudder I now look back upon the six
or seven weeks immediately succeeding the middle of
Oct. During that period I suffered intensely. My
thought & feelings were such as to give me most painful foretastes of the woes of the damned.

"It was during that period that I forwarded the
draft from Payson to Dr Coe. My conviction was that my
house was to be destroyed that night, & my family driven
forth without the possibility of obtaining shelter from
the inclemency of the weather, & the fury of our enemies;
while I myself was to be stripped of every possession of
value, & then tortured & executed in a most barbarous
manner. Under these circumstances I deemed it best to
send the draft to the Society, as there was no one here
to whom I could confide it, that it might be turned to
good account, & should any of my family survive the ill
treatment that awaited them, be, perhaps, restored to them.

"Let that one item of those weeks of wretchedness
suffice. To detail what I can ever recall of my thoughts
& feelings & doings, might not interest you, and would
certainly be painful to me.

"I now find myself without employment, & with an income so small, as to render it necessary to recall my
son from college; & that may result in his abandoning
further thoughts of the ministry, & devoting himself to
some secular pursuit. But the act that has placed me
in such circumstances was right at the time: & since
I have resigned, & that fact, through the agency of another, has been given to the churches, it is too late
[footnote continued on next page]

We have dealt in some detail with the five men of the Illinois Band who acted as agents for the American Home Missionary Society between the years 1833 and 1867. It is now possible to summarize the work of these men, and show how much they had in common with one another.

First, it will be noticed that all five were born and raised in Connecticut, and were strongly influenced by the traditional Puritanism of New England. Their early environment was rural rather than urban. Three of the men, and possibly four, underwent conversion experiences in the year 1821. At various times in their lives all five men had taught school.

Secondly, their work on the frontier was of a similar nature. Much of the time was spent in visiting feeble and destitute churches. Churches which had been newly organized must be nursed along until they could stand on their own two feet. This took time, patience, financial aid and spiritual encouragement. Although the collection of funds was not the primary task of the agent, nevertheless this aspect of their work was a very necessary one. Perhaps their most important task was to coordinate the activities of the American Home Missionary Society in New York with the actual needs and conditions of the frontier churches. Their recommendations with respect to placing missionaries, and their suggestions with regard to the allocation of funds were of utmost importance in making the Society's work effective. Even when they were not actually in the employ of the Society, they nevertheless rendered their services at all times, even though no financial remuneration was at that moment involved.

A third fact to be noted is that these men carried on their work at great personal hazard. Long and frequent trips caused great fatigue. Even the hardiest constitution was taxed by wilderness conditions. There was the constant threat of epidemics, especially in southern Illinois. The scourge of cholera was ever present. And Indians might at any time attack a lone traveller as he journeyed from one outpost of civilization to another. Lack of funds and other financial

---

[footnote continued from previous page] to retrace my steps, even though that should, on some accounts be deemed desirable. Be assured, however, that my interest in the Society & its managers, is as deep & strong as ever; & hereafter, if there be any way in which I can act for them, please command my services."

burdens were ever-pressing problems with which the missionary had somehow to cope. The combination of these several difficulties was literally exhausting, and agents of the Society found it impossible to continue for many years a work which was so demanding.

Finally, these men were missionaries of zealous devotion and unquestioned integrity. They were highly regarded by the American Home Missionary Society for they rendered to society an invaluable service. They promoted educational as well as religious enterprises, and they constantly pointed out how necessary it was to establish religious influences early in order that Christian ideals might be the very undergirding of the whole life of the settlement. Their efforts in behalf of social service and their work as explorers of a new state cannot be too highly estimated.

These members of the Illinois Band were especially outstanding in the spread of educational, moral and religious influences throughout the entire state. In a very real sense they were soldiers of the Cross.[174]

---

[174]Cf. Kofold, Carrie Prudence, _Puritan Influences in the Formative Years of Illinois History_. Transactions of the Illinois State Historical Society for the Year 1905, p. 261ff.

Massachusetts, he was brought up on a rock-bound New
England farm where the Turners taught their eight
children habits of industry, prudence, respect for
right and rights, the keeping of the Sabbath, integrity,
kindness, conscientiousness, and devotion.[2]   Young Asa
was

> . . . a good worker on the farm, and enjoyed
> work. I have heard him say that after work-
> ing all day he had driven an ox-team loaded
> with lumber to Shrewsbury, twenty miles or
> more, by night, and reached there by the open-
> ing of business in the morning. Probably he
> had aided in cutting and hauling to mill the
> logs from which the lumber was sawed. This
> training gave him a strong constitution which
> enabled him to survive his neglect of the
> laws of health while in college.[3]

The religious climate of Templeton, Massachusetts
was Unitarian, and dwelt much on the beauties of virtue
and the deformities of vice. Turner says that "the
great facts of the gospel -- sin, the atonement, re-
pentance, faith, and the new birth -- were ignored, so
far as the instructions of the pulpit were concerned.
Of these I had no conception."[4]

> There was scarcely a family in Templeton
> that observed family worship. Early in
> life it troubled me that my father did not
> have family prayers. My mother taught me

[footnote continued from previous page] correspondence
with the A.H.M.S.   Frederick Kuhns, author of A History
of Illinois Congregational and Christian Churches thinks
that Turner's Autobiography may be extant, although it
is not available. Further research may bring to light
this interesting and valuable document. It was apparently
not available, however, to Truman O. Douglas when he wrote
Builders of a Commonwealth, which contains a number of
pages dealing with Turner's work in Illinois and Iowa.

[2]Magoun, George F., Asa Turner, A Home Missionary Patriarch and His Times, p. 19. For a good brief portrait
of Turner, see Weigle, Luther A., The Pageant of America, Vol. X. p. 242.

[3]MS. Sketch, by Julius A. Reed from Magoun George F.,
p. 20. The description of Turner is by his sister, Hannah.

[4]Magoun, George F., Asa Turner, A Home Missionary Patriarch and His Times, p. 27.

in my childhood to pray. I always observed
the form, but felt that it was lip-service.
I was naturally religious. The tolling of
a bell for a death[5] filled me with awe, and
to hear the clods fall on a coffin in the
grave made me shudder. I was in bondage
through fear of death. As I grew older the
subject engrossed my mind. Finally this
thought fastened on me -- "I ought to love
the God who made me and gives me every thing
I have." I used to pray that God would manifest himself to me in visible form, or work
a miracle to make me feel that he existed.
I used to go to meeting hoping that something
would be said to awaken me to my spiritual
condition; wondered why my father didn't
seem to think more about religion, and that
professors of religion did not act as if religion were true.

I finally concluded that either the Bible was
not true, or those around me were not Christians. Still the claim to love God pressed.
I felt that nothing short of this would sat-
isfy my conscience. How to do it, or what
love was, I had no idea. To such an extent
did my obligations to love God press on me,
and the consciousness that I did not, that
I wished I could change places with any
animal, a table, or a chair, or any thing my
eye rested on, that I might get rid of my
obligations. I continued to pray, and sought
means to impress my mind. What I feared was
not the future, but my cold, dead heart. One
night as I retired I engaged in prayer as usual. Why or how I can not tell, but my heart
went up in love to God. I felt a joy I never
felt before or conceived of. I got up in the
morning feeling that I was a new creature, but
not knowing what it meant. It was a dark
night, but when my heart went up to God the
room seemed light as day. I can see now how
the room looked at that time some sixty years
since. Could I then have had some instruction from Christian friends, what a blessing
it would have been to me!

---

[5]An old New England custom which was later carried by
New England settlers to the Iowa village in which he
preached.

A little while after I read in Corinthians
that Satan "transformed himself into an angel
of light," I thought that was exactly my case.
A cloud came over me, and I wandered in dark-
ness many months; I don't remember how long.
Still I did not lose my interest in religion.
It was my chief concern.

The young people in our town were divided into
three classes -- according to age -- to attend
balls, and the minister would go to see them
dance. It was thought as proper to attend
school. But from that time I had no desire to
join in any of their amusements, nor did I feel
the need of it. I did not suppose I was a
Christian, but I wished to act in all things
so as not to dishonor religion. I felt that I
was and must be identified with it. My ideas
of religion were very crude, I may say in a
large degree instinctive, but I wished to be
numbered with religious people. This has been
my desire all my life.

When about nineteen (I do not remember the
exact date), I united with the church in my
native place. I went to the minister, Mr.
Wellington, and tried to tell him how I felt,
the exercises of my mind. But he didn't seem
disposed to hear. Didn't seem in the least
disposed to doubt my fitness to join the church.[6]

During his teens Asa Turner taught district schools
in the winter, although he still lived at home on the
farm. At one time he had eighty-five scholars, and
although the custom of the day allowed rather brutal
methods of discipline, Asa "controlled them by a look."
T.B. Hawks, one of his pupils, remembers being trodded
gently on his foot as a cure for disquietude.[7] It was
his custom to have religious exercises, and when he was
told that a minister was hired to do the praying, he
replied, "Well, gentlemen, whether it be right in the
sight of God to hearken unto you more than unto God,
judge ye."[8] There was no further objection.

---

[6]Magoun, George F., Asa Turner, A Home Missionary Patriarch and His Times, pp. 31-32.

[7]Ibid., p. 41.

[8]Ibid.

When he was twenty-two years old, he went to Amherst Academy to fit for college. Amherst College was opened the same year that Turner entered the academy. Tuition was free to candidates for the ministry, and board a dollar a week. Girls were also admitted, for one of the students in Amherst, "then uncultivated in mind and manners, of large physique, twenty-three or twenty-four years of age, and receiving her first impulse in education," was none other than Mary Lyon.[9]

> In the fall of 1823 I entered Yale College. I was an entire stranger and had never seen any one in college. My father carried me there in his buggy, gave me a bed and bedding and ten dollars. This was the amount of his contribution to my education. I had earned something winters teaching school before I commenced study, and after I was twenty-one. Before that I gave my earnings to my father. I was thrown on my resources. The college woodyard opened the way to earn a little, by sawing wood. (He often did it with perspiration dripping from his elbows.) I boarded myself and ate at "the second table," which cost from thirty-seven and a half to seventy-five cents a week. My fare was not extravagant. As I went to prayers at night I would put a little skillet in the fire with a pint of water and two tablespoonfuls of Indian meal, leaving it to boil while I attended devotions. After my return I salted it and broke in crackers, and this would make a meal. In my second year I taught school in old Guilford and boarded with Colonel Chittenden . . . .[10]

In April, 1824, he was received to communion by the college church, and later in 1828 when he was a theological student, he served as a deacon with his classmates Hale and Baldwin.[11] He was greatly respected by his classmates, and during the revival of 1826-1827 was very active in helping to win souls to Christ. His brother says of Asa's college days:

---

[9] Magoun, George F., Asa Turner, A Home Missionary Patriarch and His Times, p. 44.

[10] Ibid., pp. 45-46.

[11] Ibid., pp. 46-47.

125

He was so miserably afflicted with dyspepsia much of the time that he could not fully profit by his course of study. But sick or well, I believe that he seldom, either there or at home, omitted any feasible opportunity of getting a few frinds to meet together, and to talk to them about "the Father," and Christ and his life and words. We thought then that such persistence in these gratuitous meetings was a loss to him. But I have since thought that these experiences were the best parts of his course, and did more than all else to make him what he was, more adroit at handling men than theories about men.[12]

Turner was graduated in the class of 1827, and entered the theological seminary the same fall. Here he came under the influence of Dr. Nathaniel Taylor, who "taught a theology which could be preached."[13] The same year he also joined the Society for Christian Research,[14] and in the spring of 1830 he was graduated from the seminary, and ordained September sixth, by the New Haven West Association.[15] On September fourteenth, he started for New York, Cincinnati, and Illinois, buying a horse and carriage at Cincinnati. The trip took two months less nine days.

Quincy, Adams County, Ill., we reached November 5, in what now seems peril by land and water, as we were entire strangers to the country. We forded every stream, with one exception . . . (between Cincinnati and Quincy).
. . . The streams were very low. The day previous to the night we reached Quincy, we had passed over a large prairie which was on fire on each side of the road. On our approach to Quincy, we were to go through a strip of timber which was also on fire, making it dangerous to

[12]Magoun, George F., Asa Turner, A Home Missionary Patriarch and His Times, pp. 47-48. The brother was Jonathan Baldwin Turner who later became instructor in Illinois College.

[13]Ibid., p. 56.

[14]Records of the Society for Christian Research.

[15]Class of 1827. Yale Memorabilia Records.

pass, as trees on fire were falling on each
side. We did not know how far we were from
a habitation, but we succeeded in getting
through safely.

. . . . We stopped at Mr. Rufus Brown's (in
Quincy) the first few days. His house was
a small one at the side of the Log Tavern.
Saturday there was a horse-race among those
who came into town from the country. The
next day I preached in the log court-house.[16]

In 1820, two young men -- Willard Keyes and John
Wood had "concluded to locate temporarily about fifty
miles north of civilization." In 1821 they bought the
site for Quincy for sixty dollars, Mr. Wood walking
one hundred and twenty miles to Alton to make the deal.
The first white woman and child came in 1822, and the
first elections were held with an old tea-pot for a
ballot-box. In 1826 the first store was opened; in
1829 the first frame building was erected.[17] A creek
in the settlement was called John, the settlement itself called Quincy, and the new county, Adams.

What sort of people did Asa Turner find at Quincy?
The population was of a very mixed sort. Between 1804
and 1822, Irish, English, German and Swiss colonies
had come to Illinois. New Englanders, as a rule, went
to the northern part of the state. Many of the male
settlers were hunters. There were no schools, and most
of the population was illiterate. Many preachers of
the Gospel could not even read the Holy Scriptures.
The story is told of one preacher who preached from the
text in Revelations respecting the man who had a pair
of balances in his hand, and read it, "who had a pair
of bellowses in his hand," with which, he said, "the
wicked would finally be blown into perdition."[18]

After eight years as pastor at Quincy, Turner resigned his charge in 1838, and crossed the Mississippi
into Iowa territory, then commonly called the "Black
Hawk Purchase." He established the first Congregational
church in the state at Denmark. In Iowa he found the
fields white for harvest, but the laborers few. His

---

[16]Magoun, George F., Asa Turner, A Home Missionary Patriarch and His Times, p. 27.

[17]Ibid., pp. 75-76.

[18]Ibid., p. 79.

constant prayer and plea was for reinforcements.

In 1843 he was joined by eleven young men who had just graduated from Andover Theological Seminary. They were ordained in the little church at Denmark, and then scattered to various fields throughout the Territory. In 1848, the Iowa Band opened Iowa College at Davenport. Later, the College was moved to Grinnell, and changed its name to Grinnell College.

In 1868 Asa Turner retired from his parish. The following year, the General Association of Iowa reported nearly two hundred churches founded from Denmark. "Father" Turner's last years were spent at Oskaloosa, where he died in 1885.

Henry Herrick was born on March 5, 1803 in Woodbridge, Connecticut. His father was Reverend Claudius Herrick, "a pioneer teacher of young ladies in the higher branches, from 1808 to 1831, the date of his death; his pupils numbering some two thousand. His residence and school was on the site of the Battell Chapel." His father studied with Charles Backus, D.D., at Somers, Connecticut, where many young men trained for the ministry. This was before the regularly established divinity schools.

After fitting for College at the Hopkins Grammar School in New Haven, and Phillips Academy in Andover, Massachusetts, in 1822 Henry was graduated from Yale College.[19] He taught the following year at West Springfield, Massachusetts. For two years he was rector of the Hopkins Grammar School in New Haven. Then he studied theology for two years in Andover, and for one year in New Haven. In 1828 he began preaching. In 1830 he was ordained as an evangelist in Humphreysville, now Seymour, Connecticut, and soon afterward he went west to supply a home missionary church in Carrollton, Illinois, for the following year.

Upon arriving at Carrollton, Herrick found a Bible, tract, and temperance society already established, "but needing constant effort to make them operative."[20] He

---

[19]Record of the meetings of the Class of 1822, Yale College, 1829; cf. Congressional Quarterly, April 1864, p. 139.

[20]Herrick to Peters, September 13, 1830, from Carrollton, Illinois.

was met by the usual difficulties of ignorance, skepticism and infidelity, but Carrollton was "as interesting a field of labor as I could rationally wish."[21] Intemperance was not so prevalent as in many New England towns with which he was acquainted. Furthermore, Greene County offered many natural advantages to the settler: great quantities of wood and stone, abundant mill sites, healthy climate, and very rich soil. There were about seven thousand inhabitants in the county. Although regretting a want of regular opportunities for study, Herrick felt that his happiness was "identified with the prosperity and improvement of the country."[22] At the close of 1830, he reported to the A.H.M.S. ten Sabbath Schools established, with two hundred scholars, a Bible class, five Temperance Societies with one hundred members, forty dollars contributed to the Bible Society, twenty dollars to the Tract Society, and eighty dollars to the Colonization Society.[23] The church of Carrollton also boasted of a Singing Society.

> The Singing Society is numerous and continued interesting. The best style of singing is practised in it.[24]

This, however, met with some opposition.

> Several of the members have been brought up to esteem it dreadful wickedness to sing Watts Psalms and Hymns. They are advanced in years, have never been trained to religious effort, and are afraid of New Measures. Besides a secular preacher comes along every year to stir up their prejudices, a thing easily done in these stirring times, where many enlightened Presbyterians quake and tremble lest the Ark of the Lord should fall into the hands of the Philistines.[25]

In the spring of 1832, Herrick returned East with the hope of returning to Illinois after six months or a year. Although he felt that great good could be done at Carrollton, at the same time he said he "should probably prefer some other location."[26]

---

[21]Herrick to Peters, September 13, 1830, from Carrollton, Ill.

[22]Ibid., December 16, 1830, from Carrollton, Illinois.

[23]Ibid., March 16, 1831, from Carrollton, Illinois.

[24]Ibid., December 14, 1831 from Carrollton, Illinois.

[25]Ibid., March 19, 1832, from Carrollton, Illinois.

[26]Ibid.

On February 19, 1835 he married Sarah Wright of
Windsor, Massachusetts. He went to Knoxville, East
Tennessee, soon after, and became a principal of a
female academy. He was also principal at the Somer-
ville and Moulton Female Academy in Alabama for a short
time. Of his work in the South we know nothing. Probably he did not fare too well, for in 1840, his brother John wrote to his other brother Edward:

> I received a letter from Henry last summer,
> and rather inferred from it that he was not
> making his fortune in Alabama.[27]

In 1842 Henry returned North, spending at least
part of the next three years in New Haven, Connecticut.

In July, 1845, he accepted a call to the Presbyterian Church in Clintonville, New York. There were
about sixteen hundred inhabitants in Clintonville, and
the town had a Methodist church, a Presbyterian church,
and a large Roman Catholic constituency. The church
requested one hundred dollars from the A.H.M.S., which
was readily granted. The church was in considerable
financial difficulty, the parsonage having been rented
out in order to pay some debts. Clintonville was very
much to Herrick's liking. On July 22, 1846, he wrote:

> So far am I from complaining of this people,
> that I must say, and do say with gratitude,
> that I never have lived among a people be-
> fore that showed so great a disposition ac-
> cording to their ability to make me and my
> family comfortable in every way.[28]

The following year his commission was renewed by
the Society.

During his pastorate at Clintonville Herrick was
very busy in the temperance cause, and was also faced
with a French Roman Catholic "problem." He refers
often to the excellent cooperation of the Methodist

---

[27]John P. Herrick to Edward Claudius Herrick, November
23, 1840; the Edward Claudius Herrick papers, Sterling
Memorial Library, Yale University, New Haven, Conn.

[28]Herrick to Badger, July 22, 1846, Clintonville, New
York.

and Presbyterian groups. But Roman Catholicism was rapidly increasing, until almost half of the population was Catholic.

> . . . Our French Bible which I persuaded a man to buy has been destroyed lately. The cover was saved and the inside cut out and torn up or burnt as being a book not fit to be read. <u>Father forgive them for they know not what they do.</u> The man (who did it by instigation of his wife) is now heartily ashamed of himself.[29]

Apparently things were not going so well as Henry Herrick imagined. On August 4, 1848, his church wrote to the A.H.M.S. thanking them for their aid, but questioning the advisability of sending more. Although they liked him as a man, they felt that his preaching "was not calculated to increase the congregation" and many were anxious that he leave.[30]

At the same time he was having serious trouble with his teeth, and one eye, which had an ulcer and which the doctors had recommended "leaching with the application of nitrate of silver."[31]

In 1850 he was serving a church at Ticonderoga, New York, after spending a year in Whitehall, New York. The Congregational church at Ticonderoga had frequently changed pastors, and the people had long drawn on the American Home Missionary Society for support. Realizing that the Society might not be disposed to grant the request, the recommending committee from Crown Point, New York suggested that aid be given a little longer, because Ticonderoga was becoming an important place. After laboring two years in Ticonderoga, Herrick admitted some success, but felt that the town was hopelessly indifferent to religion. Most of the converts of his revival could show few evidences of piety several months after their conversions. He felt continually discouraged. Whether the fault lay with Ticonderoga or with Henry Herrick, it is hard to say.

---

[29] Herrick to Badger, April 25, 1848, Clintonville, New York.

[30] Clintonville Presbyterian Church to Badger, August 4, 1848.

[31] E.C. Herrick to ?, July 11, 1848. Sterling Memorial Library, Yale University, New Haven, Connecticut.

After leaving Ticonderoga he spent some time at Middlefield, New York, but being dissatisfied with Middlefield, he decided to candidate for the church at Southwick. By the year 1855, he had moved to Lawrens, in Otsego County. In 1858, he was serving the Congregational Church at Exeter Centre. The church here applied to the A.H.M.S. for aid, and sent its application to the Society's agent, Mr. Goodman. Goodman was very reluctant to endorse the application, and therefore delayed it four or five months, saying that "Mr. Herrick never does anything to build up the churches to which he ministers & it seemed very much like throwing the money away to appropriate it & the church themselves do but very little for his support."[32]

Mr. Goodman's letter eventually fell into Herrick's hands. On February 16, 1859 he wrote to Badger and said that Goodman was prejudiced in the matter because he was trying to unite the Fly-Creek church with the Exeter church. The Exeter church was very small, and probably Goodman felt that a more efficient ministry would result if the two churches became one. From Herrick's past history there is no doubt that Goodman's criticism was sound. Herrick won his point, however, and received aid from the Society.

On March 28, 1862, Herrick reported forty-eight members for his church, fourteen men, thirty-four women, and an average attendance of one hundred at church every Sunday. Herrick's pastorate lasted six years at Exeter.

In March 1865, he wrote to Badger:

My object in writing is to enquire of you of a location in the ministry for which you would think I am in some degree, fitted to which I could go in the spring. I could supply two adjoining places. My health is good & my habits active. I am good at walking and visiting and fond of missionary work in general & should not object to go into some Congregational Church.

In 1867 he moved to North Woodstock, Connecticut. Here he died on March 11, 1895.

_____

[32]S. Goodman to the A.H.M.S. The application is dated September 22, 1858.

Benoni Y. Messenger was born in Windham, Ohio in July, 1800. In 1827, he was a member of the Society for Christian Research. He was ordained evangelist at Hamden, Connecticut on May 19, 1830. He studied in the theological department of Yale University and was appointed by the A.H.M.S. about the first of July, 1830, to Illinois. He reached the new state on the twenty-fourth of August, and on October twelfth located at Edwardsville, Illinois. On the first of April, 1831, he was able to report two Sunday Schools, eighty pupils, a Bible class of thirty-seven members, one temperance society, one Bible society for the county, and a church library of one hundred books. The Sugar Creek congregation could boast one Sunday School, of thirty-five members, but no books, and one Bible class of thirty members. Marine Settlement had no church; one Sunday School of twenty pupils with twenty-eight books in its library; one Bible class with thirty-five members. Messenger also had a class of colored children consisting of eighteen or twenty, who met at his house and were instructed by his wife.

In the spring of 1832, he assisted Albert Hale at Bethel, where a notable revival was taking place. An account of this revival appeared in the Home Missionary for July, 1832.

After spending two years at Edwardsville, Messenger decided to seek another field of labor. Edwardsville had long been a place of sectarian strife, and the little church had for several years been rent with divisions. His efforts had not been entirely without success, however, Cyrus Watson says that no minister in the state had been more successful in winning souls to Jesus Christ. Messenger had the reputation of being a pious, devoted and faithful minister of the Gospel.[33]

His next pastorate was at Winchester, Naples and North Prairie. Here he found the people at first bitterly opposed to missionaries. Many of the frontiersmen were Campbellites.

> Considerable effort has been made here by the
> followers of A. Campbell, & they succeeded in
> forming (what they call) a church: their num-
> bers were few at first & such an array of truth
> has been brought to bear upon the people, & the

---

[33]Cyrus L. Watson to Peters, August 24, 1832.

errors of Campbellism held up so clearly
before their minds, that not a single individual that I have heard of has joined them
since their first meeting. Every effort that
could be devised has been made by them to get
numbers: even habitual drunkards have been
urged time & again to "go down into the watery grave" than wash away their filth & thus
become members of their self-styled church
of Christ. Most of their members do not pretend that they have ever experienced any
change of heart, & utterly deny that any
such thing is necessary to salvation.[34]

Naples he describes as

. . . a very wicked place; so much so that the
Methodists & Baptists have long since delivered
them over to saten (sic). At my second meeting
the congregation was much larger & has continually increased. The last Sabbath I was there,
it was thought there was near an hundred present.
The house was as full as it could be. Attention
& deep solemnity has increased as rapidly as the
congregation. Thoughtless men & infidels, who
have not attended a religious meeting for years
are now the regular hearers of the word of life,
& not unfrequently are the tears seen flowing
from eyes unaccustomed to weep. I have uniformly held a meeting at candle light, which
has been attended by full as many as attend in
the day time. These meetings are kept up regularly every Sab. night by F. Collins (an elder) & are well attended. I do feel that the
time as at hand when Naples will no longer be
proverbial for its wickedness. I feel that a
protracted meeting, with the Holy Ghost sent
down, would prove an incalculable blessing.
Such a meeting has been talked of, & would have
been held, but we have no house to meet in.
The house that we now occupy probably would not
accommodate one sixth of those that would attend; for it is not sufficient for those who
usually attend on the Sabbath. The Messrs
Collins are about to build a house, but we want
it now. Now the state of feeling is ripe for

---

[34]Messenger to Peters, February 25, 1833 from Winchester, Illinois.

a protracted meeting; by delaying, it may pass away. We cannot meet in the grove, it is too cold. A Sabbath School has been kept up through the winter and is doing well . . . .[35]

In the spring of 1833 he returned East because of his wife's health. He was pastor at Darien, Connecticut 1834-1835 and in South Britain, Connecticut 1835-1837, and then in Orange, Connecticut 1837-1838.

On June sixth, 1842, he was appointed by the A.H.M.S. to labor in the church at Orwell, Ohio. The church contained about forty members, who "exerted themselves to their utmost to build a small meeting house & when they had got that inclosed & the floor laid, they found themselves unable to sustain a minister even for one half the time."[36] Messenger increased the congregation to almost two hundred. He also spent half of his time laboring with the congregation at Bloomfield, Ohio, five miles south of Orwell.

In the summer of 1843 Benoni Messenger left Orwell and Bloomfield for "a wider field of labor."[37] The church was "in a very happy and flourishing condition. It pained me exceedingly to leave them."[38]

In 1845 he returned to Illinois, and became pastor of the church at Mount Sterling. Since the church drew upon the A.H.M.S. for aid, Messenger was obliged to make quarterly reports. The report dated April 1, 1846 is unimpressive. There were no hopeful conversions, none added to the church, only forty Bible and Sunday School scholars. On June first, he sent another report from Mount Sterling, of a lamentable tone:

. . . Another quarter has passed away & calls for my report. I had hoped, on this occasion, to give you an account of an interesting work of grace among my people; but alas our hopes & expectations have been blasted. There was at one time considerable feeling & our expec-

---

[35] Messenger to Peters, February 25, 1833 from Winchester, Illinois.

[36] Messenger to Hall and Badger, September 6, 1842 from Orwell, Ohio.

[37] Messenger to Badger and Hall, June 6, 1843 from Freedom, Ohio.

[38] Ibid.

tations were very much raised; -- the cloud
seemed to be rising with appearance of much
rain, we set out our buckets but it passed
by on the other side & left us "barren &
cold as Shinar's ground" . . .

The next report sounds even more forlorn. It is
dated September 1, 1846.

. . . It is with a sad heart that I seat myself for the purpose of making my third quarterly report: my anticipations have not been
realized, my hopes are blasted. I learned
soon after I entered upon my labors at Mt.
S. -- that I had engaged in one of the hardest
& most hopeless fields in the State. This
was the character given it by the brethren
around . . . .

Accordingly he moved. His next pastorate was at
Belleville, Illinois, one hundred and thirty miles
south of Mount Sterling. Belleville contained about
three thousand inhabitants. On February 1, 1847 the
church at Belleville wrote to the Executive Committee
of the A.H.M.S. requesting financial aid. They said
they expected to raise two hundred dollars, and they
desired two hundred dollars more from the Society in
order to support Messenger. Of him, all that is said
in the entire letter is: "He was recommended to us by
Brother Norton of Alton & we hope will prove an instru-
ment of great good among us." Their former pastor
had been the Reverend W.E. Chittenden who left them on
account of ill health, and the implication of the letter is that they were heartily sorry to see him go.
The Society therefore got in touch with A.T. Norton,
at Alton, and asked him to investigate the church's
application. Belleville had been aided for seventeen
years, over two thousand dollars having been granted to
the church and the Society felt that by this time the
church should do more for itself. Hall therefore asked
Norton for a confidential report.

Norton went to Belleville and investigated. His
reply deserves to be quoted:

. . . I made my enquiries of (of) three male
members of the Church, Ellis, Batz (?) & underwood (sic), being all the male members in town,
who I could find. Ellis is a prominent member
of the Church, leader of the singing, & active
in the Sabbath School. Batz is an Elder. Un-

136

derwood is a lawyer of some repute, a member
of the last Legislature. All are men of sincere, unaffected piety. I consulted them separately, proposed to them substantially the
same questions & received for substance the
same answers.

Ques. "How are you getting on in your Church
affairs?"
Ans. "Very poorly indeed."
Q. "How are you pleased with bro Messenger?"
A. "The Church likes him pretty well, not
disposed to complain. He is rather dull,
confines himself too closely to his notes,
his sermons do not seem to (sic) appropriate.
(Mrs. Ellis, a very pious intelligent lady,
said, 'I am afraid he does not look them over
during the week.')"
Q. "How have your Congregations been during
the winter?"
A. "Very small, few attend except members
of the Church. Mr. M does not call out the
people as Mr Chittenden did."
Q. "Would you feel disposed to emply (employ)
bro. Messenger another year?"
A. "No! Mr. Underwood said he felt sorry a
different arrangement had not been made for
the present year."

The above needs no comment & is beyond any
question the universal feeling in the Church.

Bro. Messenger is himself discouraged, feels
almost sorry he went to Belleville. He is
awaiting with great anxiety the result of his
application to your Committee. His chief
fear, however, seems to be that his letter
has not been received. I judge he has not
the smallest inkling of the doubts of your
Committee with respect to himself.

I asked Rev. J.M. Peck, Baptist minister at
Rock Spring, 8 miles from Belleville, what
he knew of bro Messenger. He replied that
"he had when in the country before the reputation of being the most harmless man in the
world." He seemed to be a negative character, lacking efficiency, enterprise, & industry.

A Methodist minister at my house yesterday
said, speaking of bro. M. -- & your Society's
aiding him, "I don't believe in paying the
people to have such men preach." I felt myself cornered, & could only reply "Bro M --
receives no aid at present from the H.M. Society. He has not since he had been in Belleville. He preaches there solely because the
Church have employed him."

I might say more of the same character & am
deeply grieved I can say nothing different.
I feel for bro. M. If your Committee drop
him, I do not believe he will get employment
as a minister, certainly nothing like a support. Would it not be best for somebody to
deal faithfully with him & get him to turn
farmer, or school master at once?

The best ministers here at the West have all
they can do to sustain themselves. If they
have tacked to them the drones of the East,
they will all go down together.

I hope you will write to bro. M. speedily.
The suspense he is in is painful.[39]

On May 20, 1847 Badger wrote to Messenger a short
letter expressing his regret that the Society could no
longer help him at Belleville.

In 1847, Messenger became Pastor at North Bloomfield, Ohio, and in 1850 Pastor at Mount Sterling, Illinois. From 1858 to 1866 he served as agent for the
American Bible Society in Ohio.

He died at Geneva, Ohio, on May 9, 1866 at the age
of sixty-five.[40]

Romulus Barnes was born on October 16, 1800 at
Bristol, Connecticut. He was the son of Captain Daniel
Barnes, who died when Romulus was still a boy. Young

---

[39] A.G. Norton to Badger, April 13, 1847 from Alton, Ill.

[40] A General Catalogue of the Divinity School of Yale
College, 1822-1872, p. 12.

Barnes was raised in Canton, and in 1816 became a Christian. He was graduated from Yale College in 1828, and from Yale Seminary in 1831. He was ordained on March 22, in Guilford by the East Association. In the same year he married Miss Olive Denham of Conway, Massachusetts. He joined the Yale Band sometime in 1830, and the following year went West, arriving in Illinois the first day of July. His first pastorate was at Canton, Illinois.[41]

Barnes' trip to the West was not made without some difficulties:

> . . . We have recently sustained a loss which has deprived us of all that we had except what little we brought with us in a one horse waggon. Nearly all of the things, belonging to myself & wife, were sent around by New Orleans, consisting of my library (which was very select & worth at least $200) and a hogshead & barrel containing bedding & other articles for housekeeping, clothing &c &c (worth $200 or $300 more). These things were all on board the Steam boat Fairy which recently sunk in the Mississippi River 16 or 18 miles above St. Louis. The box containing my books was raised though the box was broken & the books had been soaking in muddy water several days when I received them. The other things have not been heard from . . . .[42]

On September 13, 1828, a Presbyterian church of seven members, four of them males, had been formed in Fulton County. The church met in two places, Canton and Lewiston, and its records date from both places. In less than two years its membership had risen to eighty-six. In August, 1831, it was determined that Romulus Barnes and Lucien Farnam begin their labors in the County as the ministers of the church. These ministers were to have support by contribution collected within the county by a committee of six, each member acting in succession one month at a time during the year. In February, 1832, measures were taken for the erection of a house of worship in Canton, private houses and a school house having been up to this time

---

[41]Sketches of the Class of 1828 in _Yale Memorabilia_.

[42]Barnes to Peters, October 12, 1831, Canton, Illinois.

the only available places for assembly. A subscription
of money, labor, materials and produce to the amount of
six hundred and sixty-three dollars was obtained, the
name of Arthur Tappan of New York for one hundred dollars heading the list. A meeting of the session was
held in the new house August 11, 1833. Nothing more
definite as to the time of completing the house appears.[43]

Early in 1834 Reverend Robert Stewart became pastor
of the church at Canton. Romulus Barnes spent a year
in supplying destitute places such as Knoxville and
Farmington, and then became pastor of the newly-gathered
church at Washington (Hollands Grove), in Tazewell
County. At Washington, Barnes was handicapped by the
small constituency of his church, a lack of funds, and
no meeting house. Furthermore, the church seemed to
grow but slowly, and Barnes found it necessary to rely
continually on the A.H.M.S. for aid. In the fall of
1838, the society asked if he should not relinquish
his field.[44]

Barnes was very decidedly in favor of remaining at
Washington, however. It was the most important town
between Springfield and Ottowa. He had been advised
by Bascom, Baldwin, and Hale not to give the post up.
The "lamentable destitution of the surrounding community" seemed to call for regular preaching, and faithful
pastoral supervision.[45] He said that if he left there
would be no other "evangelical influences coming from
other sources which would promise relief."[46] Furthermore, what good he had been able to accomplish would be
undone. Finally, "it has appeared to me that the principle would lead missionaries to avoid hard fields,
however important, for fear that after laboring with
great sacrifice four or five years they must abandon
their field and lose their labor."[47]

> Br. Baldwin asked me whether there was annually
> a perceptible increase in the strength of the
> church, or in its ability to support the gospel.

---

[43]Mills, Henry, A Brief History of the Congregational
Church of Canton, Ill Oct. 3, 1876: in the church file
of the American Home Missionary Collection, Hammond
Library, Chicago Theological Seminary, Chicago, Illinois.

[44]Barnes to Badger, January 2, 1837; January 9, 1839,
and intervening correspondence.

[45]Barnes to Badger from Washington, Illinois, January 1,
1841.

[46]Ibid.

[47]Ibid.

I told him that this increase although slow
was obvious. His reply was "Then hold on."
I told him that it was very unpleasant to
me, to be under the necessity of receiving
so much aid from abroad. He replied that
in Foreign Missions it was often necessary
to support the missionaries entirely and
for many years and that Christian policy
would not allow such villages as this in
our own country to grow up without the influence of an enlightened ministry. In as
much as I had found no individual expressing an opinion at variance with this I concluded that it would be your pleasure that
I should remain here and accordingly made
up my mind to continue my labors & sacrifice as God should give strength.[48]

The Society therefore resolved to continue its aid
to him.

By the end of 1841, a church building had been completed. The membership had increased from ten to forty-
one. There was a thriving Sabbath School and a Temperance Society. Church prayer meeting was conducted in
the middle of the week, and there was also a female
praying society.[49]

In 1843, Romulus Barnes resigned from his pastorate
at Washington, and went East. Returning to Illinois in
the fall, after spending the summer in Massachusetts,
he settled at Downer's Grove in Dupage County. He stayed
here but a short time, however, and in 1844 accepted a
call to the Congregational Church of Newark, which had
been gathered the previous year. Newark was a small but
growing village; Barnes describes it as "a place of
great wickedness, but seems to give some evidence of a
disposition to retrieve its character."[50]

Much remains to be done here upon the subject
of temperance. There are three places in the
village where the "liquid poison" is sold, and
as the fruit of the trofie (sic), about a year
since, two men were shot, the same night, one
of whom soon died.

---

[48] Barnes to Badger from Washington, Illinois, Jan. 1, 1841.

[49] Barnes to Badger, Washington, Illinois, July 20, 1842.

[50] Barnes to Badger, Newark, Illinois, January 1, 1845. Cf.
also Marcus Hicks to the Society, January 23, 1845.

Infidelity has also sown over this field, the
seeds of death, a portion of which has fallen
upon a soil prepared for its reception, and
is bringing forth its appropriate fruits.

Mormonism by its cry of "persecution" by
holding forth certain bible truths till the
attention of people could be secured, and by
keeping in the background their new revelations, prophecies, miracles, &c. has also
succeeded in obtaining a footing here; . . . [51]

Sometime later he wrote:

The most that I can say in reference to the
State of things among this people is that
they are "careful and troubled about many
things" while the "one thing needful" is
far from receiving the attention which it
demands. In the Spring of the year men are
exceedingly "careful and troubled" about
getting in their seed, then they feel justified in being very "careful" in cultivat-
ing their crops, then (as at the present
time) they are of course much "troubled"
to get their grain to market, and finally
it is not the least of their troubles in
these days that they receive what they consider a very inadequate compensation for
their trouble. After all it is hard to
turn them from an undue attention to these
cares to those which would receive a most
ample reward. Oh, how hard to persuade
them to be "careful," chiefly, to secure
for themselves and others, "that good part
which shall not be taken away." Yet to
this work with whatsoever difficulties
encompassed or with whatsoever success
attended I would have "my cares and toils
be given till toils and cares shall end." [52]

His toils and cares were to end very soon. When
the American Home Missionary Society received the next
quarterly report from Newark, it was written by Mrs.
Olivia D. Barnes. Romulus Barnes had "passed to his
reward" on September 24.

---

[51] Barnes to Badger, Newark, Illinois, January 1, 1845.

[52] Barnes to Badger, Newark, Illinois, July 6, 1846.

Lemuel Foster has left us a short but interesting autobiography, half of which is written in his hand, and the other half by his wife at his dictation. Lemuel was born November 24, 1799, in Hartland, Connecticut, the second of six children. We are told that "his parents were strictly pious, they brought up their children in the nurture and admonition of the Lord, in the good old puritanic style." When he was fifteen years old he became converted at a protracted meeting, and joined the church. From that time on, he intended to devote his life to the ministry, but Lemuel's father had died when the boy was only twelve, and so it was necessary to remain on the farm. This he did until he was twenty-one, teaching school during the winter after he was seventeen. In 1820, a severe attack of typhoid fever nearly cost him his life.[53]

Foster was graduated in the class of 1828, and then spent two years in the Theological Department. His health was so bad that Nathaniel Taylor advised him to be licensed and go to work. In 1831 he was licensed by the Hartford North Association, and then was engaged as an agent of the Connecticut Bible Society for six months. On September 5, 1832 he received his commission from the American Home Missionary Society, and after marrying Miss Lydia Cowdrey of Hartland, the two drove to Springfield, Illinois, a distance of 1200 miles, in thirty travelling days. After reaching Springfield, Foster went the next day to Jacksonville, where he met old acquaintances from Yale.[54]

In September of the following year he was ordained with his classmate Bascom by the Sangamon presbytery as an evangelist. A short time afterwards, he visited Bloomingfon, in McLean County, and after preaching a number of Sabbaths, he organized a Presbyterian church there and applied to the A.H.M.S. for financial aid. Foster's pastorate at Bloomington lasted five years. Mrs. Foster opened a school in a log schoolhouse; they soon had two large school rooms full of scholars, and had to employ an additional teacher.[55]

---

[53] Foster, Lemuel, _Autobiography of Lemuel Foster_, pp. 26-27. Cf. also Sketches of the Class of 1828 in Yale Memorabilia. Foster was at Williams for a short time in 1815.

[54] Sketches of the Class of 1828 in _Yale Memorabilia_.

[55] Foster, Lemuel, _Autobiography of Lemuel Foster_, p. 12ff.

In the fall of 1838 the Fosters decided to go East for a rest, but on the eve of their departure Mrs. Foster contracted a fever, and the Fosters were forced to remain in Illinois. On November 12, Foster moved to Bethel to accept a position as principal of the Academy. Mrs. Foster taught the school at large, while Foster taught Greek and Latin and higher mathematics. He also preached at the church in Bethel which had recently been occupied by Thomas Lippincott. His preaching was not confined to one spot, however; he preached about in neighboring districts as the occasion demanded, and at Collinsville held revival meetings with considerable success. Such was his enthusiasm and self-sacrifice that in 1842 a rest became imperative. In the spring of 1840 the Fosters started East, and after a short visit returned to Bethel where Foster continued to preach and to establish churches and schools and promote education. In the latter he was somewhat hampered by the lack of a printing office, the nearest one being more than forty miles away at Alton. On going there, he found that the church in Upper Alton, although small, was destitute of a pastor, so he volunteered to supply there. Just at the critical moment he met Charles Burton, who was seeking a location. Foster succeeded in getting Burton to take the church at Bethel, and he and Mrs. Foster moved to Upper Alton in December, 1845.[56] Here they remained until 1853. Describing their stay at Upper Alton, Mrs. Foster says,

. . . We found religion at a very low ebb, & the members pretty generally inefficient. After exploring the ground, we could see very little prospect, or hope of encouragement for elevating or building up the waste places of Zion. Here he preached once on the sabbath, & supplied out in vacant places as occasion required, where we have reason to think much good was done. He employed his time mostly with his pen, he wrote for the Oberlin Evangelist & various articles for other papers, The Truth Seeker Tracts, on the sabbath cause, Temperance &c. As the sabbath was feerfully (sic) desecrated in this region, he took up the subject, Lectured, wrote & enlisted many minds by forming a society to supress (sic) the evil,

[56] Foster, Lemuel, Autobiography of Lemuel Foster, p. 22.

several Clergymen lent their influence which
produced quite a marked change in all the
region around, for the better. Again he
was a strong advocate for Temperance & had
labored for many years very efficiently in
the cause . . . which produced violent opposition by a certain class . . . he said
agitation was a favorable omen, as it led
persons to think & canvass the subject, &
as he hoped to produce a reform, which
silence & contentment could not do.[57]

In 1853 the Fosters moved to Atlanta, Illinois,
where they taught school, Mr. Foster preaching on the
sabbath. The town of Atlanta was badly divided by de-
nominationalism, but Foster succeeded in building up
a sturdy church and also a good school.

On April 12, 1859 they moved to Anurga, a small
town on the eastern branch of the Central Railroad.
Here they found a church only about three months old,
with nine members, a Methodist Church with a house, a
group of Presbyterians who worshipped in a warehouse,
and a group of Baptists who had just completed a church
building. The Baptists had incurred a heavy debt, and
were soon forced to sell. By pledging six hundred
dollars himself, and raising the rest of the money
among his church members, the Congregationalists secured the building. Foster secured the assistance of
a young minister named Winter, and "being somewhat
prejudiced in his favor proposed to him to take charge
of this church & relieve him as he had two churches in
charge for nearly four years, & needed rest."[58] But
Winter and Foster had a violent quarrel over church
polity, and Foster resigned.

On April 1, 1863 the Fosters moved to Blue Island,
where they remained for six years. Lemuel Foster continued to do the work of a pastor, although by now his
hearing had become greatly impaired. He succeeded in
building up the church and erecting a meeting house
free from debt and well-filled on Sundays.

The remainder of his life was spent at Washington
Heights. During the summer of 1872 he held protracted

---

[57] Foster, Lemuel, _Autobiography of Lemuel Foster_, pp.
22-23.

[58] _Ibid_., p. 30.

meetings, taking preliminary steps to organize a church of twenty members. Frequent preaching began to tell on his strength; he caught cold one night and complications set in. He died a few days later.

William Carter was born at New Canaan, Connecticut, December 31, 1803. His parents, Ebenezer and Rhoda Carter, were of New England ancestry, "moderate and frugal in their expenses, industrious in their habits, and devoted to the rearing and training of a large family of children for usefulness to their country and the church of God."[59] The Carter children were never allowed to be idle. William worked on the farm in summers, and in winter went to the district school. When he was sixteen years old, his father sent him to the academy in his native town, to prepare for college. His father wanted him to become a doctor, but he himself desired to enter law. His mother hoped that he would enter the ministry. William objected to this because he did not feel as though he were a Christian. He devoted himself to his studies and was about to enter college, when his father got caught in a pecuniary tangle, and lost a good deal of money. William had to forego college for the time being. He was detained two years from pursuing his studies, and for the most part had to rely on his own support while in college.[60]

In 1824 he entered Yale College, but he did not have a religious experience until his third year. He says of himself:

In 1827, my junior year in college, I was led, I trust, to a full and final consecration of myself to Christ. . . . It then seemed to me that I could not be a lawyer and such a Christian as I wanted to be. I promised the Lord I would be anything he would have me to be, -- a minister, if it was his will, and he would open the way for me. The result was that I saw no other way open.[61]

---

[59] Sturtevant, J.M., "William Carter," in the Congregational Quarterly for October, 1871, p. 498.
[60] Ibid., p. 499.
[61] Ibid., pp. 499-500.

Graduating from Yale in 1828, Carter was employed as teacher in the Hartford grammar school. His teaching was thorough and his life exemplary. After remaining at Hartford for a year and two terms, he was called to be a tutor at Yale College. At the same time he was able to study for the ministry in the theological department of the college.[62]

In the fall of 1833, after completing his studies for the ministry, he resigned his tutorship in order to go to Illinois as a member of the Yale Band. He was married in the fall to Elizabeth Bell, of Darien, Connecticut.

A few weeks after his arrival in Jacksonville, William Carter, although not an ordained minister, was invited to assist Julian Sturtevant in organizing the Congregational Church of Jacksonville. Of this infant church he soon became pastor, having been ordained evangelist by the Schuyler Presbytery in October, 1834, and during the four years that he was in Jacksonville, he built the membership of the church to about one hundred members.[63]

He resigned his pastorate at Jacksonville in 1838, and moved to Pittsfield, in Pike County, where he was to spend the remainder of his days. Of Pittsfield, Sturtevant says:

Conceive of a small village, containing a few hundred people, drawn together by the fact that that spot had been designated as the county town, without wealth, with no homes but such as had been hastily and rudely built within a few months, or at most a very few years, to meet their present necessities, without schools, or any public school system in accordance with which they could be founded; the population though so few and feeble in resources, divided into several different religious sects, and generally adhering with great tenacity to their sectarian preferences, or, still worse, feeling

---

[62]Sturtevant, J.M., "William Carter," in the _Congregational Quarterly_ for October, 1871, p. 501.

[63]Ibid., p. 503.

little interest in any religion; the large
majority of Southern origin, having those intense prejudices which slavery had been already for generations nourishing in the
Southern heart, and prepared to regard any
Northern man with suspicion; among them a
considerable number of lawyers and politicians who had been attracted thither by
the hope of achieving eminence through the
law and politics, among whom were, indeed,
some worthy citizens, but not a very few who
had all the usual vices of the selfish,
ignorant, and yet cunning demagogue. Conceive, if you can, of such a village, and
you will not be far from a true conception
of Pittsfield, and of nearly every village
in all that region, as it was in its origin.
. . . [64]

When William Carter commenced his labors with the
Pittsfield church, it was Presbyterian in its organization, and in full connection with the General Assembly. In accordance with his wishes, however, and
a large majority of its members, the church adopted a
Congregational type of polity. The change was effected quietly and without a conflict. Carter became
pastor of the church shortly after its organization,
and remained there for over twenty-seven years. In
the course of his pastorate about four hundred and
thirty members were added to the church.[65]

During the first nine years of his work in Pittsfield, Carter also had charge of the Congregational
Church at Summer Hill and Rockport, and saw that
church increase under his ministry from about a dozen
to one hundred members.

During my ministry I have been permitted to
receive to membership in the church more than
six hundred persons, by far the larger portion of them on profession of their faith. I
feel that I have been an unprofitable servant.
And yet I feel thankful that I have been able
to see even so much fruit of my labor. From

---

[64]Sturtevant, J.M., "William Carter," in the Congregational Quarterly for October, 1871, pp. 503-504.
[65]Ibid., p. 504.

the first, I think it has been my controlling
desire and prayer and labor to gather souls
into the kingdom of Christ.[66]

William Carter was also connected with Illinois
College during his entire life. About twenty years
before his death, he was called to a seat on the Board
of Trustees, which he held until his death. Although
he drew a slender salary from his church, he donated
much to Illinois College. As a trustee of the College,
he was firm and independent in his own opinion, candid
and open to conviction, and sound in judgment.[67]

In addition to serving as a trustee of Illinois
College, Carter was also a member of the Board of Directors of the Chicago Theological Seminary, punctual
in his attendance on its meetings, and deeply interested in the success of that institution. During the
last years of his life he found it very inconvenient
to attend board meetings, and resigned his position.[68]

In 1844, he, with eight other ministers and five
delegates from churches, organized the General Association of Illinois. There were then in the State but
two District Associations, and less than three thousand
members of the Congregational Church. Yet the last
General Association which he attended, and of which
he was the preacher, ranked among the most dignified
and influential of the annual Congregational gatherings.[69]

Julian Sturtevant describes William Carter as being
eminently a practical man. He was not deficient in
doctrinal preaching, but he presented his doctrines
with a practical end in view. On such questions as
temperance and slavery, he always spoke with freedom
and earnestness, but with such moderation and wisdom
as ultimately to disarm opposition. He was a diligent
student, and very much interested in the subject of
prophecy. He was a very able public speaker. In his
private life, he was eminently sociable, amiable, and

---

[66]Sturtevant, J.M., "William Carter," in the Congregational Quarterly for October, 1871, p. 505.

[67]Ibid., p. 506.

[68]Ibid., pp. 506-507.

[69]Ibid., passim.

genial. He was an earnest promoter of revivalism in his church, but did not foster a sectarian spirit. His letters reveal him as a man of sparkling vivacity and wit.[70]

For several weeks just before his death, he had been suffering from a cold, and although he could not preach he was confined to the house. On the last day of his life he arose and dressed as usual, but did not feel well. A short time later his wife found him in a dying condition. He died on February 9, 1871, at the age of sixty-nine.

John Flavel Brooks was born at Westmoreland, New York, in 1802. He was graduated from Hamilton College in 1828. In 1831 he took his degree from Yale Seminary, and was ordained by the Oneida presbytery. In 1831, he set out for Illinois; the journey from Utica, New York to Collinsville took him five weeks. He began to preach in St. Clair County, and on November 14, 1831 he decided to locate at Belleville, dividing his time between that settlement and Collinsville. Although no church had been gathered at Belleville, the church at Collinsville, by the following April had thirty-six members, a Sunday School with eighty pupils, one hundred volumes in the library, one Bible Society with twenty members, one temperance society with one hundred members, and forty-seven dollars donated to missions and education.[71]

Methodists and Baptists were the most numerous Christians at Belleville, and apparently they were opposed to a paid clergy. Hence Brooks found it very difficult to get money subscribed for his support. He was able to report little success as a preacher, so his mind kept revolving about the possibility of a teaching ministry. His school which he had recently set up now drew over sixty scholars, which was more than his wife and her brother could handle.[72] Therefore, in

---

[70]Sturtevant, J.M., "William Carter," pp. 507-512.

[71]Brooks to Peters, January 18, 1832, Collinsville, Ill.

[72]Baldwin to Peters, December 24, 1834, Jacksonville, Illinois. Brooks to Peters, January 12, 1835, Belleville, Illinois.

1835, he severed his connection with the American Home
Missionary Society, and did not resume it again until
1843. During the intervening years he taught his private school at Belleville, and in a teachers' seminary
at Waverly. In 1840 he began teaching at Springfield
Academy, Springfield, Illinois, until 1843.

While teaching in Springfield, he also preached at
various towns in Sangamon County, such as Chatham,
Mount Auburn, and Rochester. He continued to teach
in Springfield until his death on July 23, 1888.

Mason Grosvenor was born at Pomfret, Connecticut,
on September 13, 1800. He was graduated from Yale in
the class of 1827, and for one year was principal of
the academy in Greenwich, Connecticut. In 1831, he
was graduated from the theological department, and was
ordained as evangelist at Guilford on March 22. After
a year and a half of brief engagements with various
churches, he became pastor of the Congregational Church
in Ashfield, Massachusetts. In July, 1835, he was dismissed at his own request. He then supplied the pulpit in Chester and Saybrook, Connecticut. On September
28, 1836 he was installed over the Congregational Church
in Sharon, Connecticut. On June 28, 1839 he left at
his own request. In the fall of 1840 he settled in
Hudson, Ohio, and was installed over the First Congregational Church there (December 22, 1840 to July 23,
1843). For the next four years he became principal of
the Hudson Female Seminary. In 1847, he became agent
of the Western College Society, working with Theron
Baldwin, and during that time resided in Springfield,
Massachusetts, and New Haven, Connecticut. In 1853 he
went West, and taught mathematics one year at Illinois
College, and part of the following year at Beloit.
In 1855 he returned to Northern Ohio and supplied
vacant churches near his home in Hudson. In 1863 he
devoted a year to an agency for the Ohio Female College.
The following year he became the general agent in Cincinnati for the Aetna Life Insurance Company of Hartford. In 1869-1870 he moved to Jacksonville to teach
at Illinois College as Professor of Moral Philosophy
and the Evidences of Christianity. In 1880 he retired
to Englewood, New Jersey, to the home of his elder sur-
viving son, and died there on March 27, at the age of
eighty-six.

Born in Upper Middletown, now Cromwell, Connecticut,
on March 8, 1802, and ordained at Bethany, Connecticut,

in November 1832, Jairus Wilcox was the last man to become a member of the Yale Band. In June 1834, he was pastor at Victor, New York. Following this he was pastor of the church at Geneseo, Illinois from 1838 to 1844.

In June 1836, an exploring committee from Bergen, New York located the present site of Geneseo, and set apart lots for a church, parsonage and school. A public square was also plotted. On September 13, 1836, a Congregational church was organized in Bergen with thirteen members. Six days later the colonists started on their westward journey. The following May they held their first communion service in a cabin, at which time six joined the church. In July a log-and-tent school and church were erected on the square.[73] A frame church was built the following year.

In May 1838, Reverend Jairus Wilcox came on to the colony with his family, and in June was elected pastor, upon a salary of four hundred dollars. In the seminary at Yale he had promised Flavel Bascom that he would go West. It was in response to Bascom's repeated urgings that he came on. After ten days upon the lakes, he and his family arrived in Chicago. There they were met by C.K. Bartlett and Anson M. Hubbard, who moved them in. The trip from Chicago to Geneseo was arduous. When they came to Green River, they found neither bridge, ferry, nor ford. It was necessary to swim the horses over by the side of the canoe. The wagons were ferried over by setting the wheels into two canoes. On reaching Geneseo, Wilcox built a log shanty north of the village, and covered it with hay. There he lived nine months. A travelling clergyman, upon being invited to spend the night with them, declined, saying that his health and life were too valuable to be thus exposed.[74]

Jairus Wilcox arrived in Geneseo with a commission from the American Home Missionary Society amounting to three hundred dollars. This amount was reduced the

[73]Dedication of the rebuilt First Congregational Church of Geneseo, Illinois. Dedication Week, Sunday, February 22 to March 1, 1925. Church File, Hammond **Library**, Chicago Theological Seminary, Chicago, Illinois.

[74]Memorial Address and Proceedings at the Thirtieth Anniversary of the Settlement of Geneseo, Illinois, November 19 & 20, 1866. Church File, Hammond Library, Chicago Theological Seminary, Chicago, Illinois, pp. 9-10.

next year to two hundred and fifty dollars, and again to
two hundred dollars, and then to one hundred dollars,
until the church became self-supporting, having received
from source altogether eighteen hundred and fifty dollars.[75]

The colonists at Geneseo were anxious to promote
revivals. A "work of grace" occurred in the summer of
1837 before they had even secured a pastor. An early
historian of the church tells us:

> They could not wait for the more permanent
> settling of their affairs; and, as they had
> covenanted to pray for the conversion of
> every adult person in the community, God
> could not wait, for he had promised that
> if his people would bring all the tithes
> into the storehouse, he would pour out such
> a blessing that there would not be room
> enough to receive it. And he did it. In
> 1838-1839 there was another season of
> spiritual exaltation, with a similar re-
> sult -- all the youth of suitable age and
> all the adults, becoming hopeful disciples
> of Christ. In the Winter of 1841 and 1842,
> our pastor at Lyndon, Rev. E.H. Hazard,
> and our deacon, A.R. Hamilton, both of them
> dear men of God, and now with Him above,
> came here to assist Mr. Wilcox in a meeting,
> which resulted in the hopeful conversion of
> all the adults, save two men. Deacon
> Ward . . . speaks of this as a continuous
> revival for five years. Soon after this
> these three men met for a similar work at
> the log schoolhouse in Sharon, Mr. Wilcox's
> out-station, to which he had frequently
> walked across the desolate prairie, twelve
> miles, and where he had organized a Presby-
> terian church. The result was a precious
> movement, which brought in the principal
> man of the neighborhood, who, at Portland,
> Maine had been one of Dr. Payson's stony-
> ground hearers, who then, largely by his

---

[75]Memorial Address and Proceedings at the Thirtieth
Anniversary of the Settlement of Geneseo, Illinois.
November 19 & 20, 1866. Church File, Hammond Library,
Chicago Theological Seminary, Chicago, Illinois, p. 17.

own means, built a near church and a parsonage, which yet crown the hill of Sharon . . . .[76]

On November 19, 1838, the Church at Geneseo affili-
ated with the Knox Presbytery for the purpose of fellowship, local church government remaining within the
church. On April 1, 1850 this fellowship with the
presbytery was severed, the church claiming that the
General Presbyterian Assembly (New School) had failed
to take a decided stand in opposition to the system of
slavery.[77]

Wilcox was not only a good pastor, but was very
much interested in community planning. He ornamented
the public square and the streets of the town with
trees. He was very much interested in educational
enterprises, as we shall see in a later chapter. He
accomplished great good as a pioneer missionary. In
1845 he moved to Chicago to take charge of the Seamen's Bethel, in which service he was engaged until
1848. Later, he was in business in Chicago until his
death in that city, September 16, 1861 at the age of
fifty-nine.[78]

In summarizing this chapter we may say that these
members of the Illinois Band were motivated by a desire to spread Christianity in a new frontier state,
and to establish educational opportunities for their
fellow-men. Their rather unspectacular lives were
part of a great on-going process. The Puritan fathers
had left Holland, not because they did not enjoy religious freedom, but because their church had no field
for expansion and no hope of growth. They longed to
extend the area of English freedom and to plant the
church of Christ, as they understood it, where there
was an open field for its growth and productiveness.

---

[76]Memorial Address and Proceedings at the Thirtieth
Anniversary of the Settlement of Geneseo, Illinois.
November 19 & 20, 1866. Church File, Hammond Library,
Chicago, Theological Seminary, Chicago, Illinois, pp.
11-12.

[77]Ibid., p. 19.

[78]A General Catalogue of the Divinity School of Yale
College, 1822-1872.

Religious forces, because they are intangible, succeed in eluding the grasp of the historian. But they nevertheless have a very vital influence wherever they are operating. It is very difficult to measure the influence which Christianity has upon its environment, because many of its results lie beyond history. While more spectacular and transitory events were occurring, these members of the Illinois Band were quietly working to place the new state on a sure moral and religious foundation.

CHAPTER V

THE ILLINOIS BAND AND EDUCATION

The members of the Yale Band believed that evangelical religion and education must go hand in hand. They accordingly played an important role in the early history of Illinois College. The story of Illinois College has already been told very ably by Charles Henry Rammelkamp in his Illinois College, A Centennial History, and need not be repeated here.

Instruction began in Illinois College on the morning of Monday, January 4, 1830. Nine students presented themselves in "Old Beecher" before William C. Posey and Julian Sturtevant. After putting up a stove, which took about two hours, Sturtevant

> . . . addressed them a few words and among other things told them . . . what my heart felt and believed, that we had come there that morning to open a fountain for future generations to drink at. We then commended ourselves and the whole great enterprise to God in prayer. It was a season never to be forgotten, whatever the fate of the college may be. I then proceeded to inquire into the intellectual condition of my pupils. Not one of them had ever studied English grammar or geography, a few had learned the ground rules of arithmetic and two had some knowledge of the rudiments of Latin.[1]

For a while, Julian Sturtevant was the only instructor at the college. After consultation with President Day and the faculty at Yale about the matter, a call was issued to Edward Beecher, pastor of the Park Street Church, Boston, to become president of the new institution of learning.[2]

---

[1] Sturtevant to Thomas Lippincott, February 22, 1844.
[2] Minutes of the Trustees, May 29, 1830.

The earliest faculty of Illinois College consisted of five men, Edward Beecher, Julian Sturtevant, Truman Post, Jonathan Baldwin Turner, and Samuel Adams. Turner was the brother of Asa Turner. William Kirby also acted as tutor for two years between 1831 and 1833. Sturtevant taught mathematics and natural philosophy, Post was Professor of Latin and Greek, Turner was Professor of Rhetoric and Belles Lettres, and Adams, Chemistry, Mineralogy and Geology. They were all men of real ability, fired by a youthful enthusiasm which enabled them to conquer difficulties and endure hardships.[3]

At first, two distinct courses were offered, an English course and a collegiate course. The latter involved the study of Latin and Greek. Both were really of a preparatory nature. The catalogue of 1836-37 states that candidates for the freshman class were to be examined in arithmetic, geography, English grammar, Latin and Greek. The examination in Latin was to cover Adam's Latin Grammar, Virgil, Cicero's Select Orations and Sallust; in Greek, Goodrich's Greek Grammar, a Greek Reader, or Graeca Minora and Greek Testament. No students were to be received under the age of fourteen.[4]

The usual courses studied in freshman year were algebra, geometry, trigonometry, Graeca Majora with Lysias and Isocrates, Livy and Roman antiquities. Sophomores battled with plane and spherical trigonometry, mensuration, navigation, conic sections, mechanics and hydrostatics, Horace, Graeca Majora, Volume I completed, and extracts from Homer. Juniors studied ancient and modern history, a variety of subjects now called physics, Tacitus and De Officiis. Optional studies were natural philosophy, history of the Latin and Greek languages, philosophy and chemistry. Seniors were required to take intellectual and moral philosophy, logic, natural theology and evidences of Christianity, more Latin and Greek, political economy, American law and rhetoric.[5]

---

[3]Rammelkamp, Charles H., *Illinois College, A Centennial History*, Chapter III, *passim*.

[4]*Ibid.*, p. 53.

[5]*Ibid.*, pp. 53-54.

There were only a few books in the College library, which was only open for brief periods of time. Students who wished to use the library were required to pay fifty cents per term. The number of books which a student might take out depended not on the number, but on the size of the volumes. At first the library was only open for a short time on Wednesday afternoons, but in 1842, the faculty voted "that the librarian be instructed to provide for such students as may desire it, the privilege of consulting the College library daily for a compensation of two dollars a year."[6]

The college calendar was quite different from what it is today. Commencement was in September. There was no vacation during the summer, but there was recess of four weeks in the spring, and one of eight weeks in the fall, during September and October.

The cost of getting an education was not extremely high in those days. Room, board and tuition were estimated at about one hundred dollars per year. The original rates for tuition were twelve dollars for the English course and sixteen dollars for the classical course. Board and room could be obtained in private families in the village at rates varying from two dollars and a half to three dollars and a half per week. Theron Baldwin was strongly opposed to the idea of a college commons. Recalling the bread and butter rebellions at Yale, he was afraid that such outbreaks would be even more prolific in the West than at the East.[7]

The College did not secure a charter until 1835. A bill was introduced in 1831, but it met with a cold reception. Some thought that it was a scheme for uniting church and state; others suspected that it was a conspiracy of land speculators to get control of large tracts of land. "No wolf or fox would tread more carefully around a trap than do these men about our bill," complained Baldwin, "and though no one of them probably knows how Troy was destroyed, yet they appear to gather around this mysterious thing much as the Trojans did about the horse."[8] Baldwin finally secured the help of Governor Duncan, however, and an act was finally passed providing for the incorporation not only of

---

[6]Rammelkamp, Charles H., _Illinois College, A Centennial History_, p. 55.

[7]Ibid., pp. 62, 64.

[8]Baldwin to Grosvenor, January 15, 1831. The bill apparently did pass the lower house, but failed in the Senate.

Illinois College but also of three other institutions --
Alton College, later called Shurtleff, McKendree College and Jonesboro College.[9]

The trustees of Illinois College named in the act
of incorporation included Samuel D. Lockwood, William
C. Posey, John P. Wilkinson, Theron Baldwin, John F.
Brooks, Elisha Jenney, William Kirby, Asa Turner, John
G. Bergen, John Tillson, Jr., and Gideon Blackburn.
Sturtevant had retired from the board of trustees when
President Beecher was elected.[10]

Closely connected with Illinois College was the
Jacksonville Female Academy. The original idea for
establishing a school for girls came from Mrs. John
M. Ellis, who had successfully operated a school in
her own home for a number of years. The Jacksonville
Female Academy was opened in 1833, Julian M. Sturtevant having assisted in its organization. In 1903
the Academy was merged with the College, and Illinois
College became a coeducational institution.[11]

The member of the Yale Band most closely associated
with Illinois College was Julian M. Sturtevant. In
1844 he was elected president of the College, and for
the next thirty-two years he guided the destinies of
the new institution.

The first problem with which the new president
was confronted was that of the College debt. Ever
since the Panic of 1837 it had been growing, until
in 1846, the principal and interest amounted to about
$30,000. It was proposed that all the property of
the College with the exception of the thirty-three
acres which then constituted the actual campus, and
with the exception of the buildings, library, apparatus
and other equipment, should be put into a "joint stock"
and be devoted to the payment of the college debt.
Sturtevant alone opposed this as an unnecessary sacrifice.
He suggested that the lands be offered in exchange for
the bonds of the state of Illinois, which at that time
were selling far below par. He was confident, however,
that in time the state bonds would again reach par value.

---

[9] The last named apparently never began operations.

[10] Rammelkamp, Charles H., Illinois College, A Centennial
History, p. 68.

[11] Ibid., pp. 72-73.

160

But his suggestion was greeted "with a storm of sar-
casm and ridicule." Would he "sell the rich lands of
Illinois for dishonored bonds not worth the paper on
which they were printed and on which not one dime
would ever be paid?" This was the only serious matter
during his entire administration in which Sturtevant
disagreed with the trustees. Events ten years later
were to prove them wrong and him right.[12]

During the Christmas vacation of 1852, a serious
disaster occurred. The main college building was destroyed by fire, and it was only with great difficulty
that the books of the library were saved. To make
matters worse, an insurance policy of four thousand
dollars had been allowed to lapse, so that only three
thousand dollars could be recovered on the building.[13]
A new building was not completed until 1857.

The early years of Sturtevant's administration were
marked by a long, hard financial struggle. Funds for
the new building did not grow rapidly, and it occurred
to him that the College should be moved to a new location. He was apparently thinking of Quincy. Theron
Baldwin was startled by this suggestion, and warned
him that if such information were known, a reaction
might occur among the townspeople, and even less money
raised. Baldwin also pointed out the bad impression
which the trustees had made on eastern friends by al-
lowing the insurance policy to lapse. "Ten thousand
in Jacksonville worth twenty or thirty thousand elsewhere," he wired.

When the College celebrated its twenty-fifth anni-
versary in 1855, it stood on a firmer financial foot-
ing. The exercises were held on Wednesday morning,
July 11, in the First Presbyterian Church. In the
evening, friends gathered for a banquet at the Mansion
House. Asa Turner asked the blessing and among those
who responded to toasts were John M. Ellis, Truman M.
Post, Mason Grosvenor, Theron Baldwin, Richard Yates,
Edward Bates, Samuel Wolcott, President Sturtevant,
Asa Turner and Flavel Bascom.

Early in President Sturtevant's administration,
the College began to feel competition from other in-

---

[12]Sturtevant, J.M., _Autobiography_, p. 267ff.

[13]_Ibid._, pp. 270-271.

stitutions. Knox, founded in 1837, began to compete
with Illinois for both money and students, as did also
McKendree (Methodist) and Shurtleff, a Baptist college.
Other colleges such as Western Reserve, Oberlin, Wabash and Beloit, while they did not compete with Illinois for students, nevertheless were keen competitors
for eastern contributions. Illinois College looked
frequently to the Society for the Promotion of Collegiate and Theological Education at the West for funds.
Although Theron Baldwin was Secretary of this Society,
he was compelled to promote the welfare of all the
schools without showing partiality toward any.[14]

A large percentage of the College's graduates
went into the Christian ministry. During the first
twenty years, about one-half became clergymen. Two
of the classes sent their entire number into the cler-
ical profession. Nineteen per cent of the graduates
of the first twenty years went into law, and about
eleven per cent became doctors. Certainly the founders
of Illinois College must have been pleased to see that
their dreams for "the new institution of learning"
were being fulfilled.[15]

During the Civil War, Illinois College was almost
forced to close its doors.[16] During the winter of
1862-63, trouble broke out in the senior class, resulting in its disbanding. Since the president usually
taught the senior class, Sturtevant began to look
around for something else to do. It was at this time
that an intimate friend offered to pay his expenses
for a trip to England. There were many who felt that
he could greatly help the northern cause. Although
Sturtevant conversed frequently on the subject, he
seldom gave a public address. It was probably not
possible for him to accomplish much. In the fall of
1863 he had returned to Illinois for the opening of
college.[17]

---

[14]Rammelkamp, Charles H., _Illinois College, A Centennial History_, p. 191.

[15]_Ibid._, p. 193.

[16]The role of Illinois College in the slavery contro--
versy will be discussed in the following chapter.

[17]Rammelkamp, Charles H., _Illinois College, A Centennial History_, p. 211ff.

The early months of the year 1866 were devoted to efforts in behalf of the "Sturtevant Foundation," an endowment for the presidency of Illinois College. This he regarded as one of the most important undertakings of his life. Although he did not want to make Illinois College a Congregational institution, neither did he wish to have it managed by a compromise between denominations. In a memorandum to the trustees, he said:

Our conception of the college, which in the early fervor of our youth we united with others in endeavoring to found, was that it should be controlled by sound evangelical men, who could be trusted to administer it for Christ and His Church, and that in administering it they were bound to appoint to the various parts of instruction trustworthy evangelical men of the highest qualifications for their respective departments, and that beyond this they were not to be held responsible for the denominational relations of the candidate. We acknowledge and keenly feel that the trustees are bound to deal impartially with the two denominations. But by impartiality we understand that the prospects of no man for election to any place in the institution shall be damaged or benefited by the fact that he belongs to one of these denominations rather than the other.[18]

In 1876 Sturtevant resigned the presidency of the College, although he continued to occupy the chair of mental and moral philosophy. Intense and active as he was, he found it hard to relinquish any part of his life work, even though it was necessary. He spent the summers of 1877 and 1878 in New Haven, going there in April and working diligently upon the "Keys of Sect." In 1879 he remained West and delivered the semi-centennial address at Illinois College. In December 1883 he delivered an historical discourse at the semi-centennial of the Congregational Church in Jacksonville. In 1885 he was released from all duty in connection with Illinois College, and died the following year.[19]

---

[18] Sturtevant, J.M., Autobiography, pp. 330-331.
[19] Ibid., p. 333ff.

Sturtevant's entire life was closely interwoven
with Illinois College. He was a keen thinker and a
fearless leader. He was greatly admired by his students, although perhaps he was a somewhat austere man.
An alumnus of the College, who frequently opposed some
of his policies, has this to say of him:

His influence upon the minds of his students
was peculiarly stimulating. His own mind was
remarkably active and his utterances were
forceful alike in the class-room and in public. I think I never received instruction
from any other teacher whose words and
thoughts and manner were as incisive and
quickening as his. I always felt it was a
real loss to be absent from a recitation
which he conducted; and I know that such
was the general feeling of the earnest students in the college. I remember today how
his countenance kindled and his eye flashed
approval when he saw that a pupil clearly
understood and well expressed the more difficult points in the lesson, whether in
language, mathematics or philosophy. It
is not easy to overestimate the privilege
of sitting at the feet of such an apprecia-
tive teacher. Even the dull or inattentive
scholar feels the personal influence of
such an instructor.

Dr. Sturtevant taught his students to think
for themselves. Almost every professor tells
his pupils, in words, to do their own thinking.
But very few manifest real pleasure in freedom of thought on the part of their pupils
when it reveals itself in the earnest questioning of their own expressed opinions. But it
often seemed to me that Dr. Sturtevant enjoyed
the respectful boldness of a student who dared
to controvert his declared views, and gave
plausible reasons for his dissent. I never
noted a symptom of displeasure on his part, on
such an occasion, unless the pupil indicated
undue self-assertion or a lack of proper attention to the point in question.[20]

[20]Patterson, R.W., Advance, March 18, 1886. (Rammelkamp, Charles H., Illinois College, A Centennial History, p. 265.)

The plans of the Yale Band, in respect to education, were never confined to Illinois College. The Band also advocated a public school system for the state, and bent their energies in influencing public opinion in that direction.[21] There was hardly a member of the Band who was not connected directly with some school at one time or another. Frequent mention of these schools is made, although the details are often exceedingly scant.

Flavel Bascom had experience in teaching in the Academy at New Canaan, Connecticut, as a young man. He tells us that the "cause of education claimed much attention from the ministers of that day. Many an anxious consultation was held by the President, Pastors and leading members of the Chicago churches, in regard to the founding of a Theological Seminary, in that city. The project never was abandoned, but its consummation was delayed until long after I had left the city. The present Seminary of Chicago is, with some modifications, the realization of our early plan."[22]

> Beloit College, and Rockford Female Seminary, had their origin in Conventions held by Presbyterian and Congregational Ministers, of N. Illinois and Wisconsin. I attended those conventions and was made Trustee of those Institutions by the charters obtained in their respective States.[23]

When Bascom moved to Galesburg, the home of Knox College, he "found the College and the whole community in a ferment." A fierce College quarrel had broken out between Mr. Gale, founder of the College and of the community, and Mr. Blanchard, president of the College. Bascom had been elected a Trustee of the College while residing at Chicago, but had never acted in that capacity. Now that he was identified with Galesburg, he was expected to be identified with Knox College, and was at once appointed on a committee of peacemakers, to harmonize the conflicting views and interests, and bring order out of confusion. The committee succeeded in persuading the Board of Trustees to retrace its steps,

---

[21] Cf. Belting, Paul E., "The Development of the Free Public High School in Illinois to 1860," *Journal of the Illinois State Historical Society*, Vol. XI, p. 269ff.

[22] Bascom, Flavel, *Autobiography*, p. 177.

[23] *Ibid.*, pp. 177-178.

so far as to escape litigation in the courts which had
already commenced. Then by recommending candidates to
fill the existing vacancies in the Board, acceptable
to both sides, a better state of feeling was secured.
As chairman of the Executive Committee of the Board of
Trustees, during these troublous times, an amount of
labor, care and responsibility was imposed upon Bascom,
"which as Pastor of a large church, I ought not to have
borne." The large College edifice and the Female Seminary building were erected during the six years of his
Galesburg pastorate.[24]

In 1831, John F. Brooks began to preach in St. Clair
County and also taught in a private school at Belleville.
In 1837 he opened one of the first teachers' seminaries
at Waverly. In 1840 he directed the Springfield Academy and acted as principal of the public schools in the
same city. In 1886 he wrote, "the Lord gives me fair
health at the age of eighty-four and ability to hear
recitations six hours a day." He taught in Springfield
until his death in 1888.[25]

William Carter taught for a while in Hartford in
1830, and was also a college tutor at Yale. In later
years, he was one of the early directors of Chicago
Theological Seminary.

The Lemuel Fosters were also active in education.
Mrs. Foster had attended, in New Haven, the celebrated
school of Reverend Claudius Herrick, father of Henry
Herrick. In Bloomington Foster opened a school in a
log school house, and later built a "real New England
academy 28 by 42 feet with arched room." He was active in the cause of education at Bethel, and when he
moved to Atlanta in 1853 he secured a building for an
academy and taught there.[26]

---

[24]Bascom, Flavel, Autobiography, p. 195ff.

[25]One authority says that he taught Latin in the Bettie
Stuart Seminary in St. Louis. (Yale Memorabilia Records.) Cf. Belting, Paul E., "The Development of the
Free Public High School in Illinois to 1860," Journal
of the Illinois State Historical Society, Vol. XI, p. 484.

[26]Yale Memorabilia. Belting says that Foster established an academy at Jacksonville.

A good half of the Foster autobiography is in Mrs.
Foster's hand. She was also a teacher, but her spelling makes the reader skeptical of her pedagogical
[footnote continued on next page]

166

Mason Grosvenor was also active in the cause of education, although the records of his service are tantalizingly brief. After graduating from Yale in 1827 he was principal of the academy at Greenwich, Connecticut for a year, 1827-1828. He was principal of the Hudson Female Seminary in Ohio from 1843 to 1847. For the next seven years he worked with Theron Baldwin as an agent of the Western College Society, residing in Springfield, Massachusetts and New Haven, Connecticut.[27] He taught mathematics for a year in Illinois College, and he did the same during part of the next year at Beloit. In 1863 he devoted a year to an agency for the Ohio Female College. In 1870 he returned to Illinois College to become Professor of Moral Philosophy and the Evidences of Christianity, and taught here until his retirement in 1880.[28]

After graduation, Henry Herrick taught for a year in West Springfield, Massachusetts, and for two years was rector of the Hopkins Grammar School in New Haven. In 1835 he went to Knoxville, East Tennessee as principal of a female academy. He also taught for a while in Alabama. Teaching was almost a tradition in the Herrick family. His father had studied with Charles Backus at Somers, Connecticut, where many young men trained for the ministry before divinity schools were regularly established.[29] The school of Reverend Claudius Herrick was widely known, and Henry must have absorbed much of his father's valuable teaching experience.

William Kirby was a tutor at Illinois College during President Beecher's administration, presumably doing most of his work in the preparatory department.[30]

During his pastorate at Geneseo, Jairus Wilcox became greatly interested in the building of a Manual

---

[footnote continued from previous page] abilities. Samples: alternity (alternative); whoom; to (two); Isreal; their for there; endurence; periodicles; conciously; disturbence; distructive; planed (planned); presance; comence; Methidest; crices (crisis); fore (four).

[27] Yale Memorabilia. Obituary Record.

[28] Ibid.

[29] Congregational Quarterly, April 1864; Yale Memorabilia Class of 1822.

[30] Rammelkamp, Charles H., Illinois College, A Centennial History, p. 56.

Labor High School. The Legislature approved a petition for it on March 2, 1839. Wilcox made two trips to the East in its behalf and looked up its first two principals. It may be readily assumed that he was closely connected with the school until 1845, when he moved from Geneseo.[31]

While Theron Baldwin was acting as Agent for the American Home Missionary Society, he became interested in another institution which was to become famous in the state of Illinois. This was the new academy for "females" at Monticello near Alton. One of Alton's wealthiest and most respected citizens was Captain Benjamin Godfrey, a Cape Cod sea captain who had made a fortune in Mexico. Godfrey was very much interested in religious and philanthropic enterprises, and he confided to his friend Baldwin his desire to build a female academy which would educate future mothers of the state. He promised to invest from eight to ten thousand dollars on condition that Baldwin would agree to superintend the institution. Although it was necessary first to disengage himself from the American Home Missionary Society, on the first Sunday of January, 1836, he assured Captain Godfrey that he would "preach, lecture, on moral subjects, and exercise general superintendence" of the seminary.[32]

It was at about this time that a widespread interest in women's education was developing in the East. Leaving Alton in the middle of July 1837, Baldwin travelled almost five thousand miles in order to visit the great pioneers in female education. He visited Rochester, Auburn, Clinton, and Albany Seminaries in New York State; Southampton, Ipswich, and Mount Holyoke in Massachusetts; Castleton and Middlebury in Vermont. He had already met Mary Lyon, founder of Mount Holyoke two years before. Dr. Norma Adams, in her excellent sketch of Theron Baldwin and Monticello Seminary says that Miss Lyon entertained Baldwin in the front yard where she could count the wagon loads of bricks during the interview![33]

---

[31]Taylor, Ella Hume, "A History of the First Congregational Church of Geneseo," _Illinois State Historical Society Journal_, Vol. XX.

[32]Adams, Norma, _Theron Baldwin, Principal of Monticello Seminary_, pp. 16-17.

[33]_Ibid._, p. 18.

The most pressing problems with which Baldwin had
to deal were those of teaching, entrance requirements,
domestic duties, curriculum, and school equipment. He
felt that it was not desirable for a woman to be principal of a female academy, and in his journal he wrote:

> Was satisfied from my investigations that Miss
> Lyon's plan was defective in not having a gen-
> tleman at the head who should do all such things
> as would not fall within the sphere of woman.
> Miss Lyon does many such things and is compelled
> to do so and this perhaps in a measure gives
> rise to a common objection raised against her
> that she is masculine in her manners. Females
> no doubt ought to conduct the business of in-
> struction both from their adaptedness to the
> work and their cheapness -- Presidents of Col-
> leges in these days are taken up very much with
> the pecuniary concerns of the Institutions
> over which they preside. They are Agents and
> the principal labor of instruction is in the
> hands of Professors.[34]

Another problem was that of entrance requirements.
Since many of the girls were not mature enough to
handle subjects on a college level, the question arose,
Should Monticello admit students under sixteen years of
age and form a preparatory department? The idea of a
preparatory department had been cancelled at both Illinois College and Mount Holyoke, and Baldwin concluded
that "contact of little girls with mature young ladies
was unhappy -- making the younger ones bold, the older
ones less mature, and that such an arrangement was apt
to lower the character of the institution."[35]

Mount Holyoke had a domestic system. The student
body was divided into three groups; one group did

---

[34]Adams, Norma, _Theron Baldwin, Principal of Monticello
Seminary_, p. 19. Baldwin's original journal is lost.
Monticello has only the memorandum from the journal
relating to the founding of the seminary. Miss Adams'
sketch is based on the correspondence between Baldwin
and Godfrey, extracts from the "Alton Telegraph,"
Trustees' minutes and Baldwin's address.

[35]_Ibid._, p. 23.

daily tasks such as getting meals, washing dishes,
setting tables, sweeping, baking bread, making ginger-
bread, pies, etc. The second department washed
clothes and rooms. Ironing was done in the middle of
the week. The third department did extra work such
as washing floors twice each week and laundering sheets
and pillow slips. Baldwin did not accept Mary Lyon's
"system" in its entirety. Pupils at Monticello were
required to do their own washing and ironing, to take
the entire care of their own rooms and such public
rooms as were devoted to their use, and to take turns
in setting tables, but Mrs. Miriam Stoddard of Poult-
ney, Vermont, was engaged to superintend the boarding
establishment.[36]

Mrs. E.R. Steele, an easterner who visited Monticello in 1841, wrote an account of her visit for the
Alton Telegraph:

> When we entered the Academy we were shown into
> a neatly furnished parlor where we were soon
> joined by the principal of Monticello, the Rev.
> Theron Baldwin, a gentleman of great information
> and piety. He kindly explained to us the prin-
> ciples upon which the seminary was conducted and
> then offered to show us the house. Everything
> seemed arranged with the greatest order and
> neatness. The dining, school, and recitation
> rooms were large, clean, and airy; and the
> bed rooms commodious. Upon the ground floor
> was a chapel fitted up with the beautiful
> black walnut of their woods. . . . In one
> of the halls we saw a young girl upon her
> knees scrubbing in payment for her board and
> her lessons. . . . She was about fourteen
> and quite pretty; her sleeves were rolled
> up to avoid being soiled and displayed a
> plump fair arm. She did not seem abashed
> by her situation but calmly arose to give
> us room to pass, glancing a firm but modest
> eye towards us. . . . It is not usual to
> admit visitors upon cleaning days, but we
> obtained a peep into an upper gallery where
> the broom and the dust brush were keeping
> time in a merry cadence with happy young
> voices. . . . Some young ladies who had

[36]Adams, Norma, Theron Baldwin, Principal of Monticello
Seminary, pp. 20, 21.

been bred in idleness or had come from the luxurious mansions of St. Louis where slaves await their nod, were very reluctant at first to undertake these menial tasks. They were soon, however, broken in, and sing as merrily over their washtubs as the other pupils.[37]

What sort of curriculum should the new Seminary offer? Prior to the nineteenth century, female education had been mainly concerned with singing, playing musical instruments, painting, needlework, etc. Baldwin planned to introduce at Monticello an advanced course of study based upon that offered at Yale University. His first catalogue included the following departments: habits and first principles of morals and religion; rhetoric and moral and intellectual philosophy; history and moral science; mathematics and natural philosophy; vocal and instrumental. The pupils were classified as Juniors, Middlers, and Seniors, and the course was to cover three years.[38]

The original stone building which housed the Monticello Female Seminary was 110 by 44 feet, and three stories high. The two upper stories contained forty rooms, 9 or 10 by 16-1/2 feet each. The second story was divided into school room, recitation, and family rooms; the basement into kitchen, dining hall, and chapel. It was dubbed "Godfrey's Folly" by some. One honest farmer, thinking that the institution was built for profit, remarked, "Well, I reckon Captain Godfrey must make a heap of money of this!"[39]

On April 11, 1838, the school was at last ready for students. The Reverend and Mrs. Baldwin, Miss Philena Fobes, formerly a teacher at Rochester Seminary, Miss Mary Cone of Ipswich Female Seminary, Mr. and Mrs. Enoch Long of Upper Alton and sixteen pupils were present at the opening chapel service. Mrs. Baldwin, Miss Fobes, and Miss Cone served the first breakfast of coffee, bread and butter, boiled eggs, and griddle cakes.[40]

---

[37] Adams, Norma, _Theron Baldwin, Principal of Monticello Seminary_, p. 23.

[38] Ibid., p. 21.

[39] Ibid., pp 21-22.

[40] Ibid., p. 22.

As might be expected, the new Seminary was noted for its religious influence. Services were held on Sunday, and evening prayers every night in the dining hall. Scripture was read, a hymn sung, and the Principal offered prayer and led in thanksgiving. A new pupil remarked it was the "most pious" place she was ever in.[41]

The school was also noted for its scholarship. Higher mathematics, natural science, English, physiology, history, ethics and mental philosophy were taught. Music and physical education were also part of the school program.

Perhaps the most important occasion of the year was the annual public examination or anniversary day. The classes to be examined would sit upon the platform, and after their teachers had finished asking them questions, members of the audience were invited to ask questions. An editorial in the Alton Telegraph for March 1840 reads:

> We had the gratification on Wednesday last of attending the annual Examination in this Institution (Monticello Seminary) and although, owing to the very crowded state of the hall in which it was held, it was not in our power to understand distinctly all that was said, we were, nevertheless, highly pleased at the great readiness and propriety with which the youthful fair answered the numerous questions proposed to them as well as the great merit of the original compositions it was our good fortune to hear. The music was excellent and the various exercises were so conducted as to reflect the highest credit on the Principal, the Teachers, and the Pupils. We are gratified to learn that an Institution which is an honor to our State as well as to the public spirit of its worthy Founder is in a flourishing condition.

Baldwin served as principal of Monticello for seven years. In the fall of 1843 he resigned his position to become corresponding secretary of a new society known as "The Society for Promoting Collegiate and Theological

---

[41] Adams, Norma, Theron Baldwin, Principal of Monticello Seminary, p. 24.

Education at the West." At its first annual meeting, the Society announced that it was aiding five institutions: Western Reserve College, Illinois College, Wabash, Marietta, and Lane Theological Seminary. Twenty-six annual reports of the Society tell of Baldwin's efforts to save institutions of learning which would surely have failed for lack of funds.

Institutions subsequently added to the Society's list, but, like the previous five, since placed beyond the need of further assistance were Knox, Beloit, and Wittenberg Colleges, and the College of California. In 1868, the Society was aiding Pacific University, Washburn College, Iowa, Olivet, and Oberlin Colleges, and Wilberforce University.[42]

In his reports, essays, addresses, and letters covering a period of almost thirty years, Baldwin pleaded the cause of colleges in the Middle West. It was a service full of cares, anxieties, responsibilities, thankless labors, and inevitable uncertainties. A number of factors combined to make his work difficult.

He was constantly hampered by a lack of funds. The meagre resources of the Society were simply insufficient for the size of the task.

A second factor which hindered him was the fact that other causes were more popular in the public mind. People were much more willing to contribute to a Christian Tract Society, whose results, although more immediate, might be more ephemeral.

A third hindrance was the inability of the Society always to show immediate results for the money which had been allotted to the various colleges.

The weakness and the inefficiency of the institutions often hindered the popularity of the Society, and made its task of raising money more difficult.

A fifth difficulty was the size of Baldwin's salary; it was meagre, and often prevented him from doing as efficient work as might be possible.

---

[42]Twenty-fifth Annual Report, Annual Reports Western College Society, p. 58.

A sixth and final obstacle which the Society met was the charge that it spread its funds too thin. Many people felt that a wiser policy would be pursued if only one or two schools were aided until they no longer needed further help.

In spite of these numerous obstacles, Baldwin did succeed in saving numerous institutions from extinction.

There can be no doubt that his addresses, reports, and letters did much to bolster the cause. In a very real sense he may be called the Father of Western Colleges.

Sturtevant describes Baldwin as a man possessing abundant capabilities of scholarly attainment, even though he was late in beginning his student career. "When the trustees of Wabash College conferred on him the degree of Doctor of Divinity, it was generally felt that it was a fitting recognition of modest and unpretending worth."[43] His reading occupied a large range rather than centering on any one department of learning.

He was essentially a practical man. He was wise and far-seeing, and he knew human nature and how to deal with individuals. He was endowed with that sort of mental activity which makes the successful man of affairs.

Thirdly, he was a devoted servant of the spiritual interests of mankind. For many years his office was in an upper story in Wall Street. Here he could see the surging billows of speculation below. But instead of buying up Western land for his own use, he spent his time in founding and rearing struggling schools and colleges.

A fourth trait which Baldwin possessed was radiant happiness. He had a keen appreciation of all the innocent joys of domestic and social life. He was the father of a truly Christian home.

Baldwin and Sturtevant were both great men and life-long friends. Their hundreds of letters which have been preserved show how closely they worked hand in hand for the same ends. Both were indeed eminent and distinguished sons of Yale.

---

[43]Sturtevant, J.M., "Theron Baldwin," Biographical sketch in the Congregational Quarterly, April 1875, p. 416.

CHAPTER VI

THE ILLINOIS BAND AND CONGREGATIONALISM

When members of the Illinois Band first came to the Prairie State, Congregationalists and Presbyterians worked together in the establishment of churches under the "Plan of Union." But shortly after their arrival, a dissatisfaction with the Presbyterian form of church government caused a number of Congregational churches to adopt the Congregational type of polity. The ministers were as a rule greatly opposed to this, to the introduction of what seemed a new sect, though some of them were becoming increasingly attached to the simple and flexible principles of Congregationalism, believing that the multiplied sectarian divisions were largely due to too rigid and complicated systems of church government.[1] A number of events soon occurred, however, which resulted in the abrogation of the "Plan of Union" between Congregationalists and Presbyterians.

Various members of the Illinois Band played important roles in the series of events which led to the disruption of the "Plan of Union." The aim of this chapter is to show how members of the Illinois Band were at first reluctant to take the lead in establishing Congregational churches, but how they were eventually forced to assume active leadership in the spread of the new denomination. The story begins in 1831, and is carried up to the Albany Convention of 1852.

In the year 1801, the General Association of Connecticut and the General Assembly of the Presbyterian Church entered into the Plan of Union. The General Association sent a committee of three to the meeting of the General Assembly to consider the establishment of "an uniform system of Church Government, between those inhabitants of the new settlements who are attached to the Presbyterian form of church government and those who are attached to the Congregational form." The General Assembly appointed a committee of five to negotiate, of which Jonathan Edwards the Younger was the chairman. Both groups unanimously ratified the Plan.

The object of the Plan of Union was to unite efforts in evangelizing the frontier. Presbyterian churches which were served by a Congregational minister, and Congregational churches served by a Presbyterian minister were urged to adjust their relationships so that harmony and cooperation might prevail.

---

[1]Sturtevant, J.M., _Autobiography_, p. 184.

The Plan of Union made it possible to organize churches composed of both Congregationalists and Presbyterians and in these Plan of Union churches standing committees were elected to hear cases of discipline.

Many Congregationalists in Connecticut believed that Congregational polity was not suited to the nurturing of weak churches in the West. They felt that frontier conditions demanded a Presbyterian form of government, and therefore the Plan of Union was agreed upon by the mutual approbation of both parties.

It must also be remembered that Congregationalists were not primarily interested in the extension of their own denomination. They were willing to cooperate at all times with other evangelical denominations; their interest was in Christianity first, Protestantism second, and Congregationalism third.[2]

Although all of the members of the Yale Band were Congregational ministers, they spent their first years in Illinois serving Presbyterian churches. But when Congregational churches began to be formed in Illinois, almost all of the men returned to their original denominational preference.

The first Congregational Church in the state was to be at Princeton. On March 23, 1831, a group of eighteen people organized themselves into a church at Northampton, Massachusetts, with the intention of soon going west and taking up lands. This church had no connection with the Presbyterian Church or the American Home Missionary Society. It simply transplanted itself on the frontier.[3] This group of settlers came west by way of Lake Erie, then made a portage to the Illinois River. The place they had chosen for their new home lay in Putnam (now Bureau) County, and when the first group arrived there was but one inhabitant

---

[2] Kuhns, Frederick, A History of Illinois Congregational and Christian Churches, pp. 323-324 (footnote 16). Cf. also Sweet, William W., The Presbyterians, pp. 41-47; Sweet, William W., The Congregationalists, pp. 14-20; Atkins and Fagley, History of American Congregationalism, pp. 142-148.

[3] The Hampshire Colony Congregational Church: Its First Hundred Years, 1831-1931, Princeton, Illinois, 1931, pp. 9-10.

in the place. The settlement was named Greenfield,
but was later changed to Princeton.

The church had no regular pastor until early in
1834 when Lucien Farnam arrived under the auspices of
the A.H.M.S. During the Black Hawk War (1832) the
church services were interrupted, and it was not until
the first Sunday in 1834 that the church's first communion service was held. On October 21, 1835, the new
pastor was installed in a meeting house which had just
been constructed and which measured twenty-eight by
forty feet.[4] Farnam served the church until 1838, when
he was succeeded by Owen Lovejoy, the brother of the
martyred Elijah Lovejoy.

The first church actually to be formed in Illinois
was at Mendon. It was formed in the cabin of John B.
Chittenden on February 20, 1833. Chittenden was a
leader in the Congregational Church at Guilford, Connecticut. The Chittendens left Guilford on September
18, and when others joined them at the New Haven green,
Dr. Leonard Bacon, pastor of the Center Church, sped
them on their way. A contemporary, describing the
event, said that Dr. Bacon, "standing on the door step
of the house we were leaving, offered an earnest fervent prayer for Gods blessing on all the company, who
were going to the new country, that they might be kept,
and be brought safety on their way become useful in
their new home &c &c. After closing his prayer he
pronounced the benediction and the company started on
their long journey to Illinois."[5] The "Chittenden
Memoranda" tells of the adventures of the party as it
went west. The family eventually arrived at Quincy on
December 15, 1831, and here the family was urged by
Asa Turner to make its home. At Quincy, the Chittendens took a house near the "Lord's Barn," which was
used by the Presbyterians as a place of worship.
Chittenden taught a singing school -- said to be the
first class in the Military Tract. During the winter
he bought a farm one-half mile southwest of Mendon to
which he moved his family, March 14, 1832. A year
later the first Congregational church in Illinois was
formed in his cabin with eighteen charter members,
the Reverend Solomon Hardy officiating.[6]

---

[4]Lucien Farnam to Absalom Peters, Princeton, Illinois,
November 3, 1835; July 1, 1835.

[5]D.W. Clark to J.M. Sturtevant, Portland, Maine, February 26, 1885, Tanner Library, Illinois College, Jacksonville, Illinois.

[6]Spinka, Kuhns, et al., A History of Illinois Congregational and Christian Churches, pp. 22-23.

The first Protestant church to be organized in Chicago was formed on June 26, 1833. Of the first four elders of this church, three were Congregationalists. The pastor of the church was Jeremiah Porter, and under his vigorous leadership the church grew from the original twenty-six[7] to one hundred members within two and one-half years. Soon after the Chicago church was formed, Porter "passed a Sabbath at a settlement on the Du Page, thirty miles west," where he found fifteen Christians who had "transplanted New England piety into these beautiful prairies where it bids fair to flourish with strength equal to[8] that seen on the hard soil of the Green Mountains." A Presbyterian church was organized on July 13, 1833. However, a month later, discussion was under way to change the church polity to a Congregational form of government. On May 2, 1834, the change was decided upon, although it was not effected until August 1, 1834.[9] In the meantime, several other Congregational churches had been formed.

In spite of the cooperation between Congregationalists and Presbyterians in the field of home missions, all was not going well in the General Assembly of the Presbyterian Church. The Plan of Union had raised thorny problems which had not been envisaged in 1801, and friction inevitably resulted. Many of the churches which had members from both denominations were governed by "standing committees" instead of elders. Between 1820 and 1833, these "committeemen" attended meetings of the General Assembly. While their presence was not in violation of the Plan, yet their undefined status at the meetings caused some uneasiness. In 1831, the Assembly reviewed the subject of committeemen's rights, and declared that the "appointment of members of standing committees is inexpedient and of questionable con-

---

[7] Spinka, Kuhns, et al., A History of Illinois Congregational and Christian Churches, pp. 26-27.

[8] For "Records of the Naperville Church," see Sweet, W.W., The Congregationalists, pp. 116-155. The approximate location of this church was in Town 38, Range 10 East of the 3rd P.M. -- south of the present-day Naperville.

[9] "Records of the Naperville Church," see Sweet, W.W., The Congregationalists, p. 126.

stitutionality, and therefore ought not in the future to be made."[10]

This caused a storm of protest from thirty-one commissioners, who declared that the action had been taken after one-third of the commissioners had gone home; they also said that such an action was in violation of the Plan of Union. One of the protestants was Theron Baldwin. In defense of its action, the General Assembly replied (through one of its committees) that while "an appearance of a departure from the letter of the Constitution" was to be noticed, no evidence of a violation of spirit was apparent. If there was any cause for grievance, then "the only proper remedy for the supposed evil would be found in a regular proceeding to amend or annul the said treaty."[11]

The Plan of Union was a further thorn in the flesh of the General Assembly because it allowed delegates from Congregational associations of New England to attend and vote in its proceedings. In 1827 the General Assembly revoked this right, but the General Association of Massachusetts, which had accepted the Plan of Union in 1811, refused to acknowledge this revocation until 1829.[12] In 1827, the powers of the Assembly's Board of Missions were considerably enlarged, and in 1828 laymen were included in its membership.[13] In 1828 only 31 missionaries were under its care, but by 1835 it had 224 men under commission in nineteen states and territories.[14] In the meantime, however, the American Home Missionary Society had had a phenomenal

---

[10]Minutes of the General Assembly of the Presbyterian Church in the United States of America from A.D. 1821, to A.D. 1835 inclusive (Philadelphia, n.d.), p. 338.

[11]Minutes of the General Assembly of the Presbyterian Church in the United States of America from A.D. 1821, to A.D. 1835 inclusive (Philadelphia, n.d.), p. 343. Cf. Spinka, Kuhns, et al., A History of Congregational and Christian Churches in Illinois, pp. 30-31.

[12]Minutes of the General Association of Massachusetts, 1829 (Boston, 1829). Cf. Minutes of the General Assembly of the Presbyterian Church in the United States of America from A.D. 1821 to A.D. 1835, inclusive, pp. 199-200; 213.

[13]Ibid., pp. 244-245.

[14]Spinka, Kuhns, et al., A History of Congregational and Christian Churches in Illinois, p. 334, footnote 78.

growth. It increased steadily from 169 missionaries in 1826 to 676 in 1834.[15] But by 1834, two-thirds of the ministers under the A.H.M.S. were serving Presbyterian churches. The conservative Presbyterians who were presently to be called "Old School" decided that it was high time that decisive action were taken and the current system scrutinized and overhauled.

Open warfare broke out when Joshua L. Wilson launched an attack against the Society in a pamphlet in which he said that the objective of the Society was to "overthrow Presbyterianism as it now exists . . . . Every judicatory, every institution, and all the funds of the Presbyterian Church will be completely and entirely under the control of the American Home Missionary Society."

> The Congregational churches have no standard of doctrines. Every man preaches what he pleases, from Antinomianism to Universalism. . . . Home Missionary men consent to be ruled only till they can govern. . . . The Lord Jesus Christ committed the management of Christian missions to his Church. The Presbyterian Church is a Christian missionary society. The American Home Missionary Society is not an ecclesiastical, but a civil institution. By interference and importunity she disturbs the peace and injures the prosperity of the Presbyterian Church.[16]

To this blast a reply was written by Ralph Cushman, local agent for the American Home Missionary Society, entitled, An Appeal to the Christian Public. Cushman said that the whole attack was "the offspring of jealousy and suspicion." Absalom Peters even tried to quiet Wilson. But the shot had been fired.

This quarrel split the General Assembly on the question of reappointing the Board of Missions. A motion to postpone the reappointment of the Board was withdrawn. Eventually a compromise was reached which

---

[15]American Home Missionary Society, Eighth Annual Report.

[16]Four Propositions sustained against the Claims of the American Home Missionary Society, Cincinnati, 1831. Quoted from Spinka, Kuhns, et al., A History of Congregational and Christian Churches in Illinois, p. 334, footnote 82.

reappointed the Board of Missions and threw the whole problem into the laps of the local synods.[17]

A fourth point of friction between Congregationalists and Presbyterians was on doctrine. A number of Presbyterian congregations on the frontier were being served by New Englanders, particularly Yale men who had studied under Nathaniel William Taylor. Taylor had enjoined upon his students the necessity for independent thinking, and like tares in the wheat field, some of his independent thinkers were standing in Presbyterian ranks.[18] One of these men was none other than the Reverend Albert Barnes, pastor of the First Presbyterian Church of Philadelphia. Barnes was hauled before the Philadelphia Presbytery for preaching and publishing a doctrinal error in respect to Christ's atonement. Although Barnes was acquitted by the General Assembly of 1831, which resolved that the presbytery "ought to have suffered the whole thing to pass without further notice,"[19] yet there were many who thought that the Church had reached an "important and very fearful crisis."[20] Many Presbyterians wondered if their Congregational brethren were doctrinally pure.

A fifth and final factor of disturbance was the question of polity. Presbyteries receiving ministers and licentiates from other denominations felt that they had a right to examine them on questions of doctrine and order as well as Presbyterian candidates. The General Assembly would probably have preferred to remain silent on this question if the Synod of Pittsburgh in 1829 had not requested a direct answer.

The following year a committee reported to the Assembly that ministers and licentiates of other denominations ought to be examined on the constitutional questions relating to the faith and government of the Presbyterian church. It was hardly fair to its own

---

[17]Spinka, Kuhns, et al., A History of Illinois Congregational and Christian Churches, p. 33.

[18]Cf. Mead, Sidney E., Nathaniel William Taylor, 1786-1858: A Connecticut Liberal.

[19]Minutes of the General Assembly from A.D. 1821 to A.D. 1835, inclusive, 329.

[20]Spinka, Kuhns, et a., A History of Illinois Congregational and Christian Churches, p. 335, footnote 90.

constituency, the committee said, for others to be admitted without undergoing the usual examination. This would imply that all newly-ordained Congregationalists serving Presbyterian churches under the Plan of Union should become Presbyterian ministers. Writing twenty-five years later, Julian M. Sturtevant said:

> Previous to the session of the General Assembly of 1830, there were many Presbyterians in the Northwest, in the habit of acting in the true spirit of the Plan of Union. Its true spirit was not a compact by which Congregationalism was to be forever shut up in New England, but an arrangement by which, over all the great west, Presbyterians and Congregationalists might fellowship each other, in the same churches, and the same ecclesiastical bodies, each enjoying his own preference, in respect to church and government. When brethren applied for admission, with "clean papers," from Congregational bodies they were admitted without asking any questions. It was not in those times supposed that a minister from New England had become a Presbyterian, by emigrating to the west, or by joining Presbytery, but only that he wished to enter into hearty and earnest cooperation with his Presbyterian and Congregational brethren who were in the field before him. He was not therefore asked to make any new declaration of his faith in respect to church government. In May, 1830, the General Assembly passed a resolution discountenancing this practice, and it was, as a consequence, from that time discontinued, so far as I know, in all the Presbyteries.[21]

On October 9, 1830, Theron Baldwin and John Mathews reported the adoption of this new rule to the Centre Presbytery of Illinois, which had just received two Congregational ministers into its fellowship: Edward Beecher, president of Illinois College, and Asa Turner, pastor at Quincy. When the Presbytery's records were later reviewed by the Synod of Illinois, John Bergen, Old School pastor of the First Presbyterian Church of

---

[21] Congregational Herald, September 6, 1855.

Springfield, wrote:

> The Committee appointed to examine the records
> of the Presbytery of Illinois report that they
> recommend the approval of the same, with the
> following exceptions: Page 89, Edward Beecher
> was received into the Presbytery without answer-
> ing the Constitutional questions, also, page 93,
> Asa Turner was received without subscribing the
> Confession of Faith.[22]

This annoyed the Centre Presbytery, and on December
22, 1831, it replied with the following resolution:

> Whereas in this entry there is a charge against
> the Presbytery of disregarding the Recommenda-
> tion of General Assembly and particularly as it
> was expressly stated before the Synod that the
> Recommendation had been formally adopted as a
> standing rule of Presbytery at their first meet-
> ing after said Recommendation appeared, and had
> never from that time, in a single instance, been
> departed from; but that the error of Presbytery
> was not in neglecting to require assent to the
> Constitutional questions, but only, in failing
> to enter a notice of it on the minutes of Pres-
> bytery, therefore Resolved, that this Presbytery
> regrets that the Synod, especially in these
> times of unparalleled excitement and jealousy,
> should have placed on our minutes a charge so
> inconsistent with truth and justice and brotherly
> love; and as such feel ourselves called upon to
> express our entire disapprobation of the above
> proceeding, and request that the entry in ques-
> tion on our Record be corrected. Resolved that
> the stated clerk be directed to lay the above
> resolutions before Synod.[23]

But when William Kirby joined the Presbytery of
Illinois at Jacksonville on March 29, 1832, he presented a letter of dismission and recommendation from
the Association of the Eastern District of New Haven,
Co. Ct. and after answering to the Constitutional

---

[22]Manuscript Records of the Centre Presbytery, quoted
from Spinka, Kuhns, et al., A History of Illinois Congregational and Christian Churches, p. 335.

[23]Ibid., p. 335, footnote 98.

questions in the affirmative was received as a member of the Presbytery.[24]

This procedure was doubtlessly irritating to many Congregationalists. In his _Autobiography_, Julian Sturtevant says:

> In 1855 I still retained my connection with the Presbyterian Church. I had tried to be fully understood by my brethren of that denomination. My language had invariably been: "I am not a Presbyterian. I came among you as a Congregationalist, and as such I have continued with you. My connection here is fraternal rather than ecclesiastical. For years I have uniformly excused myself from voting upon questions of ecclesiastical politics. If with this understanding it is desirable that I continue with you, I shall seek no change." I had, however, always maintained my unrestrained liberty of free utterance on all subjects, religious and ecclesiastical ones not excepted.[25]

At the General Assembly of 1832, which contained a New School majority, the following resolutions were presented:

> (1) The Plan of Union of 1801 does not authorize any committeeman to sit and act in any presbytery as a ruling elder, unless he represents a church composed partly of Presbyterians and partly of Congregationalists; nor even then, unless in the express case of discipline provided for under the fourth head of that plan of union;

> (2) The Plan of Union does not authorize any private person not being a committeeman, to sit and act in any case whatever;

> (3) The Plan of Union, when truly construed, does not authorize any committeeman to sit or act in any case in any synod or in the General Assembly.

---

[24]Manuscript Records of the Centre Presbytery, quoted from Spinka, Kuhns, et al., _A History of Illinois Congregational and Christian Churches_, p. 335, footnote 99.

[25]Sturtevant, J.M., _Autobiography_, p. 273.

The Assembly finally waived these resolutions, declaring that "without expressing an opinion on the resolutions offered, it is inexpedient to consider them."[26] The Presbytery of Cincinnati under the leadership of Joshua L. Wilson, set up the Assembly of 1832 the following memorial:

> The evils of which the Presbytery complain and for which they seek a remedy, are, the introduction into Presbyterian churches of doctrines at varyance with our standards, the mutilation of our confession of Faith, and formation of new confessions, the introduction of a mixed and lax discipline and the spread of a spirit of Congregationalism through the whole Church. "Know ye not that a little leaven leaveneth the whole lump." It is believed that these evils will increase untill (sic) the General Assembly shall dissolve the Union between Congregational and Presbyterian churches -- and change their mode of correspondence from the personal to the epistolary mode.[27]

In 1837, the storm broke. Gaining a majority in the General Assembly of that year, the Old School men resolutely decided to clean house. They declared the Plan of Union at an end. They withdrew from the missionary and educational societies in which they had been associated with the Congregationalists, and exscinded four Synods which had been formed under the Plan of Union. These Synods refused to accept the excision, and for thirty-three years "Old School" and "New School" Assemblies divided the Presbyterian Church.[28]

But the formation of Congregational churches had already been under way in Illinois. In 1833 the Congregational Church at Quincy had been formed. Originally organized as a Presbyterian Church in 1830 by Asa Turner, the church had had a continued growth. Asa Turner was also a trustee of Illinois College, and

---

[26] Minutes of the General Assembly, A.D. 1821 to A.D. 1835, inclusive, pp. 354, 356.

[27] University of Chicago, Durrett Collection, Ms. No. 631, Joshua L. Wilson, from Spinka, Kuhns, et al., A History of Illinois Congregational and Christian Churhces, p. 335, footnote 103.

[28] Weigle, Luther A., The Pageant of America, Vol. X, p. 161.

in 1832 he had to go East for funds. While absent, his
pastorate was supplied by Solomon Hardy. When Solomon
Hardy examined the church records, he exclaimed that
if such records were sent up to the presbytery, "they
would be sent back at once, as they were Congregational,
and nothing Presbyterian about them."[29]   On October 10,
the church was reorganized as the First Congregational
Church of Quincy.

Since Turner's letters are no longer extant, and
his autobiography unavailable, it is necessary to rely
entirely on his biographer, George F. Magoun. The Home
Missionary, although containing some extracts from Turner's letters, says nothing about the reorganization of
the Quincy Church. Nor is there any correspondence from
the American Home Missionary Society in the Society's
letter books. Furthermore, contemporary sources are
silent on the reorganization of the Quincy church. Turner had written to someone in New York:

> My church are all Congregationalists in their
> feelings. One of our elders is gone; we can
> not find another who will be ordained. They
> claim the privilege of worshiping God accord-
> ing to the dictates of conscience. What shall
> be done? Eight or ten Congregationalists are
> around (us) who refuse to unite with us as yet.[30]

And the unpublished autobiography adds:

> It was said that Congregationalism would not
> do for the West, but after trying Presbyter-
> ianism for three years, it was thought best
> to change the polity.[31]

In his notable work on Congregationalism in Illinois
Frederick Kuhns says,

> At any rate, the movement to reorganize was not
> initiated until early summer. It is incredible,
> however, that the church was in the dark concern-
> ing Presbyterian usages, for Turner had attended

---

[29]Spinka, Kuhns, et al., A History of Illinois Congregational and Christian Churches, p. 41.

[30]Magoun, George F., Asa Turner, A Home Missionary Patriarch and His Times, p. 125.

[31]Ibid.

enough meetings of the presbytery and synod to familiarize himself with them. If, however, the church had for two years or more been Presbyterian in name only but in every other sense Congregational (as Keyes said), its records would bear out the fact and Hardy might have detected it. Perhaps the majority were long since accustomed to independency. At least the three Baptists and the three Congregationalists in the original members were Presbyterians, but five were "from the world," that is to say, had no denominational affiliation. Perhaps, as the church grew, the membership was recruited from the more prosperous element of the town, an element which frequently insists upon self-determination. Turner himself may have advised the shift much earlier. He was in the East, as we know, from the spring of 1832 to the spring of 1833. It is not known that he wrote to Hardy or that Hardy wrote to him during that year. Hardy carried on Turner's work as well as his health allowed, but for months he was unequal to the taxing duties of the pastorate. Undoubtedly the people from Quincy who had formed the Mendon church took occasion to visit their former neighbors and fellow church members; being Congregationalists, they probably exerted a considerable influence in Quincy. And William Carter stated that Chittenden was "invited to be present and counsel with them, at the reorganization of the church on the Congregational plan."[32]

Another factor was undoubtedly of importance in influencing Turner and the church at Quincy. This was the celebrated heresy trial of three members of the faculty of Illinois College in 1833. On March 28, the Presbytery of Illinois met in the house of one William J. Fraser, pastor of the Providence church of Virginia. Fraser presented charges of unsound teaching against President Edward Beecher and Professors Julian M. Sturtevant and William Kirby of Illinois College. Fraser's language was extreme and "highly injurious to

---

[32]Spinka, Kuhns, et al., A History of Illinois Congregational and Christian Churches, pp. 43-44.

the character of these three gentlemen." Accordingly,
charges of slander were preferred against Fraser. The
cases were issued at an adjourned meeting of Presbytery in Jacksonville on April 23rd. The charges of
unsound doctrine against the three brethren were not
sustained. The charge of slander, on the other hand,
was sustained, and Fraser was suspended from the func-
tions of the ministry. In both cases he gave notice
of appeal to Synod.[33]

Sturtevant declares that the trial was "humiliating
and disgusting in the extreme," even though the accused
were acquitted. But the effect of the trial on Turner
must have been considerable for he was undoubtedly in
complete sympathy with his Illinois brethren. Later,
in October 1852, Turner delivered an address in which
he said:

> Twenty-two years ago I removed to the West.
> I was taught that when I went out of New
> England I must be a Presbyterian. I had
> never in my life heard a sermon upon our
> church polity, and had never seen a line
> in print upon the subject. As I have said,
> I came to the West under the impression that
> it was necessary that I should be a Presby-
> terian; and soon after arriving there, I
> organized a church in Adams county, Illinois.
> Everything went on harmoniously for about
> two years; but soon there began to be fric-
> tion in the General Assembly itself, and our
> church members became restive: and those who
> are acquainted with the history of the times
> at the West, know the difficulties we had to
> pass through. Our religious meetings up to
> the time of Synod were like political meetings
> of the two parties. My church demanded of me
> that they should be Congregational. I hesi-
> tated some time about acceding to their wishes.
> My brethren in the ministry all opposed the
> idea. A good father sent me word, that if I
> organized a Congregational church, he must
> come out against me; and one of the Presby-
> terian fathers, whose name is revered in all
> the land, told me that if I organized a Con-

---

[33]Norton, A.T., History of the Presbyterian Church in
the State of Illinois, p. 184.

gregational church in Quincy, he would come
and preach me down. But I organized a church,
and when he came to Quincy, I told him, that
after we got down through the soil in Quincy,
we came to solid rock; that the Mississippi
had not washed away the soil, and I thought it
probably never would. According to the Plan
of Union, when a church is to be organized,
those who are to compose it are to have a
choice in regard to its form. I was, however,
reproved for giving my church its choice.
The whole feeling was that Congregationalism
must be frowned down. The blame is that New
England fathers have not taught their own
children. If they had been taught, if all
the light had been spread over the land which
is spread over it now, we should have seen an
entirely different result. . . . But time
has passed on, and now the right is granted.
And we rejoice to feel that the right is
granted from you, because in 1837, after
having organized thirteen churches in northern Illinois, composed of those who asked me
to organize them thus, on returning to New
England I tried to present myself before an
Association in Massachusetts, and they did
not know me. They regarded it as a heresy
that I should be a Congregationalist coming
from the valley of the Mississippi! I say
then that Congregationalists were to blame
in the beginning.[34]

A third factor which may have influenced the Quincy
church to become Congregational was the formation of
the Congregational church at Jacksonville. In the
winter of 1832-1833 Dr. M.M.L. Reed and Elihu Wolcott
called upon President Beecher and Professor Sturtevant
at the College to discuss a serious matter which was
taking place in Jacksonville. "Their object," says
Sturtevant in his Autobiography, "was to inform us
that thirty or forty residents of the town had resolved to organize a Congregational church, and to

------

[34]Spinka, Kuhns, et al., A History of Illinois Congregational and Christian Churches, p. 336, note 125. The
Independent, October 14, 1852. Frederick Kuhns says
that he is indebted to Professor William Warren Sweet
for making available his transcription of the proceedings of the Albany Convention.

invite us to unite in the organization. Mr. Beecher
listened, but uttered not a word of sympathy with
Congregationalism."

> He expressed his conviction that the attempt
> to establish a Congregational church in Jack-
> sonville at that time would result only in
> weakness and disaster, and kindly entreated
> them to desist from their purpose. I assured
> the gentlemen of my growing attachment to the
> principles of Congregationalism, and my be-
> lief that the time for the organization of
> such a church in our town was not many years
> distant, yet I joined with Mr. Beecher in
> deprecating immediate action. It was ob-
> vious that a sanctuary in which all, whether
> of Presbyterian or Congregational affinities,
> might assemble for worship had become an ur-
> gent necessity to the Christian cause. Sub-
> scriptions were already in circulation to
> secure such a building, and a site had been
> selected. I earnestly urged them to remain
> with the Presbyterian church and assist in
> meeting this great present want of the com-
> munity. I expressed the opinion that the
> rapid growth of the church would soon justify
> the formation of a second church, which could
> be made Congregational, and that thus their
> purpose could be accomplished without serious
> loss to the Master's cause. I assured them
> that I would then unite with them in the or-
> ganization. At the close of the interview
> they again assured us that their object had
> not been to consult us with reference to the
> propriety of the step they were about to take,
> but to invite us to go with them, and that the
> organization would none the less be effected
> without us.[35]

It is important to note that it was lay leadership
which was responsible for the formation of the Congregational church in Jacksonville. Mr. Frank J. Heinl
and Frederick Kuhns both lay stress on this. However,
it must always be remembered that the clergy could oppose such a scheme with tongue in cheek. Once such a
church was organized, men like Sturtevant and Beecher
must inevitably join it, if they were to remain consistent with their beliefs.

---

[35]Sturtevant, J.M., _Autobiography_, pp. 195-196.

Frederick Kuhns says:

> It is probable that the effects of this agi-
> tation were transmitted to Quincy by friends
> and relatives, and it is possible that a "gen-
> tlemen's agreement" was made between the two
> parties. Since the organization of the "In-
> dependent" church of Jacksonville has been
> attributed to the action of laymen, action
> in Quincy may have been taken at the behest
> of laymen. Asa Turner said that it was.

> The most reasonable conclusion is that the
> Quincy people screwed up their courage and
> took a long chance on the American Home
> Missionary Society, and that Turner, find-
> ing his congregation predisposed to reor-
> ganize and being challenged by the Synod
> to lend his sanction to this movement,
> brought suddenly to consummation their de-
> sire to take this step. On the basis of
> the evidence it cannot be said that Turner
> either initiated the action or had been
> scheming to take it. Yet his subsequent
> activities in behalf of Congregationalism
> in Illinois and in Iowa attest his devo-
> tion to its principles.[36]

In discussing the Congregational church at Quincy,
we have already touched upon the beginnings of the
Congregational church at Jacksonville. If Beecher
and Sturtevant were at first hesitant to join such
a church, it cannot be denied that the heresy trial
pushed them mightily in that direction. The group of
Congregationalists in the Presbyterian church had
hoped that Asa Turner would preach the sermon and conduct the organization of the new church. At the last
minute, however, he was unable to come, and Julian
Sturtevant was asked to take his place. This put him
in an embarrassing situation. Although he was a Congregationalist, he was also a member of the Illinois
Presbytery and of the Illinois Synod as well as a generous contributor to the current budget and building
fund of the local Presbyterian church.[37] He had ad-

---

[36]Spinka, Kuhns, et al., A History of Illinois Congregational and Christian Churches, p. 49.

[37]Ibid., p. 50.

vised against the formation of a new church, yet with the Presbyterian Church in its turmoil he was very dissatisfied, because

> . . . it seemed to lack the essentials of spiritual home for persons of New England birth and training. Others beside myself were inclined to suspect that the agitations were largely due to the constitution of that church. The controversy about the "New Haven Theology" had originated in New England, and might reasonably have been expected to produce there its most disastrous results. Yet it had there expended its utmost force without manifesting any tendency to disrupt religious society. But as soon as the agitation crossed the Hudson and extended itself in the domain of the Presbyterian Church it began to threaten a great division. Immigrants from New England expecting to unite promptly with the Presbyterian Church hesitated in the presence of so much strife. As I have already said, I came to this state with no definite opinions about church government, but the experience of the first three years had compelled me to reflect, with painful earnestness and deep solicitude, upon the foundations of the church.[38]

After a day of meditation Sturtevant finally consented to conduct the meeting to organize the Congregational church, even though to do so would put him in bad odor. "If any other body which I recognized as a Christian church had made the same request of me, I would have consented without hesitation. Why then should I decline in this instance? Especially when I knew that as soon as the organization was completed I should feel it to be my duty to cooperate with them, as with any other church, in all acts of christian worship."[39]

---

[38]Sturtevant, J.M., Autobiography, pp. 182, 193, 206.

[39]Sturtevant, J.M., The Origin of "Western Congregationalism": A Historical Discourse delivered on the Fiftieth Anniversary of the Congregational Church, Jacksonville, Illinois, December 15, 1883. Celebration of the Fiftieth Anniversary of the Organization of the Congregational Church, Jacksonville, Ill., Dec. 15 and 16, 1883 (Jacksonville, Ill., 1884), 21.

On Sunday, December 15, 1833 the "Independent Church" of Jacksonville held its first service in the Methodist house of worship. Prayer was offered by the Methodist minister and President Beecher. The sermon was preached by William Carter, another member of the Yale Band, who had arrived early in November. Carter was asked to become pastor of the new church, which he reluctantly consented to do. Carter's call was renewed at the end of the year and he remained as pastor until September 1838, during which time the membership increased from thirty-two to one hundred.[40]

Sturtevant threw his entire support behind the organization of the new church, declaring that he heartily approved the principles of government and discipline which the new church was about to adopt.

I made this last declaration very deliberately and with careful forethought. I was already fully aware that if I was to be tolerated in this community, it must be as a man of avowed Congregational predilections. I thought that I could have no better opportunity to make the declaration of my independence. I therefore made it explicitly then and there. I did it with a very clear foresight of its bearing on my reputation and influence. It was the part of manly honesty, and I have never doubted the part of true wisdom. It has decidedly tinged the complexion of my life from that day to this.[41]

What was the reaction of Theron Baldwin to the formation of this new church? He undoubtedly took a more conservative position than did Sturtevant. When John G. Bergen resigned from the Presbyterian church of Jacksonville, Theron Baldwin supplied his pulpit from time to time. The church was very anxious to have him accept a regular call, but the American

---

[40] Sturtevant, J.M., The Origin of "Western Congregationalism": A Historical Discourse delivered on the Fiftieth Anniversary of the Congregational Church, Jacksonville, Illinois, December 15, 1883. Celebration of the Fiftieth Anniversary of the Organization of the Congregational Church, Jacksonville, Ill., December 15 and 16, 1883 (Jacksonville, Ill., 1884), pp. 21, 22. Carter to Badger, Pittsfield, Illinois, January 21, 1839.

[41] Sturtevant, J.M., The Origins of Western Congregationalism, p. 22.

Home Missionary Society was even more anxious that he should remain in their employ. Absalom Peters stated the case in very plain terms; there was no one who could take Baldwin's place, it was very unwise for an agent to resign after such a short term of service, and a faithful reader of the Home Missionary had even subscribed Baldwin's salary. Baldwin was virtually forced to decline the Jacksonville call. In doing so, he made it very clear to the church how important his connection with the Society was.[42]

What was the reaction of the Society to the formation of the Jacksonville Congregational Church? They undoubtedly did not approve of it, not because the Society had any quarrel with Congregationalism per se, but because relations with the Presbyterians were already strained and this later step merely added to the tension. They would naturally frown on any attempt to disrupt the unity existing between the two denominations.[43]

---

[42] Baldwin to Peters, Jacksonville, Illinois, January 26 & 31, 1834 (Jan. 31 letter not extant); Peters to Baldwin, New York, February 25, 1834, Letter Book G, #359; Baldwin to Peters, Jacksonville, Illinois, February 10, 1834, in which Baldwin asks advice about the church call; Peters to Baldwin, New York, March 17, 1834, in which Peters urges Baldwin to decline and remain at his post as agent. Letter Book G, #417; Baldwin to Peters, Jacksonville, Illinois, June 11, 1834, where he says he declined after fully stating his reasons to the church.

[43] Peters to Baldwin, New York, February 25, 1834, Letter Book G, #359:
    "We are not much surprised, though we are very much grieved to learn that you meet with some serious difficulty, or rather embarrassment, from the conflicting prejudices entertained by some in Illinois on the subject of Church government. If it were possible, we do earnestly desire to dissuade our brethren, everywhere, not to contend & divide on this subject. And why should not this be possible? Is it not manifest to every intelligent, warm-hearted Christian of the West, that the feeling and tallent (sic) which have been expended on this subject, in some portions of the church, have been worse than wasted?
    "For ourselves, as we have looked abroad on the desolations of the land, we have been grieved by the tendency to division, in many places, on points of mere form & order, which have little to do with the spirit & [footnote continued on next page]

[footnote continued from previous page] essence of religion. We have therefore cautiously avoided taking any part in contentions of this sort, & we beg our brethren to excuse us from having anything to (do) with them. The members of both of the Presbyterian & Congregational churches should understand that the A.H.M.S. is a Society formed for the spread of the gospel through the whole land. It has no controversy in relation to the existing orders of the churches. With Congregationalism or Presbyterianism, as such, it has nothing to do, but with the churches, under both of these forms, it rejoices to cooperate in supplying (the) destitute & aiding the needy.

"The auxiliaries as well as the beneficiaries of this Society are ranged under both of these forms, & in all this we see no reasonable grounds of jealousy or suspicion, because they be all brethren. Hence we have never felt any restraint on this subject, but in many instances have granted aid to the destitute & needy, without even knowing the precise order of the church, being assured of the regular standing of the minister in one of the denominations above named. We have accordingly aided some Presbyterian churches in New England, some Congregational churches in New York, Ohio, Michigan & Illinois, & we shall doubtless continue to do so, only assuring ourselves that the churches thus aided are regularly formed, & that their position is peaceful & kind in relation to surrounding churches &c. On this subject we fully concur with you in the course which you have marked out for yourself, as our Agent. We desire that our whole influence may be pacific.

"We shall use no power to crush either Congregationalism or Presbyterianism, but exert our best endeavors to build up & extend both on their appropriate fields, & our opinion is that the appropriate field of each of these forms is just where the members of the church choose to adopt it, & can do so without contention; but, as you say, form or no form, the harmony of christian feeling must not be interrupted, nor christian communion disturbed. These principles we believe can not be too strongly urged upon the churches where there are any symptoms of division in relation to government. Especially should it be impressed upon our New England brethren, when they are a minority in the midst of a Presbyterian community, that they render a poor service to the church by getting up a contention on ch. government. We would say the same of a Congl. church. Behold! how good & how pleasant a thing it is for brethren to dwell together in unity. Love to all the brethren, Beecher, Sturtevant, &c."

195

The pastor of the new Congregational church was William Carter. He had been stationed at Winchester, Exeter, and Naples. But the Jacksonville Congregationalists had called him, and with "very strong feelings" against leaving his original field, he consented to become the pastor of the Independent church. A month later he wrote to Peters:

I arrived at Winchester Morgan Co. on the 3rd of November last, where I resided until the close of the year. My field of labor was Winchester, Exeter & Naples. I preached, however, in the last two places but once each & once at Jacksonville. During the remainder of the time I preached at Winchester. This is a flourishing little village which has sprung up within a few years. I bestowed more labor here than in the other places, hoping by continued efforts & oft repeated, I might see fruit of my labor; having but little expectation of such a result where the gospel is preached only once in 3 or 4 sabbaths. I did not however intend to neglect the other places, but give them their share in their season. I was encouraged both by the attendance & attention of the people at W -- And so I was at Exeter & perhaps should have been at Naples had it not been a stormy day.

But I have left that field with very strong feelings of regret. It pleased me as well as any I could have selected. And my feelings were very strong against leaving it, & my judgment too: but I finally yielded to the opinions of those to whom my commission referred me for advice & to my own sense of duty. Right or wrong I have left it.

You have probably heard that a new congregational church has been formed at Jacksonville. You may remember the views I once expressed to you on the general subject of forming Congregational churches in this state at present. I remain essentially of the same opinion still. This opinion I have expressed here repeatedly & endeavor to maintain.

I thought it was premature at least & better on the whole that they should remain contented & united as they were. I had conversation with

196

leading men among the Congregationalists soon
after my arrival & expressed my views more
strongly than I have ever before. But it was
too late. It was not for me to have influence
in quelling or agitating the discussion of this
question. Actum est. It was discussed & decided before I set foot on Illinois. I was told
that nothing but Divine efficiency would prevent
it. I replied that in my opinion moral influence ought. Here, except a few discussions
of the subject on principle with some of my
brethren, I have ceased my opposition; having
learned before this that if we cannot have things
as we would we must take them as they are & make
the best of them. The church was to be formed
& I was applied to, to assist in the organization
& to preach a sermon on the occasion. And who
was I, born a Congregationalist & nurtured in
the lap of Congregationalism, that I should re-
fuse. Had I done so, I should never have dared
to look my N. England brethren & Fathers in the
face again; as I hope to do if God spares my
life. Moreover I would have done the same thing
for the Methodists or Baptists or Episcopalians
or any other evangelical denomination.

A Methodist brother assisted us. Mr. Sturtevant
also aided us. Br. Baldwin went to Naples &
fulfilled an appointment of mine on that day.
The occasion was one of deep & universal interest. Even those who did not attend (the exercises were in the Methodist meeting-house! --
the largest in the place & full to overflowing)
were not without feelings of interest on the
subject. I am much mistaken if the impression
made upon the public mind was not good.

Our whole aim was to make the impression that
Christian character is everything & to incul-
cate love of this character whenever and wherever
found -- Christian love. The constitution of
this church & its articles of faith & covenant
are remarkably simple -- much like that of the
church in Yale College if you what that is.
Its terms are professedly such that any person
giving credible evidence of piety can unite
with them. And here I find myself at the head
of them endeavoring to discharge the duties of
a pastor. You will understand I presume from
what I have stated, how I could on principle,
if I thought I could be most useful here.

197

I concluded to try for a time.

(I in)tend to put my hand & my heart into the
work, not of Congregationalism but of Christ-
ianizing this people. I leave when I think
best. There are more than 30 members. They
will give me ample support. The other church
will support a minister as soon as they can get
one. Either church will now do more towards
supporting the Gospel at home & abroad than
they would both together before -- would, not
could or ought. Whilst there has been some
feeling as was to be expected, there has been
& is I think a good deal of Christian feeling
& principle exhibited on both sides: And I
have no question that they will soon settle
down into more union of feeling & action than
ever before. Considering the actual state of
things I do not know but the separation was
best. The evils here I do not believe will be
so great as has been anticipated by some. In
this respect my views have been modified. I
feel for you, though after all it won't hurt
you nor me. The people will be congregationalists if they choose & we cannot help it. The
responsibility of a change is on them. And
once established the ism is as good as any ism --
and better adapted I am persuaded to the genius
of the people & less obnoxious to their prejudices.

Both churches now I hope are praying & laboring for a revival. This communication is not
designed for the public but for you my Dear
Brother. I felt that I was bound to give you
a full statement of what has transpired -- of
my own course & my reasons for it. I may have
acted unwisely but I hope not & think not. At
least I have wished to know the path of duty.

As to compensation for the two months labor, it
is not a matter of great importance though I
think I ought to receive it -- needing it
enough I do not however set a high value on my
labors, not seeing many important results from
them. I hope & trust that you will not think
the fact of my connecting myself with this Congregational church is a reason why I should not
receive compensation. That would be an extremely
unfortunate conclusion I think. If I think I
can be useful here I may stay -- else I shall

198

quit. Will you ever take me under your patronage again? If not I will preach at my own charge while I can & then go where the laborer is deemed worthy of his hire. But you will if it be necessary, I have no doubt. I wish you would write if you please _in propria persona_ though it be but few words. With as much respect & love as ever I remain Your Brother in the Lord.[42]

A number of interesting questions may be raised from this letter. Is it possible that Theron Baldwin deliberately stayed away from the meeting lest it might seem that the American Home Missionary Society were endorsing the formation of the new church? It is hard to separate Baldwin's personal point of view from his official point of view as an agent for the Society. What was his real attitude toward the new church? How much did Sturtevant influence Carter in taking charge of the new church? Carter says that he accepted the new post with reluctance. Would he have accepted it at all, if he did not feel a group loyalty toward the Yale men who had preceded him to Illinois?

There is no comment in the _Home Missionary_ with regard to this church, nor about the organization of any Congregational churches in Illinois. Nor do we have a letter from Peters in answer to Carter's letter. It is probable that he did not write one, since the Society's correspondence is complete in the Letter Books.

Fifty years later, Sturtevant declared:

It is often said that all the conflicts and divisions of the church are instigated and urged on by ministers. That was not true in this instance. The founding of this church originated wholly with the laity. The ministers had nothing at all to do with it, except to dissuade from it. I was not consulted before the step was taken, in reference to the propriety of taking it -- I was told at the very outset that the thing was irrevocably determined on -- but only as to my own disposition to unite in the congregation. My answer was that I was in hearty sympathy with them in respect to the

---

[42]Carter to Peters, Jacksonville, Illinois, January 13, 1834.

desirableness of standing by the polity of our
fathers in our western home; but that I thought
that the division of Presbyterians and Congregationalists into two churches at that time, would
be a great calamity. I could not then favor
it. If they would wait till we were strong
enough for two churches, I would then gladly
go with them. Pres. Beecher, though equally
in sympathy with Congregational principles
with myself, took a decided stand against the
measure. They firmly replied: "The thing will
be done without you."[43]

The organization of the Independent Church of Jacksonville was the result of lay dissatisfaction within
the Presbyterian church, and when it became apparent
that a Congregational church was to be formed, Julian
Sturtevant and William Carter threw in their support.
Although other Congregational churches had previously
been formed in Illinois, this was the first church to
be organized in open violation of the Plan of Union.
It was, in a sense, the "go-ahead" signal for other
Congregationalists (particularly members of the Yale
Band) to form churches of their own polity.

Dean Luther A. Weigle, in his Commemoration Address of the One Hundredth Anniversary of the Congregational Church, Jacksonville, Illinois, December 10-
17, 1933 says:

At four major points this church contributed
definitely to the direction and development
of our common life in the nineteenth century.
These points are: (1) This church was a pioneer in the development of Congregationalism
in what was then known as the West, and it
was the first church to be organized in open
rejection and defiance of the Plan of Union
between Presbyterians and Congregationalists.
(2) It had an important share in the development of the anti-slavery movement in Illinois,
and that movement, because it brought forth
Abraham Lincoln, became of determinative significance in American history. (3) This
church, through Julian M. Sturtevant and Truman M. Post, had much to do with the movement
which led to the organization of the National

---

[43]Sturtevant, J.M., The Origin of Western Congregationalism, pp. 20-21.

Council of Congregational Churches, with the
consequent strengthening of the fellowship
of the churches, west and east, that hold the
free, democratic polity of Congregationalism.
(4) This church, again through Julian M. Sturtevant, contributed to the development in American education of the ideal of a college avow-
edly Christian in purpose and outlook, yet not
under denominational control.[44]

During the next eleven years (1833-1844) Congregationalism spread rapidly through the state. The story
has been told admirably by Frederick Kuhns in his History of Illinois Congregational and Christian Churches
and need not be repeated here. The Yale Band was in-
timately connected with this growth. Late in 1838,
Carter resigned from his pastorate in Jacksonville,
and moved to Pittsfield, where he persuaded the Presbyterian church to become Congregational in 1841. From
1838 to 1847 Kirby was pastor of the Congregational
church of Mendon. Asa Turner was directly responsible
for the formation of thirteen Congregational churches,
and became known as the Father of Congregationalism
in Iowa. Flavel Bascom later became a Congregationalist.

At least thirty-six Congregational churches were
formed between 1831 and 1837, when the Plan of Union
was abrogated. During the next six years, at least
seventy-four more churches were organized. Most of
these churches were formed in the northern part of the
state. This was due to the fact, as we shall see
later, that much of southern Illinois contained vigorous pro-slavery elements.

Nor was the spread of Congregationalism confined
to Illinois. Churches were now being established in
Indiana, Michigan, Wisconsin, and Iowa. In 1844, the
first General Association of Congregational Churches
was formed. But by 1844, Illinois was no longer a
frontier state. The tide of emigration had moved on,
and the columns of the Home Missionary began to devote
less and less space to Illinois. In the meantime,

---

[44]Weigle, Luther A., Commemoration Address of the One
Hundredth Anniversary of the Congregational Church,
Jacksonville, Illinois, December 10-17, 1933, p. 3.

Congregationalism had become an accepted fact in the Prairie State.[45]

It was not until 1852, however, that the "Plan of Union" was finally abrogated by the Congregationalists. As a result of the plight of western Congregationalism, a national convention was called at Albany, New York. The official call was sent out by the General Association of New York inviting ministers and delegates of Congregational churches in the United States to meet in Albany on October 5, 1852 as a convention. The Business Committee, of which Reverend Leonard Bacon, eminent pastor of Center Congregational Church, New Haven, was made chairman, sent out circulars before the convention assembled, announcing as main purposes of the assembly:

1. The discussion of the Plan of Union between Presbyterians and Congregationalists agreed upon by the General Assembly of the Presbyterian Church and the General Association of Connecticut, in 1801.

2. The building of church edifices in the West.

3. The system and operation of the American Home Missionary Society.

4. The intercourse between the Congregationalists of New England and those of other states.

5. The local work and responsibility of a Congregational church.

6. The bringing forward of candidates for the ministry.

7. The republication of the works of our standard theological writers.[46]

One of the results of the Albany Convention was to declare the "Plan of Union" at an end. Another result was the adoption of a resolution calling for fifty thousand dollars with which to provide a fund for the assistance of churches in the West. In response to

---

[45]Spinka, Kuhns, et al., A History of Illinois Congregational and Christian Churches, Chapter III passim.

[46]Atkins, G.G., and Fagley, Frederick L., History of American Congregationalism, pp. 196-198.

this resolution $61,891 was raised. A third result
of the Albany Convention of 1852 may be expressed in
the words of Dr. Albert E. Dunning:

> Congregationalists had discovered that their
> polity was adapted to the entire country,
> that they had a divinely appointed mission
> to give the gospel of Christ to the whole
> world, and in order to carry out this mis-
> sion it was necessary that they should know
> one another and should become affiliated as
> one body in such a manner that they could
> act intelligently and unitedly in fulfilling
> their great work.[47]

The meeting at Albany in 1852 had made no provision
for the calling of another convention. But as the
Civil War drew to a close, the churches again faced a
crisis. The need for religious and educational work
among the newly-liberated negroes, the obsolescence
of the Cambridge Platform of 1648, the lack of well-
trained ministers particularly in the growing West,
and a new sense of mission were some of the factors
which thinking Congregationalists deemed of national
concern and for which adequate provision must be made
in the future.

Definite action for calling a national council was
first formulated at the Convention of the Congregational Churches of the Northwest at its triennial meeting in Chicago in April 1864. Realizing that they
could not face their pressing needs alone without the
help of older churches of New England, they voted that
"the crisis demands general consultation, cooperation,
and concert among our churches, and to these ends, requires extensive correspondence among our ecclesiastical
associations, or the assembling of a National Congregational Convention."[48]

When the State Association of Milford met at Quincy
the following month, Reverend Julian M. Sturtevant proposed a resolution recommending that every orthodox
Congregational church in the United States be invited

---

[47]Dunning, Albert E., _Congregationalists in America_,
p. 333.

[48]Atkins, G.G., and Fagley, Frederick L., _History of_
American Congregationalism, pp. 196-198.

to send as delegates "their acting pastor or pastors and one other member and to provide if necessary for paying their expenses to and from the convention."

On November 16, 1864, fifteen states sent representatives to a preliminary meeting in New York at the Broadway Tabernacle Church. Julian Sturtevant was present, representing the State of Illinois. Five men (Messrs. Bacon, Sturtevant, Budington, Thompson, and Quint) were appointed a committee to select topics for the council and to nominate suitable persons to present matters for its consideration. Seven topics were selected:

1. The work of evangelization, in the West and South and in foreign lands.

2. Church-building.

3. Education for the ministry -- in colleges, theological seminaries, or otherwise; and ministerial support.

4. Local and parochial evangelization.

5. The expediency of issuing a statement of Congregational church polity.

6. The expediency of setting forth a declaration of the Christian faith, as held in common by the Congregational churches.

7. The classification of benevolent organizations to be recommended to the patronage of the churches.[49]

When the council met at Boston on June 14, 1865, the roll included 502 delegates, 14 honorary members, and 16 delegates from foreign countries, a total of 532 persons. Thirty-eight delegates came from Illinois, including Flavel Bascom, Edward Beecher, William Carter, Elisha Jenney, and Julian Sturtevant. Asa Turner was also there from Denmark, Iowa.

---

[49]Debates and Proceedings of the National Council, Boston, Massachusetts, June 14-24, 1865, pp. 7-8. Cf. Atkins and Fagley, History of American Congregational-ism, p. 200.

On the second day of the council (Thursday, June
15) Julian Sturtevant preached the sermon at the Mount
Vernon Church. He sounded the clarion call to spread
the Congregational teachings and principles throughout
the United States.[50]

As the business of the council proceeded, each of
the topics was taken up in order, and prominent in the
discussions were such men as Professor Bacon of Yale,
Professor Park of Andover, President Sturtevant of
Illinois, Dr. Barstow of New Hampshire, and Dr. Wolcott of Ohio.

After fulfilling its purpose as voiced in the original letter of invitation, the council adjourned
without making provisions for future meetings.

In summarizing the Albany Convention and the Council of 1865, Williston Walker says:

> The Albany Convention of 1852 had clearly
> manifested the real unity of Congregational-
> ism, East and West, and the abandonment of
> the Plan of Union gave impetus to the grow-
> ing consciousness of the denomination . . . .
> This dawning sense of the continental mis-
> sion of Congregationalism was strengthened
> by the war of the rebellion -- a crisis in
> which the Congregational churches, unlike
> the Presbyterian, found themselves substan-
> tially united in support of the triumphant
> cause. Accordingly, when the failure of
> the rebellion became probable, and it was
> evident to far-sighted observers that the
> South and Southwest would be unbarred to
> Congregationalism as never before, and that
> a new epoch in national history has opened,
> movement began having for their aim the
> gathering of a representative Convention
> wherein the churches might deliberate as to
> the best methods of improving the opportun-
> ities of the hour. . . .at the council of
> 1865 there came into being the only Declara-
> tion of Faith which a body representative of

---

[50]Congregational Quarterly, July-October 1865, p. 244.

American Congregationalism as a whole had approved since 1648 -- a distinction it still retains.[51] As compared with the Puritan symbols of two centuries before, it shows great advance in simplicity and catholicity. . . . In a statement of broad principles, rather than specific beliefs, issued on an historic occasion as a memorial rather than as a formula for permanent local use, these characteristics are not necessarily demerits; but they have operated to prevent the adoption of the Burial Hill Declaration as the creed of individual churches, and have made it to be comparatively little known and little used.[52]

[51]A new Statement of Faith was adopted by the Kansas City Convention in 1913.

[52]Walker, Williston, The Creeds and Platforms of Congregationalism, Chapter 18, pp. 553-554. 564-565.

CHAPTER VII

THE ILLINOIS BAND AND CONTEMPORARY SOCIAL ISSUES

The most important social issue of the mid-nineteenth century was the slavery controversy.

"In the study of revolutions such as the overthrow of slavery in the United States, we are apt to over-estimate the forces which appear in open conflict, and to undervalue the more tranquil influence of thought guided by the providence and the Spirit of God. The progress of anti-slavery opinion in the state of Illinois was like the sunshine. It came as the Kingdom of God always comes, and no one had reason to exclaim: 'Lo here, or, lo there!'" So wrote Julian Sturtevant in 1885.[1]

The founders and trustees of Illinois College were an important factor in the development of anti-slavery sentiment in Illinois. Since such men as President Beecher and Professor Sturtevant exercised a pronounced influence upon the early moral and educational development of Illinois, we can readily understand that their efforts in behalf of the anti-slavery movement would also bear fruit.

The early population of Illinois was made up of both Yankees and Southerners. Hardy New Englanders, coming west by way of the Great Lakes, bought land and laid out farms in northern and central Illinois. Not only was their attention attracted by the fertile expanse of the prairies, but the fact that the Northwest Ordinance of 1787 had dedicated this land to freedom must have influenced them to settle within its bounds. With them came the thought patterns, habits, and customs of New England, and an antipathy toward slavery.

But the fertile prairies of Illinois were not attractive to Yankees alone. Settlers from the slave states of Kentucky and Virginia began to pour into the southern part of the state, and although they could not bring their slaves with them, yet many of them were quite sympathetic to slavery. Some even hoped that Illinois might become a slave state, and an attempt

---

[1]Sturtevant, J.M., _Autobiography_, p. 277.

was made in 1823 and 1824 to amend the state constitution so that slavery would be permitted.

In Jacksonville, both of these emigrant groups with their varying cultures and thought patterns were well represented. On account of the views of its professors, however, the College very soon became the spearhead of the anti-slavery movement. This courageous stand was to have its price. Dr. Sturtevant always regarded the slavery issue as one of the greatest obstacles to the progress of the institution. At the fiftieth anniversary of the College, he said:

> Of the difficulties under which this college labored, in the times in which the martyr Lovejoy fell, and his printing press was thrown into the Mississippi for the advocacy of a very mild form of abolitionism, no man can form any just estimate, who was not himself an actor in those scenes. The same power that ordered and obtained the martyrdom of Lovejoy, was dogging the footsteps of the prominent teachers of this College by night and by day and ever ready to let loose upon them the dogs of war. My soul hath those times in remembrance and is humble. There are many persons who seem to have great difficulty in understanding why the progress of the College was so slow during its early history. The whole difficulty lies in their own ignorance of the facts of the case and not in any mystery which really envelops the subject. I will speak what I think. I am old enough to have a right to do so. The trustees and teachers of this College that stood by it in those bad times and saved it from extinction, have a right to the grateful remembrance of their fellow citizens. That the College did not die in that struggle is success and ought to be glory enough.[2]

The most active opponent of slavery at the College was undoubtedly President Beecher. When he first came to the state he desired a "cool, dispassionate" discussion of the subject. "I had up to this time," he wrote, "not participated at all in the public discussion

---

[2]*Rambler*, May, June, 1879.

which was so deeply exciting the nation, but had been merely an attentive and thoughtful spectator. Such was the magnitude of the subject, and such the consequences involved in its proper management, that, until the providence of God should make it my duty, I was glad to retire from the conflict, and spend my time in preparing for the hour, should it ever arrive, in which duty would allow me to be silent no longer. My views, when I came to this state, were decidedly hostile to the doctrines of immediate emancipation; and it was not until the year 1835 that I became satisfied, from a careful examination of the history of experiments on this subject, that the doctrine of gradual emancipation was fallacious, and that of immediate emancipation was philosophical and safe. From that time I felt it to be a matter of immense importance that measures should be taken, kindly, but thoroughly, to convince the slave states of the fact, and to urge claims of duty. Still, however, considering the magnitude and importance of the subject, and the interest, ignorance and prejudice to be encountered, I felt that more was to be hoped from deep and thorough discussions in a cool and dispassionate style, than from popular appeals and excitement."[3]

An event occurred in 1837 which made Beecher's stand no longer possible. Elijah P. Lovejoy, fearless advocate of a very mild form of abolitionism, was murdered by a pro-slavery mob at Alton, Illinois. Beecher could remain passive and silent no longer when the slave power began to attack freedom of speech and of the press. Beecher and Lovejoy had corresponded together when the latter was advocating the calling of a convention to found an anti-slavery society in Illinois. In 1837 Lovejoy had attended the College commencement where he had discussed at length the project for a state anti-slavery society. While Beecher had at first been unwilling to follow Lovejoy in all of his proposals, nevertheless when Lovejoy was murdered, Beecher discovered that calm, deliberate discussion of the slavery issue was impossible.

President Beecher had remained in Alton with Lovejoy to witness the storing of the press. Then Beecher

---

[3]Beecher, E., Narrative of Riots at Alton, pp. 21-22; 36-37; requoted from Rammelkamp, Charles H., Illinois College, A Centennial History, p. 105.

returned to Jacksonville several hours before the murder. When news of the tragedy arrived, the entire campus held an indignation meeting.[4]

President Beecher now came more actively to the fore in the slavery controversy. His decided stand caused the whole college to be linked with abolitionism in the pro-slavery mind. Not infrequently was he the subject of fulminations from the Missouri Republican:

> The doctor is now esteemed by every one as an abolitionist and by the mass in a much more odious light than was the conduct of the deceased Lovejoy. Upon him rests the censure due for the late violent proceedings, and morally and politically he stands answerable for the fatal consequences which have followed. His conduct in the late meeting, on the second and third instant, shows that under the specious pretext of maintaining abstract principles, he was pushing forward his friend and co-laborer to certain and inevitable destruction.
> We have ever with pride and pleasure (continued the editorial) marked the advance of Illinois College. Not that State but this and the whole West are interested in its prosperity and the sentiments and professions of those who may preside over its destiny. Many of the young men of Missouri have been sent there for their education, and under proper auspices, we trust this would continue to be the case; but with one so deeply identified with the abolition cause as the Rev. E. Beecher now is esteemed by all to be, it cannot expect either a continuance of the support of the citizens of this or of many of that state. For ourselves, we would rather see a host of such men, as we esteem the president to be, sacrificed than that the properity of the college should in the least be affected by retaining him at its head.[5]

---

[4]Rammelkamp, Charles H., Illinois College, A Centennial History, p. 110.

[5]Missouri Republican, November 18, 1837; quoted from Rammelkamp, Charles H., Illinois College, A Centennial History, p. 112.

In the meantime, Professor Jonathan B. Turner, and several of the College students were playing active parts in the Underground Railway at Jacksonville. Several slaves had been sent on their way to freedom. One night, Turner cut "a heavy hickory bludgeon from the wood pile" and went forth to aid three colored women to escape. Later, he boldly confessed his action in prayer-meeting. An effort was made to secure his arrest, but the matter was not pressed.

The attitude of Julian Sturtevant was somewhat more conservative toward the slavery problem. "Since the martyrdom of Lovejoy," says Sturtevant, "two notable events have been the way-marks of our progress." The first of these was "Uncle Tom's Cabin." The second was the formation of the Republican Party, 1854-1856. Sturtevant belonged in that large group of people who were unwilling to advocate the total and immediate abolition of slavery, but who viewed the threatened spread of slavery to free territory with growing alarm. At first he was dissatisfied with both political parties, and did not vote in a presidential election until 1848. Then, it was not Van Buren, but the party platform which secured his support. Not until the Free Soil Party nominated a candidate, could he find a political party worthy of his suffrage.[6]

It is impossible to determine whether or not Illinois College influenced Lincoln. Ann Rutledge's brother David and William Berry, Lincoln's partner at New Salem, attended Illinois College. William H. Herndon, who later became the law partner of Lincoln, failed to graduate because his father was determined to remove him from the anti-slavery influence of the faculty. The first diploma granted by the college was given to Richard Yates, who was governor of Illinois during the Civil War. Over two hundred alumni and students of Illinois College served under arms.

It is clear that Illinois College was one of the powerful anti-slavery forces in the state. Even though its stand was an important factor in hindering the College's growth, yet in spite of severe criticism and loss of patronage, the institution was ever true to its position. There can be no doubt that the College exerted an influence that powerfully molded public opinion

---

[6] Sturtevant, J.M., _Autobiography_, Chapter XX _passim_.

on the slavery issue both in the state and outside
of it.[7]

All of the members of the Illinois Band were vigorous opponents of slavery. This may readily be expected,
since Congregationalists were most ruthless in their
condemnation of the evil. They could afford to be,
for Congregationalism was almost entirely confined to
the area north of the Mason-Dixon Line, and did not
have to deal with the sin of slavery among its own com-
municants. The attitudes of various members of the
Illinois Band are characteristic of Congregationalism
as a whole. If we examine their attitude, we shall
see why Congregationalists must bear much of the blame
for making the conflict over abolition of slavery
"irrepressible."

No one opposed slavery more staunchly than did
Lemuel Foster, and, on at least one occasion, he suf-
fered physical violence as a result of his views. Mrs.
Foster records the incident in the Autobiography:

> Although Mr. F had freely expressed his views
> on that subject (slavery) in social converse,
> & likewise in our school & neighbourhood Ly-
> ceum, still the outsiders demanded a more full
> expression, saying he dare not come out fully
> if those were his views. His reply was, that
> he took the Bible for his rule & guide on this
> as on all subjects & if they desired, he would
> give it to them in a sermon on a given Sabbath.
> When the day arrived all the proSlavery element
> in a vast region around were present. Our
> church was large on the ground, but low plain,
> & cheap, every standing foot of space was occu-
> pied, big waggons were place (sic) at the win-
> dows all well filled. Mr. F. had prepared
> two long sermons & as all seemed so attentive
> (with very few exceptions) & the opportunity
> so favorable, he gave them the whole at once,
> without any recess, which occupied more than
> two hourse, (sic) he commented on every pas-
> sage on that subject within the lids of the

---

[7]Cf. Rammelkamp, Charles H., Illinois College and the
Anti-Slavery Movement. Transactions of Illinois State
Historical Society in the Illinois State Historical
Journal, 1908.

Bible. It created quite a sensation & our
people trembled for his safety. I well remember taking his arm as we left the Church,
& passing by a gang of the proSlavery rabble,
& seeing him bow to them & address them as
Gentlemen. Although many & constant were
the threats in circulation, yet we had but
one slight annoyance, & that was never known
by our friends to this day, we acted upon the
principle that the less that was said, the
sooner it would die out, while some others
suffered severily (sic) from petty disturban-
ces. Still our church continued united with
barely one exception, our principal physician
so hostile to the collered (sic) race, made
some strong demonstrations for a time but soon
found himself loosing (sic) Caste, his ardor
abated, & he became one of our warmest friends.

Not long after another season of special interest was manifest in the church when many
children & youth came forward to the anxious
seat (for we had anxious seats in those days)
some few came in from this Modern Sodom to
witness the proceedings & to ridicule, when
one young lady of the company became so deeply
impressed with a sense of her lost condition
that she came forward & manifested a deter-
mination to come out on the Lord (sic) side.
Her brother in law (with whoom (sic) she was
living) became very much engaged on hearing
of it. In a day or two . . . Mr. F called
to see & converse with her, on arriving there,
he met this brother coming in with his teem
(sic) at the same time, & emagining (sic)
his errand, pursued him with oaths & curses,
gave him one sever (sic) cut with his whip,
& finding his sister was still religiously
inclined, gave notice that a great dance
would come off at his house the next week,
this same young lady engaged in the hilarity,
took cold, was laid upon a sick bed, & before our meetings closed, death had laid
its cold hand upon her, both herself & sister
were deeply impressed, but no evidence of their
acceptance with God. That brother ever after
appeard (sic) ashamed of his conduct, but not
that repentence (sic) which leads to a life
of holiness, several came out on the Lord side

in the meeting & joined themselves with the
people of God. The church was united and
advancing . . . .[8]

The American Home Missionary Society was not infrequently faced with an unpleasant dilemma. One of
its tasks was to aid struggling Presbyterian churches
in the South, -- churches which often had slave-owners
among their members. That funds from Congregational
churches in the North should be sent to slave-owning
churches in the South was unthinkable. No one pointed
the finger more accusingly than did Flavel Bascom:

My mind is not a little exercised in regard to
our Home Missionary operations, & I have at
length determined to express my feelings to you,
& make some inquiries in respect to the plans &
prospects of your Society. You have probably
understood me to be opposed to the granting of
missionary funds, to churches which receive
selfish slaveholders to their communion. If
there are any slave owners who can make it appear that their case is so peculiar, that the
"golden rule" requires them to stand, for the
present, in the legal relation of slaveholders,
I would not object to communing with them, or
to aiding a church which receives them to its
fellowship. But I would put the burden of
proof on the slaveholder & let him clear himself from criminality, before I would recognize
him as a christian brother. I understand that
your Society practically ignores any such distinction. The fact that a church receives
slaveholders to its communion, unquestioned &
unrelented in regard to the practice of buying & selling & owning men & women, is no bar-
rier to its receiving patronage from your
Treasury, in supporting the gospel. Is it so?
You may say that you aid but a few churches of
this character & that these have but a few
slaves. But this does not alter the principle.
Do you aid any churches in which Slaveholding
is treated as a practice compatible with gospel morality? Do you say that you send gospel
to such churches in order to get the leaven of
slavery out? But the Missionary has to commence

---

[8]Foster, L., _Autobiography_, pp. 20-21.

his labors with giving his solemn sanction to
slavery as a practice worthy to be received
to the communion table. In connection with
such an act on his part, his words will not be
likely to bring about a very speedy divorce
of slavery from christianity. I have read
all your reasoning on this point with painful
interest and I am not satisfied. Very many of
your old & long tried friends in the West are
far from being satisfied. I am sincerely
sorry for the necessity which seems to exist,
for the prosecution of Home Missions outside
of your Society. I write now to inquire simply
for my own satisfaction, what are the possibilities of your future policy on the subject
of slavery . . . .

It seems to me, dear Sir, that the prominent
ministers, the large ecclesiastical & benevolent organizations, have tampered with the
Northern conscience, on the subject of slavery, until men have lost their horror of it,
as a crime, and looked at it, now, only as a
matter of political expediency. If the northern ministry & the northern churches, & the
northern benevolent Societies have treated
slavery uniformly & consistently as a stup-
endous crime northern politicians would never
have had the presumption to propose a scheme
so black as the Nebraska Bill. "We have sown
the wind" & we have reason to tremble when we
think of the harvest we are to reap. If the
church were right, the state would still be
safe, But "if the salt have lost its savor,"
alas! alas!![9]

Gilbert H. Barnes, in his book, The Anti-Slavery
Impulse, has brought the religious emphasis of the
anti-slavery movement to the foreground. And where did
the strength of political anti-slavery lie? It developed in the Middle West. It was here that party
organization crystallized. The Free-Soil Party and
the Republican Party sprang out of the West. Then they
made agreements with the East (e.g., on the protective
tariff).

---

[9] Bascom to Badger, March 9, 1854, Galesburg, Illinois.

Another important point is this: since a substantial part of the impulse for the anti-slavery movement stemmed out of a religious activity, the anti-slavery movement acquired a strong moral aspect. Barnes fails to emphasize this adequately. Even Stephen Douglas did not appreciate sufficiently the moral impetus in the anti-slavery movement. But the historian ignores this to his peril. When a movement takes on moral implications, other considerations fly out of the window. The economic interpretation, to be sure, is important, but moral attitudes may transcend purely economic considerations. This moral impulse may be traced directly to such sources as the members of the Illinois Band typify.

The same may be said for the Temperance movement. The most vigorous efforts in behalf of temperance came from the churches. The subject was discussed very frequently in letters which were written by ministers to the American Home Missionary Society. Henry Herrick especially was active in establishing temperance societies in his churches.[10] Benoni Messenger wrote "the cause of Temperance is popular. Our Merchant keeps spirit only as a medicin: (sic) & our tavern is soon to change landlords, where that is to be 'tetotal' also."[11] In 1834, Lemuel Foster reported a flourishing society of about two hundred members in Bloomington.[12] At Princeton, Flavel Bascom declared that "In the cause of Temperance I found a wide field for effort. Through the Press, in the Pulpit, and especially, in connection with a Juvenile organization called a 'Temperance Army,' I labored with tokens of good accomplished, & if, no signal victories were gained some lads were saved from intemperance and the way was prepared for greater apparent results which have since followed."[13]

One evening in April, 1840, six men in Baltimore formed themselves into a club called The Washingtonian Total Abstinence Society, and they adopted a pledge requiring total abstinence from the use of all intoxicating liquors. The movement was quick to spread, and Washingtonian Societies were organized throughout the country. Although the movement had spent its force by

---

[10]Herrick to Peters, September 13, 1830, March 16, 1831, April 21, 1846 etc.

[11]Messenger to Badger and Hall, September 6, 1842, Orwell, Ohio.

[12]Foster to Peters (or Hall), July 19, 1834, Bloomington, Illinois.

[13]Bascom, Flavel, Autobiography, pp. 229-230.

1843, over six hundred thousand drunkards are said to have professed reformation.[14]

One of the reasons why the Washingtonian movement was short-lived was that the moral principle had little to do with the reformation. Romulus Barnes noticed that the work was "done under high steam pressure."[15] Lemuel Foster "had the opportunity of lecturing before the Society frequently (so that) the cause is now looked at as a bible cause, both in its totalism, & in its sympathy for the degraded and ruined." He adds,

. . . Non-professors in t Society who had stood aloof from any religious influence lest it should be sectarian, now rejoice in this bible sanction, appeal to it strongly, & are cordially for suitable religious exercises in our meetings. The work has gone on west. During our meeting which occupied t day on Christmas & a number of evenings, several given to drunkenness signed t pledge & some 20 or thirty others. Much interest in t cause prevails.[16]

All of the members of the Illinois Band were interested and active in the cause of temperance. Nor was their activity ephemeral. Their frequent reference to the liquor problem in correspondence ranging over a number of years testifies to their continued interest in the necessity for reform.

It is interesting to examine their attitude toward war. With regard to Indian warfare, Henry Herrick is probably typical of the group when he implies that expeditions are necessary, but such circumstances are "unfavorable to every religious effort and (render) it more difficult to assemble people for a religious meeting."[17]

Opposition to the Mexican War was vigorous and unqualified. Albert Hale preached "two discourses" on

---

[14]Weigle, Luther A., _American Idealism_, Vol. X, The Pageant of America, p. 178.

[15]Barnes to Badger, April 1, 1846, Newark, Illinois.

[16]Foster to Badger, January 4, 1847, Upper Alton, Illinois.

[17]Herrick to Peters, June 22, 1831, Carrollton, Illinois. The letter is written on a huge piece of stationery.

the subject of war in the Second Presbyterian Church
of Springfield. He condemned the war as wasteful,
unnecessary, and unchristian.[18] Henry Herrick said he
had "no sort of hesitancy in regard to condemning all
aggressive war in general and this Mexican War in particular."[19] Messenger wrote that it was impossible to
excite war spirit without the spirit of alcohol, and
his reference to the enemy as "poor Mexico" clearly
shows where his sympathy lay.[20]

Attitudes toward the Civil War are quite different.
We have already seen the active role which the Band
took in the anti-slavery movement. They would therefore have no sympathy with the southern point of view.
And yet, while Benoni Messenger rejoiced that his son
had entered the army "intent on doing good," he also
sadly observed that "our churches, feble enough before,
cannot well endure such depletions." Necessary as the
irrepressible conflict might be, it was not without
its tremendous price.[21]

One of the topics frequently preached about by
frontier clergymen was the desecration of the Sabbath.
In New England, people took the Sabbath for granted;
on the frontier they did not. Romulus Barnes complained frequently of Sabbath-breaking, and condemned
hunting, travelling, open stores and even social visiting on the Sabbath. Travelling was particularly
frowned upon, and we have seen how various Band members
were careful to patronize stage-coach companies which
did not operate on the Sabbath. Benoni Messenger said
that "profanation of the Holy Sabbath" was "the crying
sin of the West."[22] John F. Brooks confessed that,

> It was painful to see professors of religion
> of various denominations which we are ac-
> customed to regard as evangelical making light

[18]Hale, Albert. Two discourses on the subject of the
Mexican War preached in Second Presbyterian Church in
Springfield, Illinois, published by the Sangamon Jour-
nal, August 1847.

[19]Herrick to the Society, July 28, 1847, Clintonville,
New York.

[20]Messenger to the Society, September 1, 1846, Mt.
Sterling, Illinois.

[21]Messenger to Badger, Galesburg, Illinois, August 11,
1862. Annual Report, March 1865.

[22]Messenger to Peters, Edwardsville, Illinois, Feb. 24, 1831.

of the holy sabbath, visiting & walking
for recreation on that day. But when such
a state of things exists we expect what we
here behold, that the unbelieving will think
it no crime to roam the prairies for summer
fruits or fields for game. Nothing is more
common than to hear guns firing on the sabbath in the village & in various directions.[23]

Perhaps the most pressing of all the social issues
which had to be faced was the problem of competing
denominations.

Congregationalists and Presbyterians got along
best with the Baptists and Methodists, although friction would frequently arise when it was necessary for
two or more groups to share the same meeting house on
alternate Sundays.

But the followers of Alexander Campbell received
much less tolerance. William Carter preached against
them and the followers of Barton W. Stone on more than
one occasion.[24] Lemuel Foster found Shelbyville "much
overrun with Campbellism and evry (sic) thing else but
religion."[25] John F. Brooks was careful to make no
unkind allusion to any other denomination, but "entered
at once upon the fundamental doctrines of the gospel."[26]
The attitude of Messenger is no doubt typical of the
feeling of many towards the Campbellites:

Considerable effort has been made here by
the followers of A. Campbell & they succeeded
in forming (what they call) a church: their
numbers were few at first & such an array of
truth has been brought to bear upon the people,
& the errors of Campbellism held up so clearly
before their minds, that not a single individual that I have heard of has joined them
since their first meeting. Every effort that
could be devised has been made by them to get
numbers: even habitual drunkards have been

[23]Brooks to Peters, Belleville, Illinois, July 14, 1832.
[24]Carter to Badger, Pittsfield, Illinois, July 29, 1846.
[25]Foster to Badger, Greenville, Illinois, March 27, 1845.
[26]Brooks to Badger, Springfield, Illinois, August 2, 1843.

urged time & again to "go down into the
watery grave" then wash away their filth
& thus become members of their self-styled
church of Christ. Most of their members
do not pretend that they have ever experienced any change of heart, & utterly deny
that any such thing is necessary to salvation.[27]

But fulminations against the Campbellites were mild
in comparison with those against the Universalists.
John F. Brooks speaks of Universalists, Infidels and
Atheists all in the same breath.[28] When the Universalists held a state convention in Washington, Illinois
in 1839, Romulus Barnes remarked that "it is perfectly
obvious that Satan has a strong hold here & means to
keep it."[29] Messenger rejoiced that the "relish for
such kind of preaching is fast dying away in nearly all
this region (Bloomfield): & that the pure & holy gospel is sought for by most of the inhabitants. I have
ever found that the best way to stay the progress of
Universalism (& indeed almost any error) is to preach
the pure gospel & take no notice of them."[30] Theron
Baldwin was equally delighted when only four people
came to hear a preacher of universal salvation.[31]

The attitude towards the Mormons is interesting.
While none of the members of the Illinois Band had
any sympathy for Mormonism, nevertheless they deplored
the persecution to which Mormons were often subjected.
We have already seen in an earlier chapter how Albert
Hale felt about the "Mormon War." He was not alone in
his feeling. William Kirby took a similar attitude.[32]
But Romulus Barnes probably speaks for the group when
he says "it is not to be supposed that men professing

---

[27]Messenger to Peters, Winchester, Illinois, February
25, 1833.

[28]Brooks to Peters, Belleville, Illinois, July 14, 1832.

[29]Barnes to Badger, Washington, Illinois, October 1, 1839.

[30]Messenger to Hall and Badger, Bloomfield, Illinois,
March 29, 1843.

[31]Baldwin to Peters, Vandalia, Illinois, December 15, 1830.

[32]Kirby to Badger, Mendon, Illinois, July 1, 1844.

even a moderate degree of intelligence can long, by
delusions so gross & palpable, be 'removed unto another gospel.'"[33]

A final problem which caused members of the Illinois Band concern was the theological innovation known
as "Oberlin Perfectionism." In brief, Oberlin Perfectionism, as defined by its chief exponent, President
Asa Mahan in his Scriptural Doctrine of Christian Perfection consisted of

the perfect assimilation of our entire character to that of Christ, having at all times
and under all circumstances, the "same mind
that was also in Jesus Christ."[34]

The American Home Missionary Society had already
refused to support missionaries of Oberlin tendencies.
At the session of 1845, the recently formed General
Association of Illinois was plunged into an acute
theological discussion. The Reverend Mr. Holmes laid
down the gauntlet when he demanded a definite answer
on the part of the Association "whether or not they
will unite ecclesiastically with the brethren of the
Oberlin school." When action was finally taken in
1846 on this question, the Association went on record
that "in the judgment of this body the interests of
religion generally and the prosperity of the Congregational churches in particular require that we should
hereafter decline receiving to membership ministering
brethren who belong to the class usually denominated
Oberlin Perfectionists." There was a large dissenting
minority. Actually, the number of Perfectionists was
much smaller than supposed. The whole controversy
eventually died out.[35]

When the American Home Missionary Society decided
not to aid men of perfectionist views, some of the
members of the Band were asked who the perfectionist

---

[33]Barnes to Badger, Newark, Illinois, January 1, 1845.

[34]Mahan, Asa, Scriptural Doctrine of Christian Perfection (1839), p. 13, from Spinka, Kuhns, et al., A History of Illinois Congregational and Christian Churches,
p. 357, Note 10.

[35]Spinka, Kuhns, et al., A History of Illinois Congregational and Christian Churches, pp. 96-98.

men were. Bascom wrote a long letter in his defense declaring that he had never knowingly recommended any man to the Society who held such views. He was indignant when accused of smuggling Perfectionists into the patronage of the Society. Furthermore, he felt that the whole controversy was assuming the proportions of a panic.[36] When William Kirby was asked by the Society whether or not it should grant aid to Reverend L. Spencer, Kirby replied that he could not find sufficient evidence for rejecting him, and added, "if your committee think differently it will happily relieve me from further responsibility."[37]

The question of "perfectionism," while it created considerable discussion and tension for a short time, soon gave way to the more pressing problem of the churches and slavery.

And now the story has been told. We have seen how the call to Christian service to labor on the frontier came to a group of men at Yale College. One by one they answered that call to spread the Christian Gospel and made the difficult trip to the West. We have seen how events in Illinois and also at Yale College worked together to lure a band of men to devote themselves to missionary and educational work on the frontier. We have noticed the backgrounds from which these men came, their common life at Yale College, and their resolution to go to Illinois under the patronage of the American Home Missionary Society. We have seen how five of these men acted as agents for the state of Illinois. We have noticed the hardships which they had to undergo, the sacrifices which they had to make, and the contributions which they were able to effect on a frontier area in the moral and religious realm. We have traced the growth of Illinois College, and have summarized briefly the work of each of the fifteen men as they went their several ways on the frontier.

We have studied the influence of the Illinois Band in the realm of education, particularly in relation to Illinois College and the Monticello Female Academy, and we have also traced the role which various members of

---

[36]Bascom to the secretaries of the American Home Missionary Society, November 8, 1842, December 29, 1842, Chicago, Illinois.

[37]Kirby to Hall, Jacksonville, Illinois, July 8, 1846.

the Illinois Band played in the disruption of the Plan of Union with the Presbyterians and the growth of Illinois Congregationalism. Finally, we have observed the attitude of the Band toward the social questions of the day, particularly the question of slavery.

Some years ago, at the unveiling of a portrait, of Dr. William Salter, in the Hall of Fame at the State Capitol in Des Moines, Iowa, Governor Cummins said in substance this: "Not the politicians, not the captains of industry, not the leaders in the great material enterprises of the state, but this man, and men of his character and class, are the men that have made Iowa what she is, a great, noble, peerless Christian commonwealth."[38]

We may say the same about the state of Illinois. Conspicuous among the builders of Illinois have been the Congregational ministers of the state. And conspicuous among the Congregational ministers was the Illinois Band. History has too often paid little attention to such men. For these reasons we have undertaken to sketch with some degree of completeness the lives of a few of the men who have had the most to do in the making of a great Commonwealth.

_____

[38]Douglass, Truman Orville, Builders of a Commonwealth, Preface.

BIBLIOGRAPHY

In the bibliography given below the attempt has been made to give practically all the sources and secondary works important for the subject covered in the preceding pages. All the main libraries and accessible collections of Chicago, New Haven, Jacksonville, Illinois, and Springfield, Illinois, and Beloit, Wisconsin have been carefully examined. There may remain some manuscript collections in Illinois which would be of value. The author is sorry that his brief stay at Jacksonville, Illinois did not permit him more time to visit with some of the people of the town, not a few of whom are descendants of members of the Illinois Band. It is hardly possible, however, that any further discoveries of material will greatly alter the conclusions which we have reached, although it would be perfectly possible to expand the material on education in detail.

In enumerating the various sources and authorities used the attempt has been made in most cases to indicate briefly the contents of the more important documents or books, wherever they are of vital bearing on the subject at hand. It is to be understood, however, that this bibliography is by no means exhaustive. Only the more important sources which have a vital bearing on the subject have been listed.

Most of the printed sources and authorities are in the Sterling Library of Yale University. With a few exceptions it may be understood that if the location of a source is not given it is to be found here.

I. CORRESPONDENCE

American Home Missionary Society Missionary Correspondence

The main source of information for this book is to be found in the correspondence of missionaries employed by the American Home Missionary Society. This consists of many thousands of letters which have been collected at the Hammond Library, Chicago Theological Seminary, Chicago, Illinois. This correspondence is filed in steel cabinets and catalogued by state, then by year, and then alphabetically. There are letters from almost every state in the Union, dating from the 1820s until the turn of the century. Although thousands of valuable letters have been saved, the collection is incomplete, as many of the letters have been destroyed.

There are about nine hundred letters from members
of the Illinois Band in this collection. To list each
letter separately would prolong this bibliography to an
undue length. The author did not keep an exact count
of the number of letters from each member of the Illinois Band, because some of the letters were only a few
lines long and were of a worthless nature. Elisha Jenney leads the list with over two hundred communications
to the American Home Missionary Society. Albert Hale
and Flavel Bascom follow with over one hundred communications. William Kirby is next with about ninety letters. Theron Baldwin has about sixty, Romulus Barnes
almost sixty, William Carter about fifty, Lemuel Foster
about forty, Jairus Wilcox twenty-five, Henry Herrick
and Julian Sturtevant about twenty each, Benoni Messenger about twenty, John F. Brooks sixteen, Mason Grosvenor and Asa Turner have only a few letters each.

American Home Missionary Society Letter Books

When the American Home Missionary Society replied
to the foregoing letters, it kept a copy of the reply
to the missionary in question in its files. These cop-
ies of letters were gathered into letter books, now
stored at the Hammond Library, Chicago Theological Seminary. Replies to missionaries number into the hun-
dred-thousands. In many cases, however, these letters
have become so faded that they are nearly if not quite
illegible. Therefore it is sometimes difficult or impossible to know what the Society wrote in reply. But
the many thousands of letters still intact are a mine
of information with regard to the Society's advice to
its missionaries on the frontier. The letters are only
arranged chronologically.

Baldwin-Sturtevant Correspondence

Numerous in quantity and also very valuable from
the historical point of view are the letters which
passed between Theron Baldwin and Julian M. Sturtevant.
These two men were very intimate friends and were constantly exchanging views on both college affairs and
the important religious and educational problems of
the day. The letters extend from the founding of the
College to the death of Theron Baldwin in the East in
1870. These letters are to be found at Illinois College, Jacksonville, Illinois.

Miscellaneous Correspondence

Among the considerable number of other letters in

226

the Illinois College archives may be mentioned more
especially the correspondence of other members of the
Illinois Band such as John F. Brooks, Asa Turner and
Mason Grosvenor, and of members of the early faculty
like President Edward Beecher, Samuel Adams and Truman
M. Post. There are not many of these letters in any
one case, but taken as a whole they are a valuable supplement to the Baldwin-Sturtevant Correspondence.

Miscellaneous Letters at Beloit College, Beloit, Wisconsin

A few letters of Theron Baldwin, Julian Sturtevant,
and Flavel Bascom may be found among the archives at
Beloit College. These letters reflect some of the
early history of Illinois College.

Miscellaneous Letters at McCormick Theological Seminary, Chicago, Illinois

Three letters from Benoni Messenger to Mr. Vail.

Miscellaneous Letters at Yale University Library, New
Haven, Connecticut

Seven letters of Henry Herrick to his brother, F.C.
Herrick, two letters of Theron Baldwin, two of Flavel
Bascom, one of Julian M. Sturtevant.

II. AUTOBIOGRAPHIES, ALBUMS, DIARIES,
LAWS, MINUTES AND RECORDS

Baldwin, Theron	Class Album Yale Memorabilia, 1827.
Bascom, Flavel	Autobiography, 278 Ms. pages, Hammond Library Vault, Chicago Theological Seminary. This val- uable manuscript is the primary source for Bascom's life and work. 1875.
Bonesteel, V.P.	Class Album Yale Memorabilia, 1827.
Cowles, H.	Class Album Yale Memorabilia, 1826.
Cowles, J.	Class Album Yale Memorabilia, 1826.

Daggett, O.E.   Class Album Yale Memorabilia, 1828.

Duncan, Mrs. Joseph   Excerpts from Diary, Illinois State Historical Journal, Volume XXI, 1928.

Foster, Lemuel & Mrs.
  Lemuel   Autobiography, Hammond Library Vault, Chicago Theological Seminary. This fascinating autobiography is a primary source on the Fosters.

Grosvenor, C.P.   Class Album Yale Memorabilia, 1827.

Hale, Albert   Class Album Yale Memorabilia, 1827.

Howe, Samuel   Class Album Yale Memorabilia, 1827.

Hubbard, O.P.   Class Album Yale Memorabilia, 1828.

Johnson, S.L.   Class Album Yale Memorabilia, 1827.

Lathrop, William   Class Album Yale Memorabilia, 1822.

Laws of Illinois College, Jacksonville 1837-1850, Illinois College.

Minutes of Phi Beta Kappa, 1826-1847, Yale College, Yale Memorabilia.

Minutes of the Faculty of Illinois College, May 1, 1835-March 26, 1843, Tanner Library, Illinois College.

Minutes of the Trustees of Illinois College, November 27, 1828.

Obituary Record, Yale College, Yale Memorabilia.

Odiorne, J.C.   Class Album Yale Memorabilia, 1826.

Porter, A.G.	Class Album Yale Memorabilia, 1822.
Putnam, D.	Class Album Yale Memorabilia, 1826.
Ripley, G.B.	Class Album Yale Memorabilia, 1822.
Smith, J.A.	Class Album Yale Memorabilia, 1826.
Townsend, D.J.	Class Album Yale Memorabilia, 1828.

Society for Christian Research, Record Book, Yale MS., November 28, 1825 to June, 1837.

Society for the Promotion of Collegiate and Theological Education of the West, Annual Reports, 1844-1870, New York, 1844. Valuable reports on the work of Theron Baldwin's work as secretary of the Society.

Records of the Chicago Presbytery, Vol. I, 1837. McCormick Theological Seminary, Chicago, Illinois.

Records of the Galena Presbytery, Vol. I, ca. 1844. McCormick Theological Seminary, Chicago, Illinois.

Records of the Meetings of the Class of 1822, Yale College. Held in 1862 and 1867; with biographical sketches of the members of the class, New Haven, 1869.

Rhetorical Society, Yale College, Records 1841-1862. See A Yale Moral Society.

Yale Missionary Society (earlier name, The Yale College Society of Enquiry Respecting Missions), organized 1818.

Record Book No. 1. Constitution; list of members, October 4, 1852, through 1864.

Record Book No. 2. Minutes, June 7, 1852 to
            November 6, 1865.

Yale Moral Society, Record Books of the,

    Book A. Transactions, April 6, 1797 through July
                22, 1819.

    Book B. Transactions, August 10, 1820 through
                March 10, 1841. Changes in
                name: became Moral and Theo-
                logical Society, July 1828;
                The Rhetorical Society, October
                22, 1834.

    Book C. Constitution of The Rhetorical Society;
                list of members, October 1834
                to October 1840.

    Book D. Revisions of Constitution; list of
                members, March 1841 to Septem-
                ber 30, 1861.

    III. SPECIAL DOCUMENTS RELATING TO CONGREGA-
            TIONAL CHURCHES IN ILLINOIS

    These documents are to be found in the Church Files
of the Hammond Library, Chicago Theological Seminary,
and consist of typewritten manuscripts of small printed
pamphlets dealing with the history of Congregational
churches in Illinois.

A Historical Sketch of Quincy, Illinois.

Chronicles of the Godfrey Congregational Church at
    Godfrey, Illinois.

Dedication of the Rebuilt First Congregational Church
    of Geneseo, Illinois. Dedication Week February
    22 - March 1, 1925.

Diamond Jubilee. First Congregational Church, Blue
    Island, Illinois.

Heinl, Frank J., (?) Sketch of the Congregational
    Church of Jacksonville, Illinois.

History of the First Congregational Church of Pitts-
    field, Illinois.

Historical Sketch of the Main Street Congregational
Church, Peoria, From the Manual of the First Congregational Church.

Hobbs, W.A. Fiftieth Anniversary of the Congegational
Church at Waverly.

Manual of the Congregational Church, Jacksonville,
Illinois, 1891.

Memorial Address and Proceedings of the Thirtieth
Anniversary of the Settlement of Geneseo, Illinois,
1866.

Our Hundredth Anniversary, First Congregational Church,
Waverly, Illinois. 1836-1936.

Pope, Thomas. Manuscript history of the Quincy Church.

Riegler, Gordon Arthur. A Century of Congregationalism
in Illinois, 1931.

Semi-Centennial Celebration, First Church of Christ,
1837-1887, Galesburg, Illinois.

Stillwell, Frederick E. History of the Mendon Congregational Church, Chicago, 1928.

IV. ARTICLES

Anderson, Paul Russell. "Quincy, An Outpost of Philosophy," Illinois State Historical Journal, Vol.
XXXIV, 1941.

Baldwin, Theron. "The Absorption of Congregationalism,"
The Congregational Quarterly, Vol. XII, 1870.

Beecher, Thomas K. "Reminiscences of 1834 and 1843,"
College Rambler (Illinois College), Jacksonville,
1893.

Belting, Paul H. "The Development of the Free Public
High School in Illinois to 1860," Illinois State
Historical Journal, Vol. XI, 1917-1918.

Chandler, Josephine C. "Dr. Charles Chandler," Illinois State Historical Journal, Vol. XXIV, 1931.

Cole, Arthur C. "Lincoln and Civil Liberty," Illinois
State Historical Journal, Vol. XIX, 1926.

231

"Collegiate and Theological Education at the West,"
The Congregational Quarterly, October 1869.

Congdon, Harriet R. "Early History of Monticello
Seminary," Transactions of the Illinois State
Historical Society, 1924.

Cowles, Henry. "Ohio Congregationalism," The Congregational Quarterly, Vol. V, 1863.

Currier, Warren & Sturtevant, Julian, et al. "Evangelization in the West and South," The Congregational Quarterly, Vol. VII, 1865.

"Death of Dr. Samuel Willard, the Oldest Member of the
Illinois State Historical Society," Illinois State
Historical Journal, Vol. VI, 1913-1914.

Dugan, Frank H. "An Illinois Martyrdom," Papers in
Illinois History, 1939, Springfield, Illinois, 1939.

"Edward Payson Kirby," Illinois State Historical Journal, Vol. X, 1917-1918.

Eversole, Mildred. "Canton College, An Early Attempt
at Higher Education in Illinois," Illinois State
Historical Journal, XXXIV, 1941.

Griffith, W.E. "The Past Three-Fourths of the Century,"
Illinois State Historical Journal, 1912.

Harrison, Ella W. "Congregational Church, Princeton,
Illinois," Illinois State Historical Journal,
Vol. XX, 1927.

Heinl, Frank J. "Congregationalism in Jacksonville
and Early Illinois," Illinois State Historical
Journal, Vol. XXVII, 1934.

_____. "Newspapers, Illinois, 1831-1832,"
Illinois State Historical Journal, Vol. XXIII, 1930.

Hildner, Ernest G. "Colleges and College Life in
Illinois One Hundred Years Ago," Papers in Illinois
History, 1942, Springfield, Illinois, 1942.

Hubbard, Anson M. "A Colony Settlement, Geneseo, Illinois, 1836-1837," Illinois State Historical Journal,
Vol. XXIX, 1936.

Humphrey, Mary E. "Springfield Home for the Friendless," *Illinois State Historical Journal*, Vol. XX, 1927.

Kofoid, Carrie P. "Puritan Influences in Illinois before 1860," Publication #10 of the Historical Library, Illinois, 1905. A brief but very suggestive article on New England influences in Illinois.

Magoun, George F. "Relative Claims of our Western Colleges," *The Congregational Quarterly*, Vol. XV, 1873.

Moore, Mrs. Clara. "The Ladies' Education Society of Jacksonville, Illinois," *Illinois State Historical Journal*, Vol. XVIII, 1925-1926.

Moore, Margaret King. "The Ladies Association for Educating Females," *Illinois State Historical Journal*, Vol. XXXI, 1938.

Muelder, Hermann Richard. "Congregationalists and Presbyterians in the Early History of the Galesburg Churches," *Papers in Illinois History, 1938*. Springfield, 1938.

_____. "Galesburg: Hotbed of Abolitionism," *Illinois State Historical Journal*, Vol. XXXV, 1942.

Oliphant, J. Orin. "The American Missionary Spirit, 1826-1835," *Church History Magazine*, 1938.

Palmer, Mrs. John M. "The Illinois State Capitol Grounds," *Illinois State Historical Society Journal*, Vol. XV, 1922.

Piper, John H. "Congregationalism in Springfield," *Illinois State Historical Journal*, Vol. XVI, 1923.

_____. "New England Dinners of the First Congregational Church of Springfield," *Illinois State Historical Journal*, Vol. XXVI, 1933.

Rammelkamp, Charles H. "Fundamentalism and Modernism in a Pioneer College," *Illinois State Historical Society Journal*, Vol. XXI, 1928.

_____. "Illinois College and the Anti-Slavery Movement," *Transactions of the Illinois State Historical Society*, 1908.

Rammelkamp, Charles H. "Original Campus of 'Old Illinois,'" College Rambler, January 10, 1918.

_____. "The Reverberation of the Slavery Conflict in a Pioneer College," Mississippi Valley Historical Review, March 1928.

Richardson, William A. "Dr. David Nelson and His Times," Illinois State Historical Journal, Vol. XIII, 1920.

Roy, Joseph E. "The Mutual Relation of Home Missions and The Christian Colleges," The Congregational Quarterly, Vol. XIX, 1877.

Ryan, John H. "A Chapter from the History of the Underground Railroad in Illinois: A Sketch of the Sturdy Abolitionist, John Hossack," Illinois State Historical Journal, 1915.

Savage, G.S.F. "Pioneer Congregational Ministers in Illinois," Illinois State Historical Journal, Vol. III, 1910.

Smith, Joe Patterson, "Charles Henry Rammelkamp," Illinois State Historical Journal, Vol. XXIV, 1931.

Smith, Theodore Clarke, "Parties and Slavery 1850-1859," Volume XVIII in the American Nation: A History, New York, 1906.

Sturtevant, Julian M. "Address at the Semi-Centennial Anniversary of the Founding of Illinois College," in College Rambler, May and June 1879. Jacksonville, Illinois, 1879. An excellent account of the early history of Illinois College.

_____. "Church and State," The Congregational Quarterly, Vol. XV, October 1873. The articles by Sturtevant are legion. This is one of the best ones.

_____. "Colleges and State Universities," The New Englander, Vol. XXXII, New Haven, 1873.

_____. "Collegiate Education at the West," The New Englander, Vol. IV, New Haven, 1845.

_____. "Denominational Colleges," The New Englander, Vol. XIX, New Haven, 1860.

Sturtevant, Julian M. "Origins of Western Congregationalism," Congregational Quarterly.

_____. "Protestantism in America," The
New Englander, November 1856, Vol. XV, New Haven.

_____. "The Claims of the Higher Sem-
inaries of Learning on the Liberality of the Wealthy,"
The New Englander, Vol. XXI, New Haven, 1862.

_____. "The Education of Heathen Na-
tions essential to the World's Conversion," The
New Englander, Vol. II, New Haven, 1843.

_____. "The True Conception of the
Christian Ministry," The New Englander, Vol. XXVII,
1868.

_____. "Theron Baldwin," (two parts),
The Congregational Quarterly, Vol. XVII, 1875. This
is our best source for the life of Theron Baldwin,
written by his most intimate friend.

_____. "William Carter," The Congrega-
tional Quarterly, Vol. XIII, October 1871.

Sweet, William W. "Bishop Matthew Simpson and the
Funeral of Abraham Lincoln," Illinois State Historical Journal, Vol. VII, 1914.

Taylor, Ella Hume. "A History of the First Congregational Church of Geneseo," Illinois State Historical Journal, Vol. XX, 1927.

"The Seventy-Fifth Anniversary of the Founding of Monticello Seminary at Godfrey, Illinois," Illinois
State Historical Society, Vol. VI, 1913.

Thrapp, Russell F. "Early Religious Beginnings in
Illinois," Illinois State Historical Journal,
Vol. IV, 1911.

West, Edward William. "Memoirs. Records of Events in
the Life and Times of Edward William West, Belleville, Illinois A.D. 1895," Illinois State Historical Journal, Vol. XXI, 1928.

Willard, Samuel. "Reminiscences of Illinois College
in 1836," Rig Veda 1895. Illinois College,
Jacksonville.

Wood, William Dustin. "Illinois College at the Half
    Century," Illinois State Historical Journal, Vol.
    XVIII, 1925.

V. PERIODICALS

Collections of the Illinois State Historical Library,
    Vol. I to Vol. XXXII, Springfield, Illinois, 1903.

Illinois State Historical Journal, Vol. I 1908 --
    Springfield, Illinois. Very excellent and valuable
    periodical for local Illinois history.

Mississippi Valley Historical Review, Vol. I 1914-1915
    (Vol. XXX 1943-1944), Cedar Rapids, Iowa, 1905.

The Congregational Quarterly, Vol. I 1859 - Vol. XX
    1878, New York 1859.

The Congregational Year Book, Vol. I 1854, New York,
    1854.

Proceedings of the Mississippi Valley Historical Asso-
    ciation, Vol. I 1907-1908, Cedar Rapids, 1909.

The Home Missionary (American Home Missionary Journal),
    Vol. I 1828 -- New York, 1829. A monthly magazine
    which featured the reports of missionaries on the
    frontier in the employ of the Society.

The New Englander, Vol. I 1843 - Vol. LVI 1892, New
    Haven, 1843.

Transactions of the Illinois State Historical Society,
    Vol. I 1895(?) - Vol. XLIII, 1936.

Williams, William W. A Magazine of Western History,
    Vol. I, 1884, Vol. XIV, 1891. National Magazine,
    Vol. XV-XIX, 1893. Cleveland, 1884.

VI. PAMPHLETS, SERMONS, ADDRESSES, DISCOURSES AND MISCELLANY

Adams, Norma. "Theron Baldwin, Principal of Monti-
    cello Seminary, 1838-1843," Godfrey, Illinois,
    1939. Pamphlet. An excellent sketch of Baldwin
    as principal of the Female Academy.

Baldwin, Theron. Autobiographical pamphlets 1826-1829;
    a list of 21 colleges in which Baldwin is said to
    have had a part. Yale Memorabilia.

Baldwin, Theron. Monticello Female Seminary. Photostat copy of announcement of opening. Illinois State Historical Library, Springfield, Illinois.

_____. "Historical Sketch of the Origin, progress, and wants of Illinois College," New York, 1832. College Pamphlets. Vol. 1908.

Barton, Charles B. "The founders and founding of Illinois College," pamphlet at Illinois College.

Bascom, Flavel. "A Historical Discourse on Galesburg, Ill," Illinois State Historical Library, Springfield, Illinois.

_____. "History of the First Congregational Church," Princeton, Illinois.

Brooks, John F. "Six Original Sermons, 1830, 1831, 1832, 1837, 1838, 1844," Illinois State Historical Library, Springfield, Illinois.

Carter, Thos. B. and Grant, John C. "The Second Presbyterian Church of Chicago, June 1, 1842 - June 1, 1892."

Carter, William. "A Reply to Wm. Thomas, Exposition and defense of the fugitive slave law," 1851. Winchester, Illinois (printed by Western Unionist).

Coffin, Nathaniel. "Origin and Progress of Illinois College," April 30, 1847 (pamphlet), Illinois College.

Emery, S.H. "A Memorial of the Congregational Ministers and Churches of the Illinois Association," Quincy, Illinois, 1863.

Goodrich, Chauncy A. "Revivals of Religion in Yale College," Quarterly Register, February 1838. College pamphlets, Vol. 1543.

Hale, Albert. "Two discourses on the subject of the war between the United States and Mexico; preached in the Second Presbyterian Church, in Springfield, Illinois," 1847 (pamphlet).

Meese, William A. "The Beginnings of Illinois," pamphlet; privately printed, 1904.

Parrish, George R. "A History of the Congregational Association of Southern Illinois," Chicago, no date.

Patterson, R.W. "Early Society in Southern Illinois," a lecture read before the Chicago Historical Society, October 19, 1880, Chicago, 1881.

Savage, G.S.F. "Flavel Bascom," Vol. 50 in Biographical Pamphlets, 1890.

Sturtevant, Julian M. Address delivered by Julian M. Sturtevant at the Morgan County Old Settlers' Reunion, Jacksonville, Illinois, August 17, 1871. Tanner Library, Illinois College.

_____. "American Colleges," an address delivered by J.M. Sturtevant at his inauguration as President of Illinois College, June 25, 1845 (pamphlet 32 pp).

_____. An address in behalf of the Society for the Promotion of Collegiate and Theological Education at the West, New York, 1853. College pamphlets, Vol. 1776.

_____. "American Emigration," a discourse in behalf of the American Home Missionary Society, New York, 1857. (pamphlet 34 pp).

_____. "Funeral Sermon for William Carter," Congregational Quarterly, 1871.

_____. Historical Discourse at Quarter Century Celebration at Illinois College (pamphlet), Illinois.

_____. "Scrap-book," Articles by and about J.M. Sturtevant collected by Lucy Sturtevant, 1919. 28 pp. folio.

_____. Sermon delivered before the National Council at Boston on June 15, 1865, Congregational Quarterly, Vol. VIII, July-October 1865.

_____. "The Memory of the Just," A sermon commemorative of Reverend William Kirby, New York, 1852. Contains valuable source material on Kirby.

Sturtevant, Julian M. "The Lessons of Our National Conflict," An Address to the alumni of Yale College at their annual meeting, July 24, 1861.

_____. "The Relation of the Congregational Churches of the Northwest to Collegiate Education," The New Englander, New Haven, January 1871.

The College Rambler, Jacksonville, Illinois, 1878. A nearly complete file of this student periodical is in the college library.

Thrift, Charles T. "Frontier Missionary Life," Scottdale, Pennsylvania, 1937.

Waggener, Halley Farr. "Baptist Beginnings in Illinois," Dissertation in Swift Library, 1928, University of Chicago, Chicago, Illinois.

Wayland, John T. "The Theological Department in Yale College, 1822-1858," Ph.D. dissertation, 1933. Yale University.

Weigle, Luther A. Commemoration Address of the One Hundredth Anniversary of the Congregational Church, Jacksonville, Illinois, December 10-17, 1933.

VII. BOOKS

Alvord, Clarence Walworth (ed.). The Centennial History of Illinois. 5 vols. Springfield, Illinois 1918-1920; published by Illinois Centennial Comm.

Angle, Paul McClelland. Here I Have Lived. A history of Lincoln's Springfield 1821-1865. Springfield, Illinois, 1935. The Abraham Lincoln Association.

Anderson, Charles P. Illinois in History 1818-1918. Chicago, 1918. University of Chicago Press.

Andreas, A.T. History of Chicago from the Earliest Period to the Present. Chicago, 1884. A.T. Andreas, Publisher.

_____. History of Cook County, Illinois from the Earliest Period to the Present Time. Chicago, 1884. A.T. Andreas, Publisher.

Atkins, Gaius Glenn and Fagley, Frederick L. _History of American Congregationalism_. Boston, 1942. The Pilgrim Press.

Bacon, Theodore D. _Leonard Bacon_. Yale University Press, New Haven, 1931.

Ballance, C. _The History of Peoria, Illinois_. Peoria, 1870. Printed by N.C. Nason.

Barnes, Gilbert H. _The Anti-Slavery Impulse_. New York, 1933. Appleton-Century Co.

Bateman, Newton and Selby, Paul. _Historical Encyclopedia_. 2 vols. Chicago, 1902. Munsell Pub. Co.

Blanchard, Rufus. _A History of Illinois to accompany an historical map_. Chicago, 1883. National School Furnishing Co.

Boggess, Arthur C. _The Settlement of Illinois 1778-1830_. Chicago, 1908. Published by Chicago Historical Society.

Brink, W.R. et al., Publishers. _A History of Schuyler and Brown Counties_, 1882.

Brown, William H. _An historical sketch of the early movement in Illinois on Slavery_. Chicago, 1865. Steam press of Church, Goodman, and Donnelley.

Calkins, Ernest Elmo. _They Broke the Prairie_. New York, 1937. Charles Scribner's Sons.

Cartwright, Peter. _Autobiography_. New York, 1857. Hunt & Eaton.

Chapman, Charles C. (ed.). _History of Fulton County_. Peoria, 1879. C.C. Chapman & Co.

_____. _History of Knox County Illinois_. Chicago, 1878. C.C. Chapman & Co.

Clark, Dan Elbert. _The West in American History_. New York, 1937. Thomas Y. Crowell Company.

Clark, J.B. _Leavening the Nation_. New York, 1903. The Baker and Taylor Co.

Dexter, Franklin B. _Biographical Notices of Graduates of Yale College_ (issued as a supplement to the

obituary record), New Haven, 1913. Henry Holt
and Company.

Douglass, Truman O. <u>Builders of a Commonwealth</u>. 12
vols. Typewritten Ms. Swift Library, University
of Chicago, Chicago, Illinois. Carbon copy made
from original in possession of Iowa State College.

_____. <u>The Pilgrims of Iowa</u> (Swift Lib-
rary, University of Chicago), Boston, 1911. The
Pilgrim Press.

Dunning, Albert E. <u>Congregationalists in America</u>.
New York, 1894. J.A. Hill and Company.

Eames, Charles M. <u>Historic Morgan and Classic Jack-
sonville</u>, 1855. <u>Jacksonville Daily Journal</u>
Printing Office.

Eaton, Edward Dwight, et al. <u>Historical Sketches of
Beloit College</u>. New York, 1928. A.S. Barnes
and Company.

Fergus Co., Historical Series, Chicago, 1885. Fergus
Printing Company.

Ford, Thos. <u>A History of Illinois 1818-1847</u>. Chicago,
1854, edited by Milo Milton Quaife. Chicago,
1945. S.C. Griggs & Co.

Fox, Dixon Ryan (ed.). <u>Sources of Culture in the Middle West</u>. New York, 1934. D. Appleton Century Co.

Gerhard, Fred. <u>Illinois as it is</u>. Chicago, 1857.
Keen and Lee.

Goodykoontz, Colin Brummit. <u>Home Missions on the Amer-
ican Frontier</u>, with particular reference to the
Home Missionary Society. Caldwell, Idaho, 1939.
The Caxton Printers, Ltd.

Haines, Selden. <u>A Biographical Sketch of the Class
of 1826, Yale College</u>. Utica, New York. 1866.

Harlow, Ralph Volney. <u>A History of the United States</u>.
New York, 1936. H. Holt and Company.

Hubbard, Oliver P. <u>Biographical Sketches of the Class
of 1828</u> in Yale College and College Memorabilia.

241

Humphrey, Grace. _Illinois. The Story of the Prairie State_. Indianapolis, 1917. Bobbs-Merrill Company.

Hurlbut, Henry H. _Chicago Antiquities_. Chicago, 1881. Privately printed.

Illinois College Bulletin, Catalog Number March 1944. Jacksonville, Illinois.

Johnson, Charles Beneulyn. _Illinois in the Fifties_. Champaign, 1918. Flanigan-Pearson Co.

Latourette, Kenneth Scott. _A History of the Expansion of Christianity_. 7 vols. New York, 1937-1945. Esp. Vol. 4. Harper and Brothers.

Magoun, George F. _Asa Turner, A Home Missionary Patriarch and His Times_. This is the definitive work on Asa Turner. Very valuable. Boston and Chicago Congregational Sunday School and Publishing Society, 1889.

Mason, Edward G. _Early Chicago and Illinois_. Chicago, 1890. Fergus Printing Co.

Matson, N. _Reminiscences of Bureau County_. Princeton, Illinois, 1872. Republican Book and Job Office.

Matthews, Lois Kimball. _The Expansion of New England_. Boston, 1909.

McClurg, A.C. & Co. _Illinois_. A descriptive and historical guide compiled and written by the Federal Writers Project of the Work Project Administration for the State of Illinois. Chicago, 1939.

Mead, Sidney E. _Nathaniel William Taylor, 1786-1858. A Connecticut Liberal_. Chicago, The University of Chicago Press, 1942.

Moses, John. _Illinois, Historical and Statistical_. 2 vols. Chicago, Fergus Printing Co., 1889.

Murray, Williamson & Phelps, eds. _The History of Adams County, Illinois_. Chicago, Blakely, Brown and Marsh, Printers. 1879.

Nevins, Joseph Allen. _Illinois_. Oxford Press, New York, 1917.

Norton, A.T. <u>History of the Presbyterian Church in the State of Illinois.</u> Vol. I (Vol. II never published). St. Louis, W.S. Bryan, 1879.

Otis, Philo Adams. <u>The First Presbyterian Church (1833-1900)</u>. A history of the oldest organization in Chicago, with biographical sketches of the ministers & extracts from the choir records. Chicago, C.F. Summy Co., 1900.

Pease, Theodore Calvin. <u>The Frontier State 1818-1848.</u> <u>The Centennial History of Illinois</u>, Vol. II. Springfield, Illinois, Illinois Centennial Commission, 1918.

_____. <u>The Story of Illinois</u>. Chicago, A.C. McClurg & Company, 1925.

Peck, John N. <u>A Gazetteer of Illinois</u>. Jacksonville, Illinois. R. Goudy, 1834.

Pierce, Bessie Louise. <u>A History of Chicago</u>. 2 vols. Vol. I, 1673-1848; Vol. II, 1848-1871. New York, Alfred A. Knopf, 1937.

Pooley, William Vipond. <u>The Settlement of Illinois from 1830 to 1850</u>. Madison, Wisconsin, Bulletin of the University of Wisconsin, no. 220, 1908.

Porter, Jeremiah. <u>The Earliest Religious History of Chicago</u>. Chicago, 1884.

Post, T.A. <u>Truman Marcellus Post</u>. Boston and Chicago, 1891. Congregational Sunday School and Publishing Society.

Purcell, Richard J. <u>Connecticut in Transition 1775-1818</u>. Baltimore, Maryland, Washington, American Historical Association, 1918.

Quincy Illustrated: <u>A Sketch of Early Quincy</u>, published by <u>The Quincy Daily Journal</u>, Quincy, Illinois, 1889.

Rammelkamp, Charles H. <u>Illinois College, A Centennial History, 1829-1929</u>. New Haven, Yale University Press, 1928. An excellent tome on the early history of Illinois College; an invaluable source of information.

243

Richmond, C.W. and Vallette, H.F. A History of the County of Du Page, Illinois, containing an account of its early settlement and present advantages, a separate History of the Several Towns, etc. Chicago, Scripps, Bross & Spears Co., 1857.

Salter, William. Sixty Years and Other Discourses, with Reminiscences. Boston and Chicago, The Pilgrim Press, 1907.

Sellon, Charles J. History of Galesburg. Galesburg, Illinois. 1857. J.H. Sherman, Printer.

Seventh General Catalogue of the Divinity School of Yale College, 1822-1888. New Haven, 1889.

Shedd, Clarence P. Two Centuries of Student Christian Movements. New York, Association Press, 1934.

Siebert, Wilbur H. The Underground Railroad for the Liberation of Fugitive Slaves. Annual Report of the American Historical Association, 1895. Washington, D.C., 1894.

Smith, George Washington. History of Illinois and her People. 6 vols. Chicago and New York, The American Historical Society (no date).

_____. A History of Southern Illinois. A Narrative Account of its Historical Progress, its People and its Principal Interests. 3 vols. Chicago, Lewis Publishing Co., 1912.

Smith, Theodore Clarke. The Liberty and Free Soil Parties in the Northwest. New York, Longmans, Green & Company, 1897.

Spinka, Matthew et al. A History of Illinois Congregational and Christian Churches. Chicago, The Congregational and Christian Conference of Illinois, 1944. A very valuable source of information. The chapters by Frederick Kuhns were of particular aid with regard to the Illinois Band and the growth of Congregationalism.

Sturtevant, Julian M. Autobiography. New York, F.H. Revell Company, 1896. This is the primary source for the life and work of Julian Sturtevant.

Sweet, William Warren. *Religion on the American Frontier, 1783-1850*. Vol. III, *The Congregationalists*. Chicago, The University of Chicago Press, 1939.

Tanner, Henry. *History of the rise and progress of the Alton riots*. Buffalo, Printing House of J.D. Warren, 1878.

_____. *The Martyrdom of Lovejoy*. Chicago, Fergus Printing Co., 1881.

Thwaites, Reuben Gold. *Early Western Travels 1748-1846*. 32 vols. Cleveland, A.H. Clark Company, 1904.

Thwing, Chas. F. *A History of Higher Education in America*. New York, D. Appleton and Company, 1906.

Turner, Frederick J. *The Significance of Sections in American History*. New York, H. Holt & Company, 1932.

_____. *The Frontier in American History*. New York, H. Holt & Company, 1920.

Waite, Frederick Clayton. *Western Reserve University*. The Hudson Era. Cleveland, Western Reserve University Press, 1943.

Walker, Williston. *A History of the Congregational Churches in the United States*. Vol. III. The American Church History Series, The Christian Literature Co., New York, 1894.

_____. *The Creeds and Platforms of Congregationalism*. New York, G. Scribner's Sons, 1893.

Webster, Martha P. *The Story of Knox College 1837-1912*. Galesburg, Illinois. Wagoner Printing Co., 1912.

Weigle, Luther A. *American Idealism*. Vol. X, in *The Pageant of America*. New Haven, Yale University Press, 1928.

Willard, Samuel. *Brief History of Early Education in Illinois*.

Woestemeyer, I.F. and Gambrill, J.M. *The Westward Movement*. A Book of Readings on Our Changing Frontiers. New York, Appleton-Century Company, 1939.

Wright, Henry B. et al. *Two Centuries of Christian Activity at Yale*. New York, G.P. Putnam's Sons; The Knickerbocker Press, 1901.

245

285.1773
W734

Lincoln Christian College

70577

DATE DUE

DEMCO 38-297